Version 4.0

EXPLORING LOTUS® FOR WINDOWS™

Robert T. Grauer

▼

Maryann Barber

University of Miami

Prentice Hall, Englewood Cliffs, New Jersey 07632

Library of Congress Cataloging in Publication Data

Grauer, Robert T. [date]
    Exploring Lotus for Windows / Robert T. Grauer, Maryann Barber.
    p. cm
    Includes index.
    ISBN 0-13-079518-6
    1. Lotus (Computer programs)   I. Barber, Maryann   II. Title.
QA76.76.W56G835 1994
005.4'3—dc20   94-147
                                              CIP

Lotus is a registered trademark of Lotus Development Corporation
and Windows is a trademark of the Microsoft Corporation.

Acquisitions editor: P. J. Boardman
Editorial /production supervisor: Greg Hubit Bookworks
Interior and cover design: Suzanne Behnke
Production coordinator: Patrice Fraccio
Managing editor: Mary Cavaliere
Developmental editor: Harriet Serenkin
Editorial Assistants: Renee Pelletier / Dolores Kenny

©1994 by Prentice Hall, Inc.
A Simon & Schuster Company
Englewood Cliffs, New Jersey 07632

Printed in the United States of America
10 9 8 7 6 5 4 3

ISBN 0-13-079518-6

Prentice Hall International (UK) Limited, *London*
Prentice Hall of Australia Pty. Limited, *Sydney*
Prentice Hall of Canada Inc., *Toronto*
Prentice Hall Hispanoamericano, S.A., *Mexico*
Prentice Hall of India Private Limited, *New Delhi*
Prentice Hall of Japan, Inc., *Tokyo*
Simon & Schuster Asia Pte. Ltd., *Singapore*
Editora Prentice Hall do Brasil, Ltda., *Rio de Janeiro*

Contents

3

Spreadsheets in Decision Making: What If? 77

4

Graphs and Charts: Delivering a Message 119

5

Data Management: File Maintenance, Queries, and Cross-tabulations   163

Appendix A: SmartIcons   205

Index   209

Preface

Exploring Lotus for Windows 4.0 is one of several books (modules) in the Prentice Hall *Exploring Windows* series. Other modules include *WordPerfect 6.0, Word for Windows 6.0, Microsoft Excel 5.0,* and an introductory module, *Exploring Windows 3.1.* The books are independent of one another but possess a common design, pedagogy, and writing style intended to serve the application courses in both two- and four-year schools.

Each book in the series is suitable on a stand-alone basis for any course that teaches a specific application; alternatively, several modules can be bound together for a single course that teaches multiple applications. The introductory component, *Exploring Windows 3.1,* assumes no previous knowledge and includes an introductory section for those who have never used a computer.

The *Exploring Windows* series will appeal to students in a variety of disciplines including business, liberal arts, and the sciences. Each module has a consistent presentation that stresses the benefits of the Windows environment, especially the common user interface that performs the same task in identical fashion across applications. Each module emphasizes the benefits of multitasking, demonstrates the ability to share data between applications, and stresses the extensive on-line help facility to facilitate learning. Students are taught concepts, not just keystrokes or mouse clicks, with hands-on exercises in every chapter providing the necessary practice to master the material.

The *Exploring Windows* series is different from other books, both in scope and in the way the material is presented. Students learn by doing. Concepts are stressed and memorization is minimized. Shortcuts and other important Windows information are consistently highlighted in the many boxed tips that appear throughout the series. Every chapter contains an average of two directed exercises at the computer, but equally important are the less structured end-of-chapter problems that not only review the information but extend it as well. The end-of-chapter material is a distinguishing feature of the entire series, an integral part of the learning process, and a powerful motivational tool for students to learn and explore.

FEATURES AND BENEFITS

➤ *Exploring Lotus for Windows* presents concepts, as well as keystrokes and mouse clicks, so that students learn the theory behind the applications. They are not just taught what to do but are provided with the rationale for why they are doing it, enabling them to apply the information to additional learning on their own.

➤ No previous knowledge is assumed on the part of the reader. A fast-paced introduction brings the reader or new user up to speed immediately.

➤ Practical information, beyond application-specific material, appears throughout the series. Students are cautioned about computer viruses and taught the importance of adequate backup. The *Exploring Windows* module, for example, teaches students to extend the warranty of a new computer and points out the advantages of a mail-order purchase.

- Problem solving and troubleshooting are stressed throughout the series. The authors are constantly anticipating mistakes that students may make and tell the reader how to recover from problems that invariably occur.
- Tips, tips, and more tips present application shortcuts in every chapter. Windows is designed for the mouse, but experienced users gravitate toward keyboard shortcuts once they have mastered basic skills. The series presents different ways to accomplish a given task, but in a logical and relaxed fashion.
- A unique Buying Guide in the introductory module presents a thorough introduction to PC hardware from the viewpoint of purchasing a computer. Students learn the subtleties in selecting a configuration—for example, how the resolution of a monitor affects its size, the advantages of a local bus, and the Intel CPU processor index.

ACKNOWLEDGMENTS

We want to thank the many individuals who helped bring this project to its successful conclusion. We are especially grateful to our editor at Prentice Hall, P. J. Boardman, without whom the series would not have been possible, and to Harriet Serenkin, the development editor, whose vision helped shape the project. Gretchen Marx of Saint Joseph College produced an outstanding set of Instructor Manuals. Greg Hubit was in charge of production. Deborah Emry, our marketing manager at Prentice Hall, developed the innovative campaign that helped make the series a success. Delores Kenny helped coordinate all phases of the project.

We also want to acknowledge our reviewers, who through their comments and constructive criticism made this a far better book.

Lynne Band, Middlesex Community College
Stuart P. Brian, Holy Family College
Jerry Chin, Southwest Missouri State University
Dean Combellick, Scottsdale Community College
Paul E. Daurelle, Western Piedmont Community College
David Douglas, University of Arkansas
Raymond Frost, Central Connecticut State University
James Gips, Boston College
Wanda D. Heller, Seminole Community College
Ernie Ivey, Polk Community College
Jane King, Everett Community College
John Lesson, University of Central Florida
Alan Moltz, Naugatuck Valley Technical Community College
Delores Pusins, Hillsborough Community College
Gale E. Rand, College Misericordia
David Rinehard, Lansing Community College
Marilyn Salas, Scottsdale Community College
Sally Visci, Lorain County Community College
David Weiner, University of San Francisco
Jack Zeller, Kirkwood Community College

A final word of thanks to the unnamed students at the University of Miami who make it all worthwhile. And, most of all, thanks to you, our readers, for choosing this book. Please feel free to contact us with any comments and suggestions. We can be reached most easily on the Internet.

Robert T. Grauer
RGRAUER@UMIAMI.MIAMI.EDU

Maryann Barber
MBARBER@UMIAMI.MIAMI.EDU

INTERNATIONALIZE YOUR EDUCATION!!

Join International Business Seminars on
an Overseas Adventure

EARN COLLEGE CREDIT
GAIN INTERNATIONAL EXPERTISE
INTERACT WITH TOP LEVEL EXECUTIVES
VISIT THE WORLD'S GREATEST CITIES
May 30, 1994–June 23, 1994

VISIT ORGANIZATIONS SUCH AS: Procter & Gamble Italia, NATO,
The European Parliament, Elektra Breganz, Philip Morris, Allianz Insurance,
Deutsche Aerospace, Digital Equipment, Coca-Cola, G.E. International,
Ernst & Young, Esso Italiana, Guccio Gucci, Targetti Lighting,
University of Innsbruck & British Bankers Association.

PRENTICE HALL INTERNATIONAL BUSINESS SCHOLARSHIP 1994

Prentice Hall and International Business Seminars have joined forces to create a scholarship for students to study and travel in Europe in the summer of 1994. We believe that in today's global business environment students should be exposed to as many different cultures as possible. Although many campuses reflect diversity in both their students and faculty, nothing can replace the educational value of learning about a continent, country, or city first hand.

Each professor may sponsor one student to apply for the scholarship by writing a letter of recommendation and providing the student the application guidelines below.

You can receive more information on the PH Business Scholarship and/or additional travel programs with International Business Seminars by contacting your local Prentice Hall representative or International Business Seminars, P.O. Box 30279, Mesa, Arizona 85275, Telephone: (602) 830-0902; Fax: (602) 924-0527.

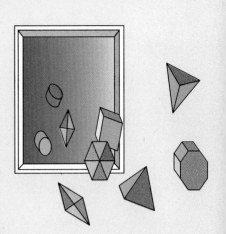

Introduction to Lotus for Windows: What Is a Spreadsheet?

CHAPTER OBJECTIVES

After reading this chapter you will be able to:

1. Explain the concept of a common user interface and its advantage in learning a new application.
2. Describe the basic mouse operations; use a mouse and/or the equivalent keyboard shortcuts to select commands from a pull-down menu.
3. Discuss the function of a dialog box; describe the different types of dialog boxes and the various ways in which information is supplied.
4. Access the on-line help facility and explain its various capabilities.
5. Describe a spreadsheet and suggest several potential applications.
6. Describe how the rows and columns of a spreadsheet are identified, and how its cells are labeled.
7. Distinguish between a label and a value; explain the use of formulas and functions within a spreadsheet.
8. Open and print an existing spreadsheet; add and delete rows and columns in an existing spreadsheet.
9. Use SmartIcons as shortcuts to execute common commands.

OVERVIEW

This chapter provides a broad-based introduction to spreadsheets and Lotus for Windows. It begins, however, with a discussion of basic Windows concepts, applicable to Windows applications in general, and to Lotus for Windows in particular. The emphasis is on the common user interface and consistent command structure that facilitate learning within the Windows environment. Indeed, you may already know much of this material, but that is precisely the point; that is, once you know one Windows application, it is that much easier to learn the next.

The second half of the chapter introduces the spreadsheet, the microcomputer application most widely used by managers and executives. Our intent is to show the wide diversity of business and other uses to which the spreadsheet model can be applied. We draw an analogy between the spreadsheet and the accountant's ledger, and derive a second example from an instructor's grade book. The chapter also covers fundamentals of spreadsheets, discussing how the rows and columns of a spreadsheet are labeled, the difference between a value and a label, and the ability of a spreadsheet to recalculate itself after a change is made.

The two hands-on exercises in the chapter enable you to apply all of the material at the computer, and are indispensable to the learn-by-doing philosophy we follow throughout the text.

THE WINDOWS DESKTOP

The *desktop* is the centerpiece of Microsoft Windows and is analogous to the desk on which you work. There are physical objects on your real desk and there are *windows* (framed rectangular areas) and *icons* (pictorial symbols) on the Windows desktop. The components of a window are explained within the context of Figure 1.1, which contains the opening Windows screen on our computer.

Your desktop may be different from ours, just as your real desk is arranged differently from that of your friend. You can expect, however, to see a window titled Program Manager; you may or may not see other windows within Program Manager, for example, the WPWin 6.0 and Lotus Applications groups shown in Figure 1.1.

Program Manager is a special program crucial to the operation of Windows. It starts automatically when Windows is loaded and it remains active throughout the session; closing Program Manager closes Windows. Program Manager is in essence an organizational tool that places applications in groups (e.g., WPWin 6.0 and Lotus Applications), then displays those groups as windows or group icons.

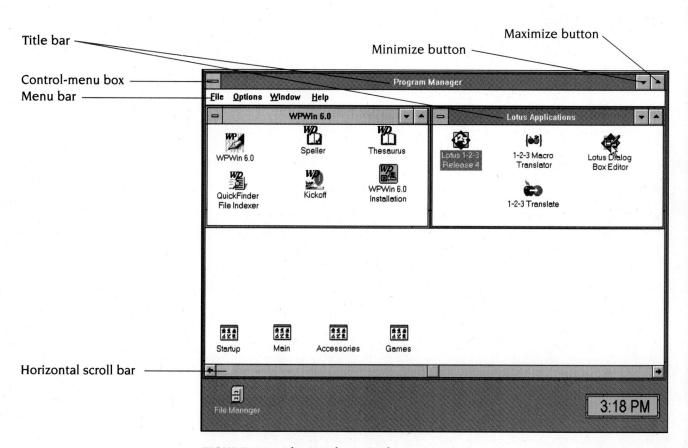

FIGURE 1.1 The Windows Desktop

Regardless of the windows that are open on your desktop, every window contains the same basic elements: a title bar, control-menu box, and buttons to maximize, minimize, or restore the window. The **title bar** displays the name of the window; e.g., Lotus Applications in Figure 1.1. The **control-menu box** accesses a pull-down menu that lets you select operations relevant to the window. The **maximize button** enlarges the window so that it takes the entire desktop, whereas the **minimize button** reduces a window to an icon (but keeps the program active in memory). A **restore button** (a double arrow not shown in Figure 1.1) appears after a window has been maximized and returns the window to its previous size (the size before it was maximized).

Other elements, which may or may not be present, include a horizontal and/or vertical scroll bar and a menu bar. A horizontal (vertical) **scroll bar** will appear at the bottom (right) border of a window when the contents of the window are not completely visible. A **scroll box** appears within the scroll bar to facilitate moving within a document. A **menu bar** is found in the window for Program Manager, but not in the other windows. This is because Program Manager is a different kind of window, an application window rather than a document window.

An **application window** contains a program (application). A **document window** holds data for a program and is contained within an application window. The distinction between application and document windows is made clearer when we realize that Program Manager is a program and requires access to commands contained in pull-down menus located on the menu bar.

Common User Interface

One of the most significant benefits of the Windows environment is the **common user interface** imposed on all applications. This means that if you already know one Windows application, even one as simple as the Paintbrush accessory, it will be that much easier to learn Lotus for Windows, because all applications work basically the same way. In similar fashion, it will take less time to master WordPerfect once you know Lotus, because both applications share a common menu structure with consistent ways to select commands from those menus.

Consider, for example, Figures 1.2a and 1.2b, which display windows for Lotus and WordPerfect, respectively. The applications are very different, yet the windows have many characteristics in common; you might even say that they have more similarities than differences, a remarkable statement considering the programs were developed by different companies and accomplish very different tasks. There is a document window (Untitled) within the application window for Lotus, and in similar fashion, a document window (Document1—unmodified) within the application window for WordPerfect.

The application windows for Lotus and WordPerfect contain the same elements as any other application window: a title bar, menu bar, control-menu box, and minimize, maximize, and restore buttons. The menu bars even contain some of the same menus—for example, File, Edit, View, Tools, Window, and Help menus, with consistent commands in both applications. Both File menus contain the commands to open and close a file, both Edit menus have commands to cut, copy, and paste text; and so on. The means for accessing the pull-down menus are also consistent: click on the menu name (see mouse basics later in the chapter) or press the Alt key plus the underlined letter of the menu name, such as Alt+F to pull down the File menu.

WORKING IN WINDOWS

The next several pages take you through the basic operations common to Windows applications in general, and to Lotus for Windows in particular. You may

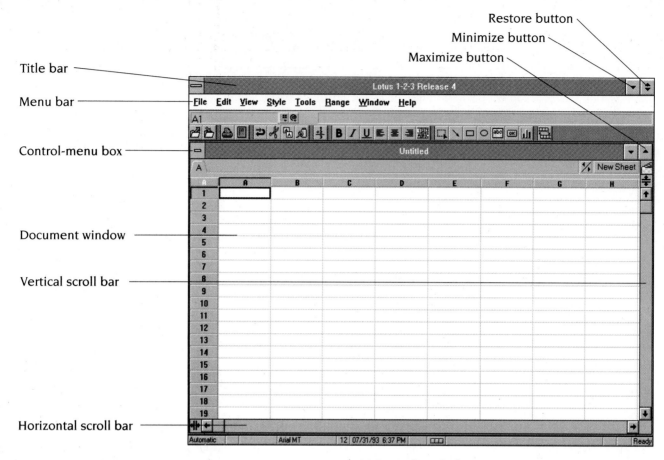

Title bar

Menu bar

Control-menu box

Document window

Vertical scroll bar

Horizontal scroll bar

Restore button

Minimize button

Maximize button

(a) Lotus for Windows

FIGURE 1.2   Common User Interface

already be familiar with much of this material, in which case you are already benefiting from the common user interface. We begin with the mouse and describe how it is used to access pull-down menus and to supply information in dialog boxes. We also emphasize the on-line help facility, which is present in every Windows application.

The Mouse

The mouse (or track ball) is essential to Lotus for Windows as it is to all Windows applications, and you must be comfortable with its four basic actions:

➤ To *point* to an item, move the mouse pointer to the border of the item.
➤ To *click* an item, point to it, then press and release the left mouse button.
➤ To *double click* an item, point to it, then quickly click the left mouse button twice in succession.
➤ To *drag* an item, move the pointer to the item, then press and hold the left button while you move the mouse to a new position.

The mouse is a pointing device; move the mouse on your desk, and the *mouse pointer*—typically a small arrow head—moves on the monitor. The mouse pointer assumes different shapes according to the nature of the current action: a double arrow when you change the size of a window, an I-beam to insert text, a hand to jump from one help topic to the next, or a circle with a line through it to indicate that an attempted action is invalid.

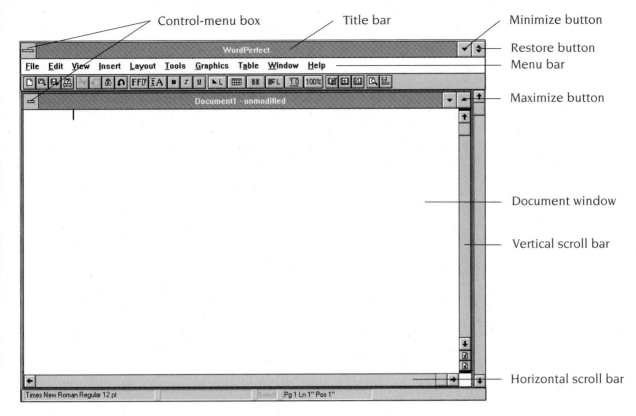

(b) WordPerfect for Windows

FIGURE 1.2 Common User Interface (continued)

The mouse pointer will also change to an hourglass to indicate Windows is processing your last command, and that no further commands may be issued until the action is completed. The more powerful your computer, the less frequently the hourglass will appear; and conversely, the less powerful your system, the more you will see the hourglass.

PICK UP THE MOUSE

It seems that you always run out of room on your real desk, just when you need to move the mouse a little further. The solution is to pick up the mouse and move it closer to you. The pointer will stay in its present position on the screen, but when you put the mouse down, you will have more room on your desk in which to work.

Windows is designed for a two-button mouse, but the vast majority of operations are done with a single (primary) button. A right-handed person will hold the mouse in his or her right hand and click the left button, whereas a left-handed individual may hold the mouse in the left hand and click the right button. If this sounds complicated, it's not, and you can master the mouse with the on-line tutorial provided in Windows. (See step 2 in the hands-on exercise on page 17.)

Note, too, that although Lotus for Windows is designed for a mouse, it provides keyboard equivalents for almost every command, with SmartIcons providing still other ways to accomplish the most frequent operations. You may (at first) wonder why there are so many different ways to do the same thing, but you will come to recognize the many options as part of Windows' charm. The most appropriate technique depends on personal preference, as well as the specific situation.

If, for example, your hands are already on the keyboard, it is faster to use the keyboard equivalent. Other times, your hand will be on the mouse and that will be the fastest way. It is not necessary to memorize anything, nor should you even try; just be flexible and willing to experiment. The more you practice, the more the various techniques will become second nature.

MOUSE TIP FOR LEFTIES

You can customize the mouse to reverse the actions of the left and right buttons. Double click on the **Main group icon** in Program Manager, double click on the **Control Panel icon,** and double click on the **Mouse icon** to bring up the appropriate dialog box.

Pull-down Menus

Pull-down menus, such as those in Figure 1.3, are essential to all Windows applications. A pull-down menu is accessed by clicking on the menu name (within the menu bar) or by pressing the Alt key plus the underlined letter in the menu name—for example, Alt+H to pull down the Help menu. Menu options (commands) are executed by clicking on the command once the menu has been pulled down or by typing the underlined letter—for example, S to execute the Search command in the Help menu. You can also bypass the menu entirely if you know the equivalent keystrokes shown to the right of the command when the menu is pulled down—for example, Ctrl+X, Ctrl+C, and Ctrl+V in the Edit menu to cut, copy, and paste text, respectively. A *dimmed command* (e.g., the Arrange command within the Edit menu) indicates that command is not currently executable; some additional action has to be taken for the command to become available.

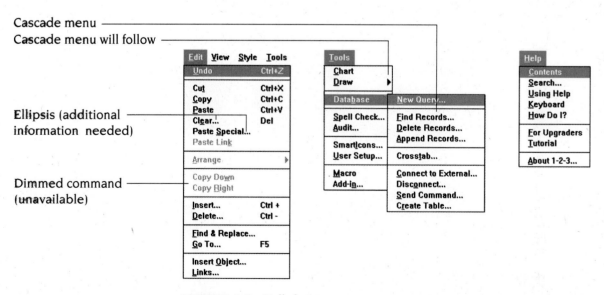

FIGURE 1.3 Pull-down menus

An arrowhead after a command indicates a *cascade menu* will follow with additional choices; for example, clicking on the Database command in the Tools menu produces the cascade menu shown in the figure.

Other commands are followed by an *ellipsis* (. . .) to indicate that more information is required to execute the command; for example, selection of the Insert or Delete command in the Edit menu requires the user to specify the appropriate item. The additional information is entered into a dialog box, which appears immediately after the command has been selected.

Dialog Boxes

A *dialog box* appears when additional information is needed to execute a command—that is, whenever a menu option is followed by an ellipsis. There are, however, different ways to supply that information, which in turn leads to different types of dialog boxes as shown in Figure 1.4.

Option buttons indicate mutually exclusive choices, one of which must be chosen, such as portrait or landscape as shown in Figure 1.4a. *Check boxes* are used if the options are not mutually exclusive and several options can be selected at the same time, such as Worksheet frame, Grid lines, and Drawn objects as in Figure 1.4a. The individual options are selected (cleared) by clicking on the appropriate check box.

A *text box* indicates that specific data is required, such as the margin specifications in Figure 1.4a or the file name in Figure 1.4b. Some text boxes are initially empty and display a flashing vertical bar to mark the insertion point for the text you enter. Other text boxes will already contain an entry, in which case you can click anywhere in the box to establish the insertion point and then edit the entry.

An *open list box,* such as the list of file names in Figure 1.4b, displays the available choices, any one of which is selected by clicking on the desired item. A *drop-down list box,* such as the list of available drives or file types, conserves space by showing only the current selection; click on the arrow of a drop-down list box to produce a list of available options.

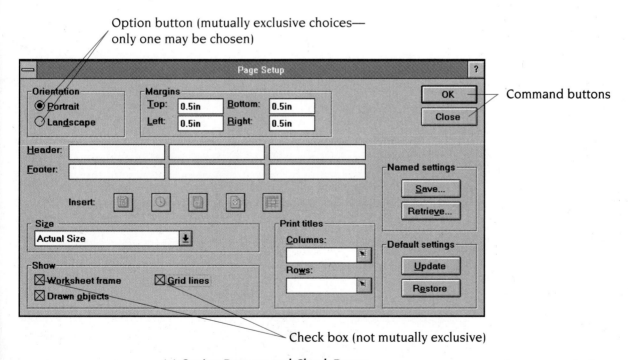

(a) Option Buttons and Check Boxes

FIGURE 1.4   Dialog Boxes

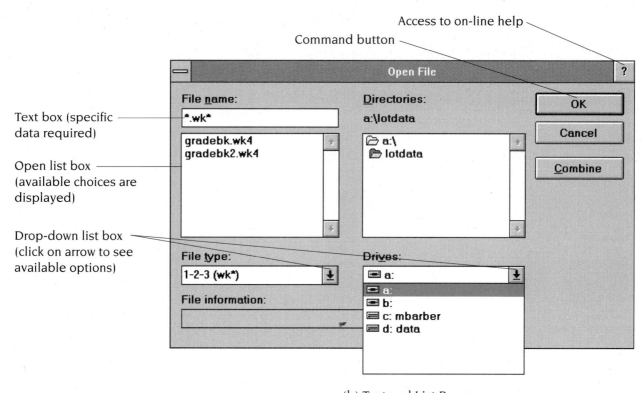

Access to on-line help

Command button

Text box (specific data required)

Open list box (available choices are displayed)

Drop-down list box (click on arrow to see available options)

Open File

File name:
.wk

gradebk.wk4
gradebk2.wk4

File type:
1-2-3 (wk*)

File information:

Directories:
a:\lotdata

a:\
lotdata

Drives:
a:

a:
b:
c: mbarber
d: data

OK
Cancel
Combine

(b) Text and List Boxes

FIGURE 1.4 Dialog Boxes (continued)

Both dialog boxes in Figure 1.4 contain one or more **command buttons** to initiate an action. The function of the command button is generally apparent from its name; for example, Cancel will return to the previous screen with no action taken. OK accepts the information and closes the dialog box.

On-line Help

All Windows applications provide extensive **on-line help,** which is accessed by pulling down the **Help menu** or by pressing the F1 function key. The various capabilities within the help facility are illustrated in Figure 1.5, which displays a help window from Lotus for Windows.

A help window contains all of the elements found in any other application window: a title bar; minimize and maximize or restore buttons; a control-menu box; and optionally, a vertical or horizontal scroll bar. There is also a menu bar with additional commands available through the indicated pull-down menus. The **help buttons** displayed near the top of the help window enable you to move around more easily; you can click a button to perform the indicated function.

The **Contents button** displays an overall list of topics as shown in Figure 1.5a. Use the mouse to click any topic within the window to produce a subsidiary window with additional information.

The **Search button** lets you search for help on a specific topic. Typing a key word in the text box of Figure 1.5b positions you on a highlighted term within the open list box. You can then double click the highlighted item for a list of available topics for the key word you entered. Highlight the desired topic and click the Go To command button to see the actual help text.

Control-menu box   Help buttons   Title bar   Minimize button

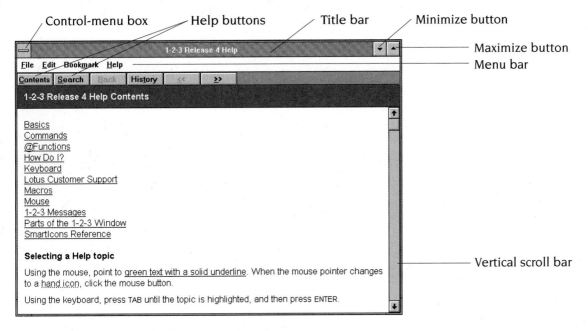

Maximize button
Menu bar

Vertical scroll bar

(a) Help Contents Window

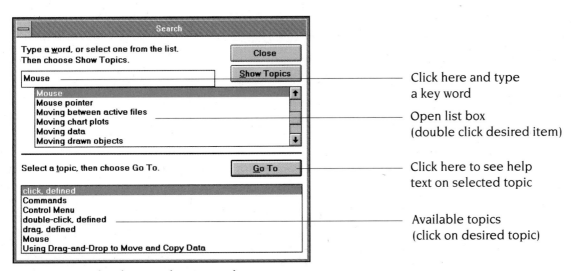

Click here and type
a key word

Open list box
(double click desired item)

Click here to see help
text on selected topic

Available topics
(click on desired topic)

(b) The Search command

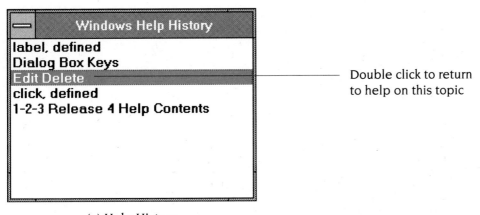

Double click to return
to help on this topic

(c) Help History

FIGURE 1.5   On-line Help

The **Back button** returns you directly to the previous help topic. The **History button** is more general as it displays a list of *all* topics selected within the current session, as shown in Figure 1.5c; you can return to a previous topic by double clicking on the topic.

HELP QUESTION MARK

On-line help is available in every dialog box by clicking the **question mark** at the right of the title bar. Press the **Esc key** to exit help and return to the dialog box.

INTRODUCTION TO SPREADSHEETS

A spreadsheet is the computerized equivalent of an accountant's ledger. As with the ledger, it consists of a grid of rows and columns that enables you to organize data in a readily understandable format. Figures 1.6a and 1.6b show the same information displayed in ledger and spreadsheet format, respectively.

"*What is the big deal?*", you might ask. The big deal is that after you change an entry (or entries), the spreadsheet will, automatically and almost instantly, recompute the entire spreadsheet. Consider, for example, the profit projection spreadsheet shown in Figure 1.6b. As the spreadsheet is presently constructed, the

	Profit Production		1	2	3	4	5	6	
1	Unit Price			20					1
2	Unit Sales			1,200					2
3	Gross Sales			24,000					3
4									4
5	Costs								5
6	Production			10,000					6
7	Distribution			1,200					7
8	Marketing			5,000					8
9	Overhead			3,000					9
10									10
11	Total Cost			19,200					11
12									12
13	Net Profit			4,800					13

(a) The Accountant's Ledger

FIGURE 1.6   The Accountant's Ledger

Original unit price

	A	B
1	PROFIT PROJECTION	
2		
3	UNIT PRICE	20
4	UNIT SALES	1200
5	GROSS SALES	24000
6		
7	COSTS	
8	PRODUCTION	10000
9	DISTRIBUTION	1200
10	MARKETING	5000
11	OVERHEAD	3000
12	TOTAL COSTS	19200
13		
14	NET PROFIT	4800

(b) Original Spreadsheet

	A	B
1	PROFIT PROJECTION	
2		
3	UNIT PRICE	22
4	UNIT SALES	1200
5	GROSS SALES	26400
6		
7	COSTS	
8	PRODUCTION	10000
9	DISTRIBUTION	1200
10	MARKETING	5000
11	OVERHEAD	3000
12	TOTAL COSTS	19200
13		
14	NET PROFIT	7200

Increase in unit price

Affected formulas recomputed

(c) Modified Spreadsheet

FIGURE 1.6   The Accountant's Ledger (continued)

unit price is $20, producing gross sales of $24,000 and a net profit of $4,800. If the unit price is increased to $22 per unit, the spreadsheet recomputes every formula, adjusting the values of gross sales and net profit. The modified spreadsheet of Figure 1.6c appears automatically on your monitor.

With a bottle of whiteout or a good eraser the same changes could also be made to the ledger. But imagine for a moment a ledger with hundreds of entries, many of which depend on the entry you wish to change. You can appreciate the time required to make all the necessary changes to the ledger by hand. However, the same spreadsheet, with hundreds of entries, will be recomputed automatically by the computer. And the computer will not make mistakes. Herein lies the big advantage of computer spreadsheets: the ability to make (or consider making) changes, and to have the computer carry out the recalculation faster and more accurately than could be accomplished manually.

The Professor's Grade Book

A second example of a spreadsheet, one with which you can easily identify, is that of a professor's grade book. The grades are recorded by hand in a notebook, which is nothing more than a different kind of accountant's ledger. Figure 1.7 contains both manual and spreadsheet versions of a grade book.

Figure 1.7a shows a handwritten grade book as it has been done since the days of the little red schoolhouse. For the sake of simplicity, only five students are shown, each with three grades. The professor has computed class averages for

(a) The Professor's Grade Book

	Test 1	Test 2	Final	Wgt Avg*
Adams	100	90	81	88
Baker	90	76	87	85
Glassman	90	78	78	81
Moldof	60	60	40	50
Walker	80	80	90	85
Class Average	84.0	76.8	75.2	

*Note: Final counts double

(a) The Professor's Grade Book

Original Grade

	A	B	C	D	E
1	Student	Test 1	Test 2	Final	Wgt Average
2					
3	Adams	100	90	81	88.0
4	Baker	90	76	87	85.0
5	Glassman	90	78	78	81.0
6	Moldof	60	60	40	50.0
7	Walker	80	80	90	85.0
8					
9	Class Average	84.0	76.8	75.2	

(b) Original Grades

Grade changed

	A	B	C	D	E
1	Student	Test 1	Test 2	Final	Wgt Average
2					
3	Adams	100	90	81	88.0
4	Baker	90	76	87	85.0
5	Glassman	90	78	78	81.0
6	Moldof	60	60	40	50.0
7	Walker	80	80	100	90.0
8					
9	Class Average	84.0	76.8	77.2	

Affected formulas recomputed

(c) Modified Spreadsheet

FIGURE 1.7 The Professor's Grade Book

each exam, as well as a semester average for every student, in which the final counts *twice* as much as either test; for example, Adams' average is equal to: (100+90+81+81)/4 = 88.

Figure 1.7b shows the grade book as it might appear in a spreadsheet, and is essentially unchanged from Figure 1.7a. Walker's grade on the final exam in Figure 1.7b is 90, giving him a semester average of 85 and producing a class average on the final of 75.2 as well. Now consider Figure 1.7c, in which the grade on Walker's final has been changed to 100, causing the class average on the final to go from 75.2 to 77.2, and Walker's semester average to change from 85 to 90. As with the profit projection, a change to any entry within the grade book automatically recalculates all dependent values as well. Hence, when Walker's final exam was regraded, all dependent values (the class average for the final as well as Walker's semester average) were recomputed.

As simple as the idea of a spreadsheet may seem, it provided the first major reason for managers to have a personal computer on their desks. Essentially, anything that can be done with a pencil, a pad of paper, and a calculator can be done faster and far more accurately with a spreadsheet.

Row and Column Labels

A spreadsheet is divided into rows and columns, with each row and column assigned a label. Rows are given numeric labels ranging from 1 to a maximum of

8,192. Columns are assigned alphabetic labels from column A to Z, then continue from AA to AZ and then from BA to BZ and so on, until the last of 256 columns is reached.

The intersection of every row and column forms a **cell,** with the number of cells in a spreadsheet equal to the number of rows times the number of columns. The professor's grade book in Figure 1.7, for example, has 5 columns labeled A through E, 9 rows numbered from 1 to 9, and a total of 45 cells. Each cell has a unique **cell address;** for example, the cell at the intersection of column A and row 9 has the address A9. The column label always precedes the row label in the cell address.

THE THIRD DIMENSION

A Lotus spreadsheet can be extended to a third dimension with up to 256 worksheets in a single file. Each worksheet is identified with a letter from A to Z, then continuing with AA to AZ, BA to BZ, and so forth. The complete cell address includes the worksheet letter followed by a colon; A:A1 would indicate cell A1 in worksheet A. We will, however, omit the worksheet letter unless we refer to a worksheet other than worksheet A.

Cell Contents

Figure 1.8 shows an alternate view of the professor's grade book that displays the **cell contents** rather than the computed values; that is, it displays the formulas and other entries in individual cells that give the spreadsheet its ability to recalculate all values whenever an entry changes. Every cell in a spreadsheet contains either a **value** or a **label.** A value may be used in a calculation, a label may not.

The simplest value is a constant—that is, a number—which is entered into a cell with or without formatting; examples are 100, $100, or 100%. A value may also be derived from a formula or a function. (Dates are also considered values and are discussed in Chapter 3.)

A **formula** is a combination of numbers, cell references, arithmetic operators, and/or functions, that displays the result of a calculation. A formula typically begins with a plus sign or left parenthesis, but other characters are also possible. (See boxed tip on formulas versus labels on page 15.)

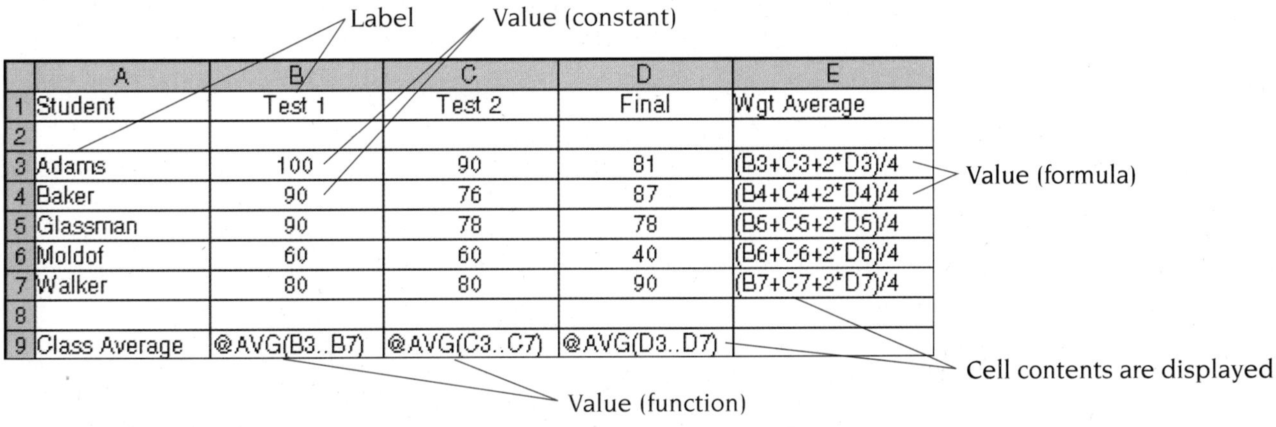

Label   Value (constant)

	A	B	C	D	E
1	Student	Test 1	Test 2	Final	Wgt Average
2					
3	Adams	100	90	81	(B3+C3+2*D3)/4
4	Baker	90	76	87	(B4+C4+2*D4)/4
5	Glassman	90	78	78	(B5+C5+2*D5)/4
6	Moldof	60	60	40	(B6+C6+2*D6)/4
7	Walker	80	80	90	(B7+C7+2*D7)/4
8					
9	Class Average	@AVG(B3..B7)	@AVG(C3..C7)	@AVG(D3..D7)	

Value (formula)

Cell contents are displayed

Value (function)

FIGURE 1.8 The Professor's Grade Book (cell formulas)

Consider, for example, the formula in cell E3, (B3+C3+2*D3)/4, which computes Adams' weighted average for the semester. The formula is built in accordance with the professor's rules for computing a student's weighted average, which counts the final twice as much as either exam. (Lotus uses the symbols +,−, *, /, and ^ to indicate addition, subtraction, multiplication, division, and exponentiation, respectively, and follows the normal rules of arithmetic precedence. Any expression in parentheses is evaluated first. Exponentiation is done next, then multiplication or division in left-to-right order, then addition or subtraction also in left-to-right order.)

The formula in cell E3 takes the grade on the first exam (in cell B3), plus the grade on the second exam (in cell C3), plus two times the grade on the final (found in cell D3), and divides the result by four. The fact that we enter a formula for the weighted average rather than a constant means that should any of the individual grades change, all dependent results will also change; this in essence is the basic principle behind the spreadsheet and explains why when one number changes, various other numbers throughout the spreadsheet are changed as well.

A formula may also include a *function*, or predefined computational task, such as the @*AVG function* in cells B9, C9, and D9. The function in cell B9, for example, @AVG(B3..B7), is interpreted to mean the average of all cells starting at B3 and ending at B7, that is, the average of cells B3, B4, B5, B6, and B7. You can appreciate that functions are often easier to use than the corresponding formulas, especially with larger spreadsheets (for example, classes with many students).

A label is a descriptive entry that begins with a *label prefix* to determine the position of the label within the cell. An apostrophe left-justifies the label, a caret centers the label, and a quotation mark right-justifies the entry. The various label prefixes and the displayed results are shown in Figure 1.9.

You need not, however, type an apostrophe to left-justify a label as that is the default prefix. In other words, Lotus assumes that any entry beginning with a letter is a label and automatically supplies the apostrophe for you. You can change the alignment of an existing label by entering a different prefix or by the appropriate command from the pull-down Style menu. (The latter is discussed in Chapter 2.)

THE REPEAT CHARACTER

A label that has the backward slash as its label prefix repeats until it fills the entire cell; for example, \X will fill the entire cell with Xs, whereas \ABC repeats the character string ABC.

	Label Prefix	Displayed Value
Apostrophe	'ABC	ABC
Quotation mark	"ABC	ABC
Caret	^ABC	ABC
Backward slash	\ABC	ABCABCABCABCAB(

FIGURE 1.9 Label prefixes

FORMULAS VERSUS LABELS

A formula must begin with a number or one of the following characters: +,−, =, ., @, (, #, $. Any other character causes the entry to be treated as a label. (B1+B2) and +B1+B2 are both formulas and cause Lotus to add the contents of cells B1 and B2. B1+B2, entered without the leading plus sign or left parenthesis, is treated as a label and displayed as such in the cell.

LOTUS FOR WINDOWS

Figure 1.10 displays the professor's grade book as it is implemented in Lotus for Windows, which shares the common user interface present in all Windows applications. The desktop contains an application window for Lotus and a document window within Lotus for the specific spreadsheet. Both windows have been maximized, and the title bar of the spreadsheet has been merged into the title bar of the application window. You should also recognize many of the elements described earlier in the chapter—for example, minimize and restore buttons, a menu bar, horizontal and vertical scroll bars, and control menu boxes.

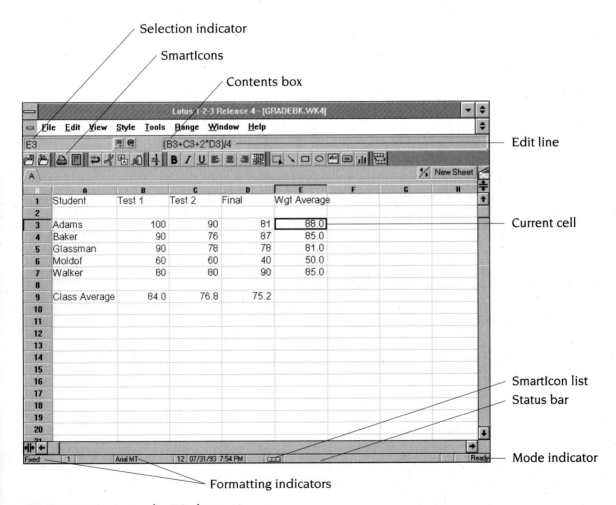

FIGURE 1.10   Lotus for Windows

Figure 1.10 resembles the grade book shown earlier, but it includes several other elements that enable you to create and/or edit the spreadsheet. Observe, for example, the heavy border around cell E3, indicating that it (cell E3) is the *current cell* and that any actions taken at this point will affect the contents of cell E3. The current cell can be changed in different ways, such as by clicking on a different cell, or by using the arrow keys to move to a different cell.

The displayed value in cell E3 is 88.0, but as indicated earlier, the cell contains a formula to compute the weighted average rather than the number itself. The contents of the current cell, (B3+C3+2*D3)/4, are displayed in the *contents box* on the *edit line.* The address of the current cell, cell E3 in Figure 1.10, appears in the *selection indicator* at the extreme left of the edit line.

Several other elements of Figure 1.10 bear mention. A series of *SmartIcon*s is displayed below the menu bar. Each SmartIcon is a shortcut corresponding to a command from a pull-down menu; for example, you can click the printer icon to print a spreadsheet rather than pull down the File menu and click the *Print command.* There is absolutely no requirement to use SmartIcons, but you will appreciate their ability to save time as you become more proficient in Lotus.

The *status bar* at the bottom of the spreadsheet keeps you informed of what is happening as you work within Lotus. It displays the type of formatting in effect for the current cell (Fixed in the example), the type face and point size (Arial 12 point), the date and time, and an indication of the spreadsheet's status; for example, Ready indicates that Lotus is waiting for you to enter data or select a command.

LEARNING BY DOING

We come now to the first of two hands-on exercises, which implement our learn-by-doing philosophy. The initial exercise shows you how to load Windows and practice with the mouse, then directs you to load Lotus for Windows and retrieve the professor's grade book from the data disk that accompanies this text. The data disk expedites the way in which you learn, especially at the beginning, as you can experiment with an existing spreadsheet. The exercise has you explore the various elements on the screen, then directs you to change individual student grades and view the resulting recalculation. The exercise also instructs you to print the spreadsheet and to save the changes you make.

HANDS-ON EXERCISE 1:

Introduction to Lotus for Windows

Objective: To load Windows and Lotus for Windows and to retrieve and print an existing spreadsheet. The exercise also introduces you to the data disk that accompanies the text and reviews basic Windows operations: pull-down menus, dialog boxes, and the use of a mouse.

Step 1: Load Windows

➤ Type **WIN,** then press the **enter key** to load Windows if it is not already loaded.

➤ The appearance of your desktop will be different than ours, but it should resemble Figure 1.1 at the beginning of the chapter.

➤ You will most likely see a window containing Program Manager, but if not, you should see an icon titled Program Manager near the bottom of the screen; double click on this icon to open the Program Manager window.

Step 2: Master the mouse
- ➤ A mouse is essential to the operation of Lotus for Windows as it is to all Windows applications.
- ➤ The easiest way to practice is with the mouse tutorial found in the Help menu of Windows itself.
- ➤ Click the **Help menu.**
- ➤ Click **Windows Tutorial.**
- ➤ Type **M** to begin, then follow the on-screen instructions.
- ➤ Exit the tutorial when you are finished.

ABOUT PROGRAM MANAGER

If you are unable to find the on-line tutorial, it may be because you are using an older version of Windows—perhaps Windows 3.0 rather than Windows 3.1. Pull down the **Help menu** and select **About Program Manager** to display information about the program, including the release in use. A similar screen is available for every Windows application.

Step 3: Install the data disk
- ➤ Do this step *only* if you have your own computer and want to copy the files from the data disk to the hard drive.
- ➤ Place the data disk in drive A (or whatever drive is appropriate).
- ➤ Pull down the **File menu.**
- ➤ Click **Run.** Type **A:INSTALL** in the text box.
- ➤ Click **OK.** Follow the on-screen instructions.

Step 4: Load Lotus for Windows
- ➤ Double click the icon for the group containing Lotus for Windows if that group is not already open.
- ➤ Double click the *program icon* for **Lotus for Windows.**
- ➤ Click the **maximize button** (if necessary) so that the application window containing Lotus for Windows takes the entire screen.
- ➤ Click the **maximize button** in the document window (if necessary) to produce a screen similar to Figure 1.11a. (You will not see the dialog box until you complete step 5.)

Step 5: Retrieve a spreadsheet
- ➤ Pull down the **File menu.**
- ➤ Click **Open** to produce a dialog box similar to the one in Figure 1.11a.
- ➤ Click the arrow for the Drives drop-down list box. Click the appropriate drive, drive C or drive A.
- ➤ Double click the **LOTDATA** directory to make it the active directory.
- ➤ Double click **GRADEBK.WK4** to retrieve the spreadsheet for this exercise.

Step 6: The current cell and contents box
- ➤ Click in cell **B3,** the cell containing Adams' grade on the first test.
- ➤ Cell B3 is now the current cell and is surrounded by a heavy border; the selection indicator on the edit line indicates the current cell (B3), and the contents box immediately to the right displays its contents (100).

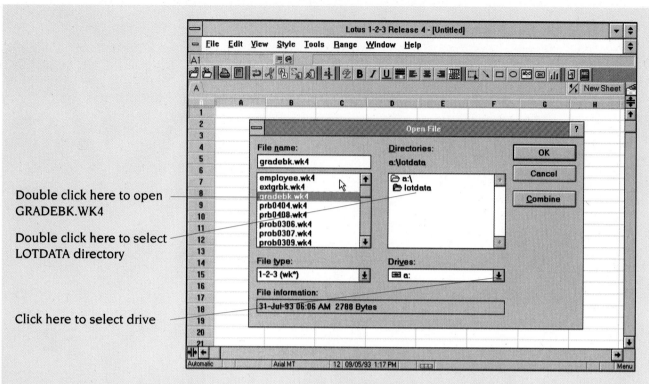

Double click here to open
GRADEBK.WK4

Double click here to select
LOTDATA directory

Click here to select drive

(a) Retrieving a Spreadsheet (steps 4 and 5)

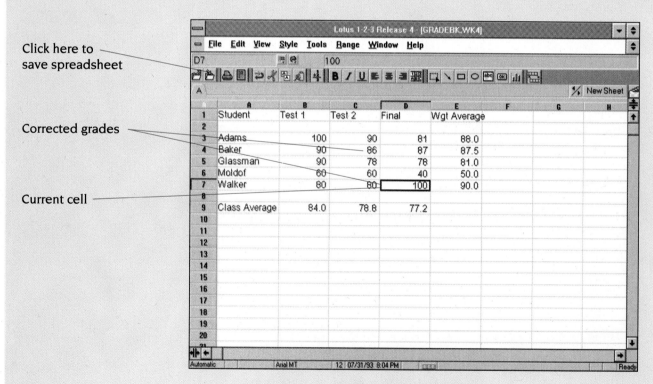

Click here to
save spreadsheet

Corrected grades

Current cell

(b) What If? (step 7)

FIGURE 1.11 Hands-on Exercise 1

- ➤ Click in cell **B4** (or press the **down arrow key**) to make it the current cell. The selection indicator indicates cell B4, while the contents box indicates a grade of 90.
- ➤ Click in cell **E3,** the cell containing the formula to compute Adams' weighted average; the spreadsheet displays the computed average of 88.0, but the contents box displays the formula, (B3+C3+2*D3)/4, to compute that average.
- ➤ Continue to change the current cell (with the mouse or arrow keys) and notice how the selection indicator and contents box change to reflect the current cell.

Step 7: Experiment (what if?)
- ➤ Let's assume that an error was made in recording Baker's grade on the second test.
- ➤ Click in cell **C4,** the cell containing this particular grade.
- ➤ Enter a corrected value of **86** (instead of the previous entry of 76). Press the **enter key.**
- ➤ The effects of this change ripple through the spreadsheet, automatically changing the computed value for Baker's average in cell E4 to 87.5. The class average on the second test in cell C9 changes to 78.8.
- ➤ Change Walker's grade on the final from 90 to **100.** Walker's average in cell E7 changes to 90.0, while the class average in cell D9 changes to 77.2.
- ➤ Your spreadsheet should match Figure 1.11b.

Step 8: Save the modified spreadsheet
- ➤ It is very, very important to save your work periodically during a session.
- ➤ Pull down the **File menu.** Click **Save** to save the changes. (Alternatively, click the **Save SmartIcon,** which is the second icon from the left.)

SMARTICONS

To determine the function of a SmartIcon, **press and hold the right mouse button** as you point to the icon; a description of the icon will appear at the top of the screen to the left of the title bar.

Step 9: Print the spreadsheet
- ➤ Pull down the **File menu.**
- ➤ Click **Print** to produce a dialog box requesting information about the Print command as shown in Figure 1.11c.
- ➤ Click the **Page Setup command button,** which produces the additional window in Figure 1.11c.
- ➤ Check the **Worksheet frame** and **Grid lines** check boxes.
- ➤ Click the **OK command button** to return to the Print window.
- ➤ Click the **OK command button** to print the spreadsheet.
- ➤ Save the spreadsheet.

Step 10: Exit Lotus
- ➤ Pull down the **File menu.**
- ➤ Click **Exit** to exit Lotus and return to Program Manager.

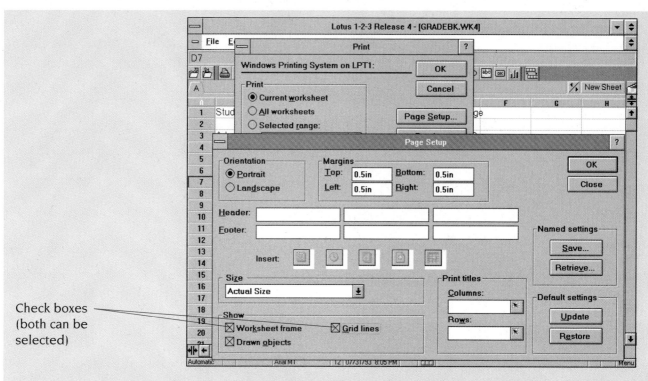

Check boxes
(both can be
selected)

(c) The Print and Page Setup Commands (step 9)

FIGURE 1.11   Hands-on Exercise 1 (continued)

Step 11: Exit Windows
➤ The consistent command structure within Windows means that the same
  operation is accomplished the same way in different applications; that is, you
  exit Program Manager in essentially the same way that you exit from any
  other application.
➤ Pull down the **File menu** in Program Manager.
➤ Click the **Exit Windows** command.
➤ You will see an informational message indicating that you are leaving Windows.
➤ Click the **OK command button** to exit.

MODIFYING THE SPREADSHEET

We trust that you completed the hands-on exercise without difficulty and that you
are more confident in your ability than when you began. The exercise was not
complicated, but it did accomplish several objectives and set the stage for a second exercise, which follows shortly.

Consider now Figure 1.12, which contains a modified version of the professor's grade book. Figure 1.12a shows the grade book at the end of the first hands-
on exercise and reflects the changes made to the grades for Baker and Walker.
Figure 1.12b shows the spreadsheet as it will appear at the end of the second exercise. Several changes bear mention:

   1. One student has dropped the class and two other students have been added.
      Moldof appeared in the original spreadsheet in Figure 1.12a, but has some-

how managed to withdraw; Coulter and Davis did not appear in the original grade book but have been added to the spreadsheet in Figure 1.12b.

2. A new column, containing the student's major, has been added for every student.

The implementation of these changes is accomplished through the combination of the Insert and Delete commands that enable you to add and/or remove rows or columns as necessary. The important thing to realize is that cell addresses in the existing formulas are adjusted automatically to account for the changes brought about by the addition (deletion) of rows and columns.

Consider, once again, the formula to compute Adams' weighted average, which is contained in cell E3 of the original grade book, but in cell F3 in the modified grade book. The original formula in Figure 1.12a referenced cells B3, C3, and D3 to obtain the grades on test 1, test 2, and the final; the revised formula in Figure 1.12b reflects the fact that a new column has been inserted, and references cells C3, D3, and E3. The change in the formula is made automatically by Lotus without any explicit action on the part of the user (other than to insert the new column).

In similar fashion, the formulas to compute the class averages appear in row 9 of the original spreadsheet and reflect the entries in rows 3 through 7, inclusive. The revised spreadsheet has a net increase of one student, which automatically moves the formulas containing the @AVG function to row 10. It also adjusts the @AVG function to use values from rows 3 through 8 in order to accommodate the additional student.

	A	B	C	D	E	
1	Student	Test 1	Test 2	Final	Wgt Average	
2						
3	Adams	100	90	81	88.0	——— Formula references
4	Baker	90	86	87	87.5	cells B3, C3, and D3
5	Glassman	90	78	78	81.0	
6	Moldof	60	60	40	50.0	——— This row will be deleted
7	Walker	80	80	100	90.0	
8						
9	Class Average	84.0	78.8	77.2	———	Averages entries in rows 3–7

(a) After Hands-on Exercise 1

Column B was added

	A	B	C	D	E	F	
1	Student	Major	Test 1	Test 2	Final	Wgt Average	
2							
3	Adams	CIS	100	90	81	88.0	⎤ Formula references
4	Baker	MKT	90	86	87	87.5	⎦ cells C3, D3, and E3
5	Coulter	ACC	85	95	100	95.0	⎫
6	Davis	FIN	75	75	85	80.0	⎬ New rows added
7	Glassman	CIS	90	78	78	81.0	⎭
8	Walker	CIS	80	80	100	90.0	
9							
10	Class Average		86.7	84.0	88.5	———	Averages entries in rows 3–8

(b) After Hands-on Exercise 2

FIGURE 1.12 The Modified Grade Book

Required Commands

The *Insert command,* located in the Edit menu, adds a new row or column (or multiple rows and columns) to the spreadsheet. Any cell reference used in an existing formula is adjusted automatically to account for the additional rows or columns. For example, if cell B6 contained the formula +B2+B3 and a new row was inserted between rows 2 and 3, the formula in cell B6 (now B7) would become +B2+B4.

The *Delete command,* also in the Edit menu, removes a row or column (or multiple rows or columns) from the spreadsheet. Cell references are adjusted automatically, as with the Insert command; for example, if cell B6 contains the formula +B2+B3 and row 1 is deleted, the formula in cell B6 (now B5) becomes +B1+B2.

The ensuing exercise also requires the Open and Save commands found in the File menu. The *Open command* brings a copy of the spreadsheet from disk into memory; the *Save command* does the opposite and copies the spreadsheet in memory to disk. The *Save As command* saves the spreadsheet under a different name, and is useful when you want to retain a copy of the original spreadsheet prior to making changes. The initial execution of the Save command (as well as every execution of the Save As command) requires you to enter a filename from one to eight characters; the extension WK4 is assigned automatically.

HANDS-ON EXERCISE 2:

Modifying a Spreadsheet

Objective To retrieve an existing spreadsheet, insert and delete rows and columns, then save the revised spreadsheet; to demonstrate the Undo command and on-line help. Use Figure 1.13 as a guide in doing the exercise.

Step 1: Retrieve the spreadsheet
➤ Repeat the necessary steps from step 4 in the previous exercise to load Lotus for Windows.
➤ Click the **Open folder SmartIcon** or pull down the **File menu** and click **Open.**
➤ You will see a dialog box similar to that of Figure 1.11a from the previous exercise.
➤ Click the arrow for the Drives drop-down list box. Click the appropriate drive, drive C or drive A, depending on whether you installed the data disk.
➤ Double click the **LOTDATA** directory to make it the active directory.
➤ Double click on **GRADEBK.WK4** to retrieve the spreadsheet from the first exercise.

DISPLAYING THE SMARTICONS

If you do not see the SmartIcons it is because a prior user changed the view preferences. Pull down the **View menu,** click **Set View Preferences,** and check the **SmartIcons box** to display the icons. If the icons are in a different position (e.g., at the side or bottom of the spreadsheet), pull down the **Tools menu,** click **SmartIcons,** then choose the appropriate position from the drop-down **Position list box.**

Step 2: The Save As command

➤ Pull down the **File menu.**

➤ Click **Save As** to produce the dialog box of Figure 1.13a, which requests the new name of the file.

➤ Type a filename from one to eight characters, such as **GRADEBK2** (the WK4 extension is added automatically).

➤ Press the **enter key.**

➤ There are now two identical copies of the file on disk: GRADEBK.WK4, which we supplied, and GRADEBK2.WK4, which you just created.

➤ The title bar of the document window reflects the latter name.

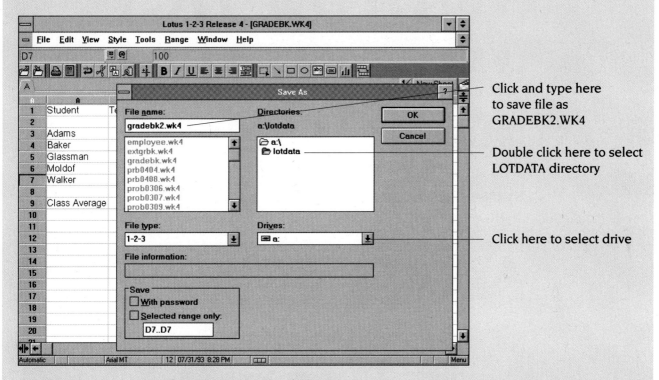

Click and type here
to save file as
GRADEBK2.WK4

Double click here to select
LOTDATA directory

Click here to select drive

(a) The Save As Command (step 2)

FIGURE 1.13 Hands-on Exercise 2

Step 3: Delete a row

➤ Moldof has somehow obtained a retroactive withdrawal and managed to drop the course.

➤ Click anywhere in **row 6** (the row containing Moldof's grades).

➤ Pull down the **Edit menu.**

➤ Click **Delete** as shown in Figure 1.13b.

➤ Click **Row** in the dialog box for the Delete command.

➤ Click **OK** to delete row 6.

➤ Moldof has disappeared from the grade book, and the class averages (now in row 8) have been updated automatically to reflect the fact that Moldof is gone.

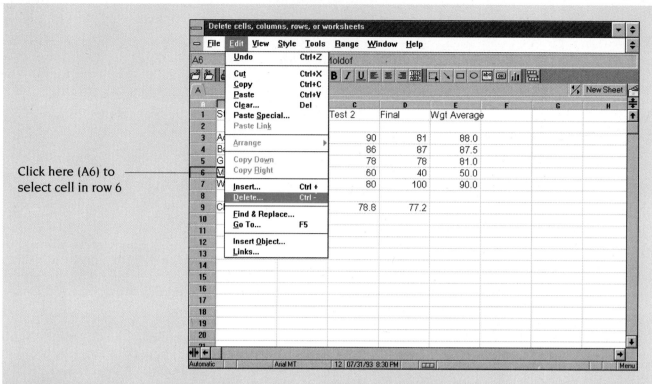

Click here (A6) to
select cell in row 6

(b) Deleting a Row (step 3)

FIGURE 1.13   Hands-on Exercise 2 (continued)

Step 4: The Undo command
➤ Pull down the **Edit menu.**
➤ Click **Undo** to reverse the last command and put Moldof back into the spreadsheet.
➤ Click anywhere in row 6, and this time delete Moldof for good.

EXECUTE COMMANDS QUICKLY

The quickest way to select a command from a pull-down menu is to point to the menu name, then drag the pointer (i.e., press and hold the left mouse button) to the desired command and release the button. The command is executed when you release the button.

Step 5: Insert a row
➤ Click in cell **A5** (the cell containing Glassman's name). Look at the contents box within the control panel; an apostrophe appears as a label prefix to indicate that the label is left-justified within cell A5.
➤ Pull down the **Edit menu.**
➤ Click **Insert.**
➤ Click **Row** as in Figure 1.13c.
➤ Click **OK** to add a row above the current row.
➤ Row 5 is now blank (it is the newly inserted row) and Glassman (who was in row 5) is now in row 6.

- All other rows have been adjusted, as have the functions to compute the class averages at the bottom of the spreadsheet.
- Enter the name and the test grades for **Coulter, 85, 95,** and **100,** as in Figure 1.13d.
- Click in cell **E5** and enter the formula to compute the weighted average, **(B5+C5+2*D5)/4.**
- Click the **Save SmartIcon** or pull down the **File menu** and click **Save** to save the changes made to this point.

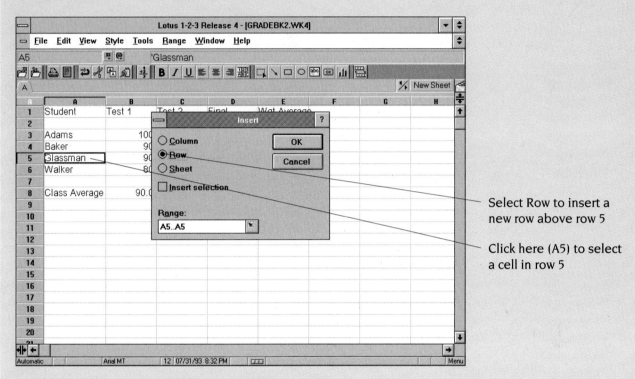

(c) Inserting a Row (step 5)

FIGURE 1.13 Hands-on Exercise 2 (continued)

SAVE YOUR WORK

We cannot overemphasize the importance of periodically saving a spreadsheet, so that if something goes wrong, you won't lose everything. Nothing is more frustrating than to lose hours of effort due to an unexpected problem in Windows or to a temporary loss of power. Save your work frequently, at least once every 15 minutes. Click the **Save SmartIcon** or pull down the **File menu** and click **Save.** Do it!

Step 6: Insert a second row
- Click anywhere in **row 6,** the row that now contains Glassman's grades.
- Pull down the **Edit menu** a second time and follow the steps to insert a new row.
- Type **Davis** in cell A6. (Glassman has moved to row 7.)

Enter data for
Coulter in row 5

Glassman now in row 6

Enter formula in cell E5
(B5 + C5 + 2* D5)/4

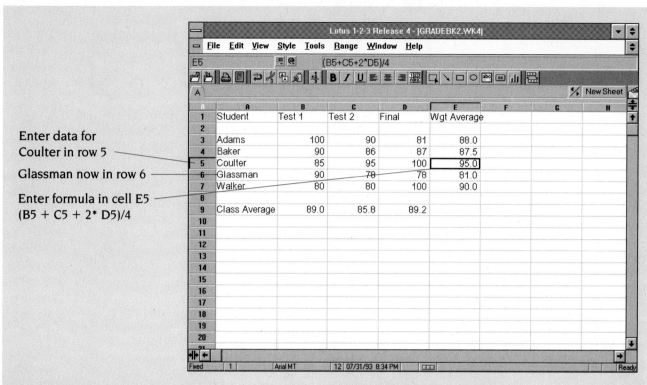

(d) The New Student (step 5)

FIGURE 1.13   Hands-on Exercise 2 (continued)

➤ Enter Davis' grades **75, 75,** and **85** in cells B6, C6, and D6, respectively.
➤ Enter the formula to compute Davis' weighted average in cell E6.
➤ Save the spreadsheet.

INSERTING ROWS AND COLUMNS

Click the row label (or drag the mouse over multiple row labels), then
pull down the **Edit menu** and click **Insert.** A new row (or series of rows)
will be inserted automatically. Use the same technique to insert a column.
You can also click a row or column label with the **right mouse button** to
produce a shortcut menu, bypassing the Edit menu. Click **Insert** and the
row or column is inserted automatically.

Step 7: Add a column
➤ Click anywhere in **column B.**
➤ Pull down the **Edit menu.**
➤ Click **Insert.**
➤ Click **Column.**
➤ Column B is now blank (it is the new column) and all existing columns have
been moved to the right; the grades for test 1 are now in column C, the
grades for test 2 in column D, and so on.
➤ Note that the formulas for weighted average have been adjusted to accom-
modate the additional column; for example, the entry in cell F3 is now
(C3+D3+2*E3)/4.

➤ Click in cell **B1.** Type **Major.** Press **Enter.**
➤ Enter the students' majors as shown in Figure 1.13e. Press the **down arrow key** after entering each major to move to the next cell.
➤ Save the spreadsheet.

Step 8: On-line help
➤ Pull down the **Help menu.**
➤ Click **Search.**
➤ Type **SmartIcon**s in the text box as shown in Figure 1.13e.
➤ Double click **SmartIcon**s in the open list box to display the available topics.
➤ Double click **SmartIcons reference** in the second list box to produce the information screen of Figure 1.13f. Read the information and make notes as necessary.
➤ Double click the **control-menu box** in the help screen to exit help and return to the spreadsheet.

HELP TIPS

You can print the contents of any help screen by pulling down the **File menu** and clicking on the **Print Topic** command. You can also increase the amount of on-screen information (eliminating the need to scroll through the help window) by clicking on the maximize button.

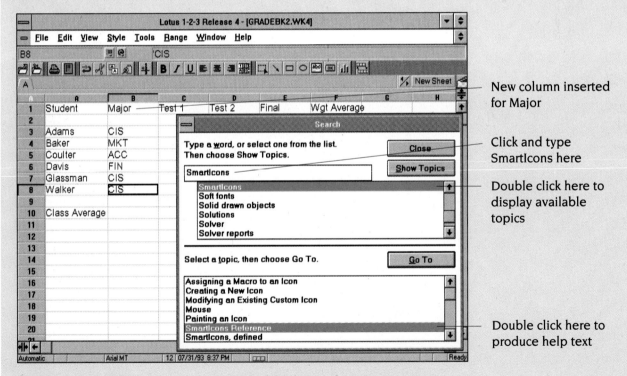

(e) Adding a Column (step 7) and On-line Help (step 8)

FIGURE 1.13   Hands-on Exercise 2 (continued)

Double click here to exit Help and return to spreadsheet

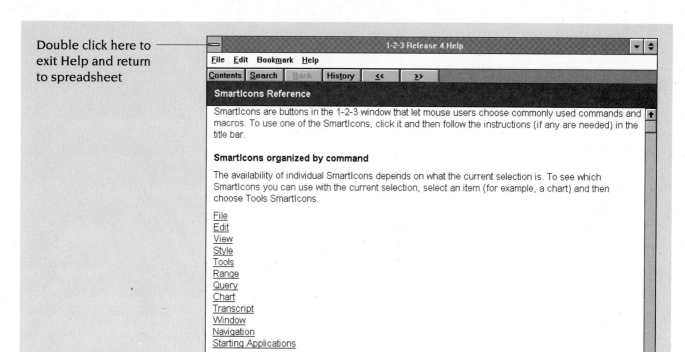

(f) On-line Help (step 8)

FIGURE 1.13   Hands-on Exercise 2 (continued)

Step 9: Print the revised spreadsheet
➤ Click the **Save SmartIcon** to save the spreadsheet a final time.
➤ Click the **Printer SmartIcon** to print the revised spreadsheet.
➤ Exit Lotus (and Windows) as you did at the end of the previous exercise.

SUMMARY

The common user interface ensures that all Windows applications are similar in appearance and work basically the same way, with common conventions and a consistent menu structure. It provides you with an intuitive understanding of any application, even before you begin to use it, and means that once you learn one application, it is that much easier to learn the next.

The mouse is essential to Lotus for Windows as it is to all Windows applications. Keyboard equivalents are provided for virtually all operations. Smart-Icons offer yet another way to execute common commands. On-line help provides detailed information about all aspects of Lotus.

A spreadsheet is the computerized equivalent of an accountant's ledger. It is divided into rows and columns, with each row and column assigned a label. The intersection of every row and column forms a cell.

Every cell in a spreadsheet contains either a value (a number, formula, or function) or a label. A value may be used in a calculation, a label may not. A label contains text (descriptive information) and begins with a label prefix.

The Insert and Delete commands add or remove rows or columns as necessary. The Open command copies a spreadsheet from disk into memory; the Save command does the opposite and copies the spreadsheet in memory to disk.

Key Words and Concepts

Application window	Edit line	Point
Back button	Ellipsis	Print command
Cascade menu	File menu	Program icon
Cell	Formula	Program Manager
Cell address	Function	Pull-down menu
Cell contents	Help menu	Ready mode
Check box	Help buttons	Restore button
Click	History button	Save command
Command button	Icon	Save As command
Common user interface	Insert command	Scroll bar
Contents box	Label	Scroll box
Control-menu box	Label prefix	Search button
Current cell	List box	Selection indicator
Delete command	Maximize button	SmartIcons
Desktop	Menu bar	Status bar
Dialog box	Minimize button	Text box
Dimmed command	Mouse pointer	Title bar
Document window	On-line help	Undo command
Double click	Open command	Value
Drag	Open list box	Window
Drop-down list box	Option button	

Multiple Choice

1. Which of the following will execute a command from a pull-down menu?
   (a) Clicking on the command once the menu has been pulled down
   (b) Typing the underlined letter in the command
   (c) Both (a) and (b)
   (d) Neither (a) nor (b)

2. The File Open command:
   (a) Brings a spreadsheet from disk into memory
   (b) Brings a spreadsheet from disk into memory, then erases the spreadsheet on disk
   (c) Stores the spreadsheet in memory on disk
   (d) Stores the spreadsheet in memory on disk, then erases the spreadsheet from memory

3. The File Save command:
   (a) Brings a spreadsheet from disk into memory
   (b) Brings a spreadsheet from disk into memory, then erases the spreadsheet on disk
   (c) Stores the spreadsheet in memory on disk
   (d) Stores the spreadsheet in memory on disk, then erases the spreadsheet from memory

4. What is the significance of three dots next to a menu option?
   (a) The option is not accessible
   (b) A dialog box will appear if the option is selected
   (c) A help window will appear if the option is selected
   (d) There are no equivalent keystrokes for the particular option

5. What is the significance of a menu option that appears faded (dimmed)?
   (a) The option is not currently accessible
   (b) A dialog box will appear if the option is selected
   (c) A help window will appear if the option is selected
   (d) There are no equivalent keystrokes for the particular option

6. Which of the following elements may be found within a help window?
   (a) Title bar, menu bar, and control-menu box
   (b) Minimize button and maximize or restore button
   (c) Vertical and/or horizontal scroll bars
   (d) All of the above

7. Which of the following is true regarding a dialog box?
   (a) Option buttons indicate mutually exclusive choices
   (b) Check boxes imply that multiple options may be selected
   (c) Both (a) and (b)
   (d) Neither (a) nor (b)

8. Which of the following correctly matches the label prefix with the indicated alignment?
   (a) An apostrophe and right justification
   (b) A quotation mark and left justification
   (c) Both (a) and (b)
   (d) Neither (a) nor (b)

9. In the absence of parentheses, the order of operations is:
   (a) Exponentiation, addition or subtraction, multiplication or division
   (b) Addition or subtraction, multiplication or division, exponentiation
   (c) Multiplication or division, exponentiation, addition or subtraction
   (d) Exponentiation, multiplication or division, addition or subtraction

10. Once a spreadsheet has been created, you can easily:
    (a) Add new rows and/or columns
    (b) Delete existing rows and/or columns
    (c) Both (a) and (b) above
    (d) Neither (a) nor (b) above

11. The entry @AVG(A4..A6):
    (a) Is invalid because the cells are not contiguous
    (b) Computes the average of cells A4 and A6
    (c) Computes the average of cells A4, A5, and A6
    (d) None of the above

12. What is the effect of typing F5+F6 into a cell *without* a beginning equal sign or other arithmetic operator?
    (a) The entry is equivalent to the formula +F5+F6
    (b) The cell will display the contents of cell F5 plus cell F6
    (c) The entry will be treated as a label and display the literal value F5+F6
    (d) The entry will be rejected by Lotus, which will signal an error message

13. A spreadsheet is superior to manual calculation because:
    (a) The spreadsheet computes its entries faster
    (b) The spreadsheet computes its results more accurately
    (c) The spreadsheet automatically recalculates its results whenever cell contents are changed
    (d) All the above

14. The cell at the intersection of the second column and third row has the address:
    (a) B3
    (b) 3B
    (c) C2
    (d) 2C

15. Assume that you have just completed an entry for cell J6, then press the up arrow key twice, and the left arrow key once. The new current cell is:
    (a) I8
    (b) I4
    (c) K8
    (d) K4

ANSWERS

1. c	**6.** d	**11.** c
2. a	**7.** c	**12.** c
3. c	**8.** d	**13.** d
4. b	**9.** d	**14.** a
5. a	**10.** c	**15.** b

EXPLORING LOTUS

1. Use Figure 1.14 to identify the elements of a Lotus for Windows screen by matching each element with the appropriate number.

    ____ Restore button
    ____ Control-menu box
    ____ SmartIcons
    ____ Scroll bar
    ____ Current cell
    ____ Minimize button

    ____ Contents of the current cell
    ____ Contains the Insert and Delete commands
    ____ Contains the Open and Save commands
    ____ Status bar

2. The Common User Interface: Answer the following with respect to Figures 1.2a and 1.2b that appeared earlier in the chapter.
    a. Which pull-down menus are common to both Lotus and WordPerfect?
    b. How do you access the Edit menu in Lotus? in WordPerfect?
    c. How do you open a file in Lotus for Windows? Do you think the same command will work in WordPerfect as well?
    d. Which icons correspond to the Open and Save commands in Lotus? Which icons correspond to the Open and Save commands in WordPerfect?

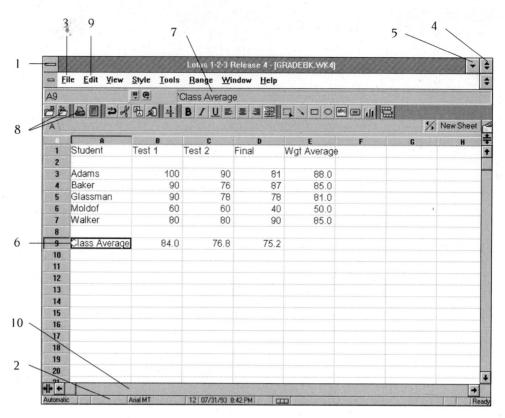

FIGURE 1.14 Screen for Problem 1

e. What do your answers to parts a through d tell you about the advantages of a common user interface? What do the answers imply about applications from different vendors?

3. Troubleshooting: The informational messages in Figure 1.15 appeared (or could have appeared) in response to various commands issued during the chapter.

a. Which command produced the message in Figure 1.15a? What action is necessary to correct the indicated problem?

b. The message in Figure 1.15b is produced when the user exits Lotus, but only under a specific circumstance. When will that message be produced? When would No be an appropriate response to this message?

c. The message in Figure 1.15c appeared in response to a File Open command. What is the most likely reason for the error?

d. The message in Figure 1.15d also appears in response to a File Open command. What corrective action needs to be taken?

4. Exploring Help: Answer the following with respect to Figure 1.16:

a. What is the significance of the scroll box that appears within the scroll bar?

b. What happens if you click on the down (up) arrow within the scroll bar?

c. What happens if you press the maximize button? Might this action eliminate the need to scroll within the help window?

d. How do you print the help topic shown in the window?

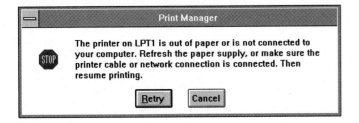

(a) Informational Message 1

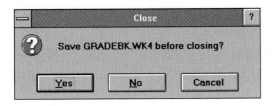

(b) Informational Message 2

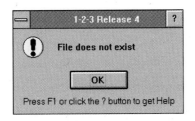

(c) Informational Message 3

(d) Informational Message 4

FIGURE 1.15   Informational Messages for Problem 3

5. Design a spreadsheet that would be useful to you. You might want to consider applications such as an annual budget, the cost of a stereo or computer system, the number of calories you consume (burn) in a day, calculation of federal income tax, and so on. The applications are limited only by your imagination.

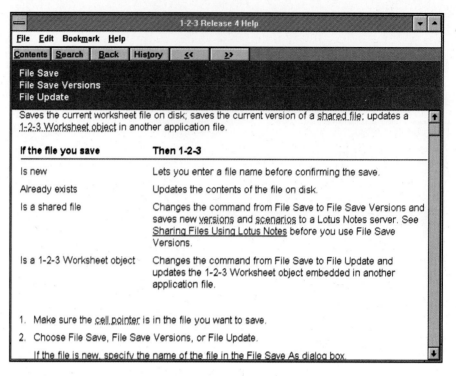

FIGURE 1.16 Help Screen for Problem 4

6. Figure 1.17 contains a simple spreadsheet showing the earnings for Widgets of America, before and after taxes. The cell values in cells B6, B7, and B9 may be produced in several ways, two of which are shown below. For example:

	Method 1	Method 2
Cell B6	10000–4000	+B3–B4
Cell B7	.30*6000	+.30*B6
Cell B9	6000–1800	+B6–B7

Which is the better method and why?

	A	B
1	Widgets of America	
2		
3	Revenue	10000
4	Expenses	4000
5		
6	Earnings before taxes	6000
7	Taxes	1800
8		
9	Earnings after taxes	4200

FIGURE 1.17 Spreadsheet for Problem 6

7. Answer the following with respect to the screen in Figure 1.18, which depicts the use of a spreadsheet in a simplified calculation for income tax.

a. Is the application window for Lotus maximized?

b. Is the document window containing the spreadsheet maximized?

c. What is the current cell?

d. What are the contents of the current cell?

e. Assume that the income in cell B2 changes to $125,000. What other numbers will change automatically?

f. Assume that an additional deduction for local income taxes of $3,000 is entered between rows 9 and 10. Which formula, if any, has to be explicitly changed to accommodate the new deduction?

g. Which formula(s) will change automatically after the row containing the additional deduction has been added to the spreadsheet?

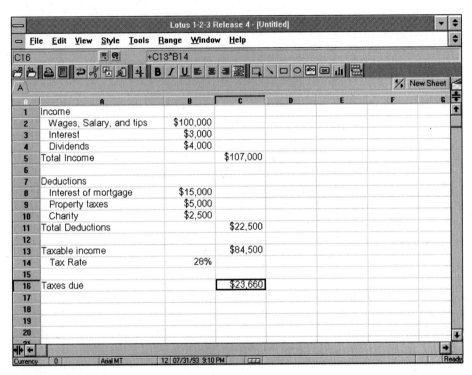

FIGURE 1.18 Spreadsheet for Problem 7

8. Return to the grade book at the end of the second hands-on exercise and implement the following changes:

a. The professor has decided to weigh test 1, test 2, and the final equally, rather than counting the final as two exams.

b. A new student, Milgrom, must be entered on the roster with grades of 88, 80, and 84, respectively.

c. Baker is to be dropped from the class roll.

d. Enter the label, *Grading Assistant,* followed by your name somewhere in the spreadsheet.

e. Print the spreadsheet after all modifications have been made and submit it to your instructor.

9. Figure 1.19 contains a simple profit projection in the form of a spreadsheet that you are to implement in Lotus for Windows. *Be sure to enter formulas rather than numbers where appropriate—for example, in the cells containing gross income, total material cost, total labor cost, total cost, and gross profit.*

a. Add your name somewhere in the spreadsheet and identify yourself as a financial planner. Print the spreadsheet as it appears in Figure 1.19, then implement the following modifications.

b. Change the selling price in cell B4 to 6, which should automatically change several other numbers in the spreadsheet—for example, the gross income in cell B5.

c. Add an overhead expense in cell B12 of $1000 (enter an appropriate label in cell A12), then change the formula in cell B13 to accommodate the additional expense.

d. Assume a tax rate of 30 percent. Enter the formula to compute the anticipated tax in row 16 and the after-tax profit in row 17.

e. Assume that the numbers in column B are for 1994. Create a corresponding forecast for 1995 in column C. Assume that the number of units sold will be 10 percent higher, and that the selling price and all other costs increase by 8 percent.

f. Add column D for 1996, using the same anticipated rates of change.

g. Print the spreadsheet a second time after completing the modifications in parts b through f. Submit both versions of the printed spreadsheet (in part a and part g) to your instructor.

	A	B
1		
2	Income	
3	Number of units	1500
4	Selling price	8
5	Gross income	12000
6		
7	Expenses	
8	Material cost per unit	4
9	Total material cost	6000
10	Labor cost per unit	1
11	Total labor cost	1500
12		
13	Total cost	7500
14		
15	Gross Profit	4500

FIGURE 1.19 Spreadsheet for Problem 9

10. Create a spreadsheet that shows your income and expenses for a typical month according to the format in Figure 1.20. Enter your budget rather than ours.

a. Enter your name in cell A1.

b. Enter the text **Monthly Income** in A3 and the corresponding amount in B3.

c. Enter the text **Monthly Expenses** in A5.

d. Enter at least 5 different expenses in consecutive rows, beginning in A6, and enter the corresponding amounts in column B.

	A	B
1	Maryann Barber's Budget	
2		
3	Monthly income	1000
4		
5	Monthly expenses	
6	Food	250
7	Rent	350
8	Utilities	100
9	Phone	20
10	Gas	40
11	Total Expenses:	760
12		
13	What's left for fun:	240

FIGURE 1.20   Spreadsheet for Problem 10

e. Enter the text **Total Expenses** in the row immediately below your last expense item and then enter the formula to compute the total in the corresponding cell in column B.

g. Skip one blank row and then enter the text ***What's left for fun*** in column A and the formula to compute how much money you have left at the end of the month in column B.

h. Insert a new row eight. Add an additional expense that you left out, entering the text in A8 and the amount in B8. Does the formula for total expenses reflect the additional expense? If not, change the formula so that it does.

i. Change the amount of your monthly income to reflect the fact that you now have a part-time work study position. Do you now have more money left at the end of the month? Did the formula indicating the amount left recompute automatically to reflect the increased income in cell A3?

j. Why did the formula in step h not reflect the change made, while the formula in step i did reflect the change made?

Case Studies

Buying a Computer

You have decided to buy a PC and have settled on a minimum configuration consisting of an entry-level 80486, with 4MB of RAM, and a 100MB hard disk. You would like a modem if it fits into the budget, and you need a printer. You also need software: DOS, Windows, a Windows-based word processor, and a Windows-based spreadsheet. You can spend up to $2,500 and hope that, at today's prices, you can find a system that goes beyond your minimum requirements, such as a system with a faster processor, 8MB of RAM, and a 200MB hard disk. We suggest you shop around and look for educational discounts on software and/or a suite of applications to save money.

Create a spreadsheet based on real data that presents several alternatives. Show different configurations from the same vendor and/or comparable systems from different vendors. Include the vendors' telephone numbers with their estimates. Bring the spreadsheet to class together with the supporting documentation in the form of printed advertisements.

Portfolio Management

A spreadsheet is an ideal vehicle to track the progress of your investments. You need to maintain the name of the company, the number of shares purchased, the date of the purchase, and the purchase price. You can then enter the current price and see immediately the potential gain or loss on each investment as well as the current value of the portfolio. Retrieve the STOCKS.WK4 spreadsheet from the data disk, enter the closing prices of the listed investments, and compute the current value of the portfolio.

Accuracy Counts

The UNDERBID.WK4 spreadsheet on the data disk was the last assignment completed by your predecessor prior to his unfortunate dismissal. The spreadsheet contains a significant error, which caused your company to underbid a contract and assume a subsequent loss of $100,000. As you look for the error, don't be distracted by the attractive formatting. The shading, lines, and other touches are nice, but accuracy is more important than anything else. Write a memo to your instructor describing the nature of the error. Include suggestions in the memo on how to avoid mistakes of this nature in the future.

Planning for Disaster

This case has nothing to do with spreadsheets per se, but it is perhaps the most important case of all, as it deals with the question of backup. Do you have a backup strategy? Do you even know what a backup strategy is? You had better learn, because sooner or later you will wish you had one. You will erase a file, be unable to read from a floppy disk, or worse yet suffer a hardware failure in which you are unable to access the hard drive. The problem always seems to occur the night before an assignment is due. The ultimate disaster is the disappearance of your computer, by theft or natural disaster (e.g., Hurricane Andrew). Describe in 250 words or less the backup strategy you plan to implement in conjunction with your work in this class.

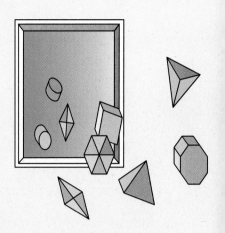

2

Gaining Proficiency: Copying, Moving, and Formatting

CHAPTER OBJECTIVES

After reading this chapter you will be able to:

1. Explain the importance of isolating assumptions within a spreadsheet.

2. Define a cell range; select and deselect ranges within a spreadsheet.

3. Copy and/or move cells within a spreadsheet; differentiate among relative, absolute, and mixed addresses.

4. Format a spreadsheet to include boldface, italics, shading, and borders; change the font and/or alignment of a selected entry.

5. Change the width of a column; explain what happens if a column is too narrow to display the computed result.

6. Print a spreadsheet to show either the computed values or the cell contents.

7. Use the Page Setup command to print a spreadsheet with or without gridlines and/or row and column headings; preview a spreadsheet before printing.

8. Use the status bar to format a spreadsheet; describe the use of SmartIcons within Lotus.

OVERVIEW

This chapter continues the grade book example of Chapter 1. It is perhaps the most important chapter in the entire text as it describes the basic commands to create a spreadsheet. We begin with the definition of a cell range and the commands to build a spreadsheet without regard to its appearance. We focus on the Copy command and the difference between relative and absolute addresses. We stress the importance of isolating the assumptions within a spreadsheet so that alternative strategies may be easily evaluated.

The second half of the chapter presents formatting commands to improve the appearance of a spreadsheet after it has been created. You will be pleased with the dramatic impact you can achieve with a few simple commands, but we emphasize that accuracy in a spreadsheet is much more important than appearance.

The two hands-on exercises are absolutely critical if you are to master the material. As you do the exercises, you will realize that there are many different ways to accomplish the same task. Our approach is to present the most basic way first and the shortcuts later. You will like the shortcuts better, but you may not remember them and hence you need to understand the underlying concepts. You can always find the necessary command from the appropriate menu, and if you don't know the menu, you can always look to on-line help.

A BETTER GRADE BOOK

Figure 2.1 contains a much improved version of the professor's grade book. The most obvious difference is in the appearance of the spreadsheet, as a variety of formatting commands have been used to make it more attractive. The exam scores and weighted averages are centered under the appropriate headings, which have been set in boldface and italics. Shading is also used to emphasize different areas of the spreadsheet, and a title has been added (in a larger typeface) to indicate the course and semester.

Scores are centered

Title added ─────────

Weight of test 1 explicitly entered and then used in formula to compute the student's average

Shading used for emphasis

	A	B	C	D	E
1		CIS 120 - Spring 1994			
2					
3	Student	Test 1	Test 2	Final	Average
4	Costa, Frank	70	80	90	82.5
5	Ford, Judd	70	65	80	73.8
6	Grauer, Jessica	90	80	98	91.5
7	Kinzer, Jessica	80	78	98	88.5
8	Krien, Darren	85	70	95	86.3
9	Moldof, Adam	75	75	80	77.5
10					
11	Class Averages	78.3	74.7	90.2	
12					
13	Exam Weights	20%	25%	50%	

FIGURE 2.1   A Better Grade Book

The most *significant* difference, however, is that the weight of each exam is indicated within the spreadsheet, and further, that the formulas to compute the student averages are based on these values. In other words, the professor can change the contents of the cells containing the exam weights and see immediately the effect on the student averages.

This is one of the most important concepts in the development of a spreadsheet and enables the professor to explore alternative grading strategies. The professor may notice, for example, that the class did significantly better on the final than on either of the first two exams. She may decide to give the class a break and increase the weight of the final relative to the other tests. What if she increases the weight of the final to 60% and decreases the weight of the other tests? What if she decides that the final should count 70%? The effect of these changes is seen instantly simply by entering the new exam weights in the appropriate cells at the bottom of the spreadsheet.

CELL RANGES

Every command in Lotus operates on a cell, or group of cells, known as a **range**. The range may be as small as a single cell or as large as the entire spreadsheet. It may consist of a row or part of a row, a column or part of a column, or a rectangle consisting of multiple rows and columns. In any event, the cells within a range are specified by indicating the diagonally opposite corners, typically the upper-left and lower-right corners of the rectangle—for example, cells A1 through E13 (A1..E13) to indicate the entire spreadsheet in Figure 2.1.

The easiest way to select a range is by dragging the mouse; that is, click at the beginning of the range, press and hold the left mouse button as you move to the end of the range, then release the button. Once selected, the range is highlighted and its cells are affected by any subsequent command. The range remains highlighted until another range is defined, or you click another cell anywhere on the spreadsheet.

DEFINING A RANGE WITH THE KEYBOARD

To define a range with the keyboard, move to the first cell in the range such as the cell in the upper-left corner. Press the **F4 key** to anchor the cell pointer, then move the arrow keys over the remaining cells. Press the **enter key** to complete the range.

COPY COMMAND

The **Copy command** duplicates the contents of a cell, or range of cells, and saves you from having to enter the cell contents individually. It is much easier, for example, to enter the formula to compute the test average once and copy it for the remaining tests, rather than explicitly entering it for every test.

Figure 2.2 indicates how the Copy command can be used to duplicate the formula to compute the class average. The cell(s) that you are copying from, cell B11, is called the **source range,** and the cells that you are copying to, cells C11 to D11, are the **destination** (or target) **range.** The formula is not copied exactly, but adjusted as it is copied, to compute the correct average for the respective tests.

The formula to compute the average on the first test was entered in cell B11 as @AVG(B4..B9). This formula references the cell seven rows above the cell containing the formula (i.e., cell B4 is seven rows above cell B11) as well as cell B9,

	A	B	C	D	E	
1			CIS 120 - Spring 1994			← Absolute address
2						
3	Student	Test 1	Test 2	Final	Average	
4	Costa, Frank	70	80	90	+$B$13*B4+$C$13*C4+$D$13*D4	← Source range
5	Ford, Judd	70	65	80	+$B$13*B5+$C$13*C5+$D$13*D5	
6	Grauer, Jessica	90	80	98	+$B$13*B6+$C$13*C6+$D$13*D6	
7	Kinzer, Jessica	80	78	98	+$B$13*B7+$C$13*C7+$D$13*D7	← Destination range
8	Krien, Darren	85	70	95	+$B$13*B8+$C$13*C8+$D$13*D8	
9	Moldof, Adam	75	75	80	+$B$13*B9+$C$13*C9+$D$13*D9	
10						
11	Class Averages	@AVG(B4..B9)	@AVG(C4..C9)	@AVG(D4..D9)		← Relative address
12						
13	Exam Weights	0.25	0.25	0.5		

Source range   Destination range

FIGURE 2.2   The Copy Command

which is two rows above the formula. When the formula in cell B11 is copied to C11, it is adjusted so that the cells referenced in cell C11 are in the same relative position as those referenced by the formula in cell B11—that is, seven and two rows above the formula itself. Thus the formula in cell C11 becomes @AVG(C4..C9), and in similar fashion, the formula in cell D11 becomes @AVG(D4..D9).

Figure 2.2 also shows how the Copy command is used to copy the formula for a student's weighted average, from cell E4 (the source range) to cells E5 through E9 (the destination range). This is slightly more complicated than the previous example, because the formula is based on a student's grades, which vary from one student to the next, and on the exam weights, which do not. The cells referring to the student's grades should adjust as the formula is copied, but the addresses referencing the weights should not.

The distinction between cell references that remain constant versus cell addresses that change is made through a dollar sign. An **absolute reference** remains constant throughout the copy operation and is specified with a dollar sign in front of the column and row designation, such as $B$13. A **relative reference,** on the other hand, changes during a copy operation and is specified without dollar signs, such as B4. (A **mixed reference** uses a single dollar sign to make the row relative and the column absolute—as in $A5—or vice versa, to make the row absolute and the column relative, as in A$5. Mixed references are not discussed further.)

Consider, for example, the formula to compute a student's weighted average as it appears in cell E4 of Figure 2.2:

+$B$13*B4+$C$13*C4+$D$13*D4

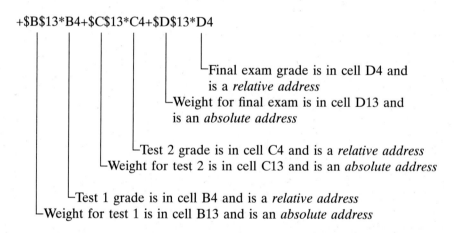

Final exam grade is in cell D4 and is a *relative address*
Weight for final exam is in cell D13 and is an *absolute address*

Test 2 grade is in cell C4 and is a *relative address*
Weight for test 2 is in cell C13 and is an *absolute address*

Test 1 grade is in cell B4 and is a *relative address*
Weight for test 1 is in cell B13 and is an *absolute address*

The formula in cell E4 uses a combination of relative and absolute addresses to compute the student's weighted average. Relative addresses are used for the exam grades (found in cells B4, C4, and D4) and change automatically when the formula is copied to the other rows. Absolute addresses are used for the exam weights (found in cells B13, C13, and D13) and remain constant from student to student.

The copy operation is implemented by using the Windows **clipboard** and a combination of the Copy and **Paste commands** from the Edit menu. The contents of the source range are copied to the clipboard from where they are pasted to the destination range. The contents of the clipboard change with each subsequent Copy command, but are unaffected by the Paste command; you can execute the Paste command several times in succession, to paste the contents of the clipboard to multiple locations in a document.

MOVE COMMAND

The **Move command** is not used in the grade book, but its presentation is essential for the sake of completeness. The Move command transfers the contents of a cell (or range of cells) from one location to another. After the move is completed, the cells where the move originated (that is, the source range) are empty. This is in contrast to the Copy command, where the entries remain in the source range and are duplicated in the destination range.

A simple move operation is depicted in Figure 2.3a, in which the contents of cell A3 are moved to cell C3, with the formula in cell C3 unchanged after the move. In other words, the Move command simply picks up the contents of cell A3 (to add the values in cells A1 and A2), and puts it down in cell C3. The source range, cell A3, is empty after the Move command has been executed.

Figure 2.3b depicts a situation where the formula itself remains in the same cell, but one of the values it references is moved to a new location—that is, the entry in A1 is moved to C1. The formula in cell A3 is adjusted to follow the moved entry to its new location, so the formula is now +C1+A2.

The situation is different in Figure 2.3c as the contents of all three cells—A1, A2, and A3—are moved. After the move has taken place, cells C1 and C2 contain the 5 and the 2, respectively, with the formula in cell C3 adjusted to reflect the movement of the contents of cells A1 and A2. Once again the source range (column A) is empty after the move is completed.

Figure 2.3d contains an additional formula in cell B1, which is *dependent* on cell A3, which in turn is moved to cell C3. The formula in cell C3 is unchanged after the move because *only* the formula was moved, *not* the values it referenced. The contents of cell B1 were changed even though cell B1 never moved, because cell B1 refers to an entry (A3) that was transferred to a new location (C3).

Figure 2.3e shows that the specification of an absolute address has no meaning in a Move command. Absolute addresses are treated exactly the same as relative

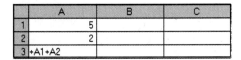

	A	B	C
1	5		
2	2		
3	+A1+A2		

	A	B	C
1	5		
2	2		
3			+A1+A2

Contents of A3 moved to C3

(a) Example 1 (only cell A3 is moved)

	A	B	C
1	5		
2	2		
3	+A1+A2		

	A	B	C
1			5
2	2		
3	+C1+A2		

Contents of A1 moved to C1

Cell address adjusts to follow moved entry

(b) Example 2 (only cell A1 is moved)

	A	B	C
1	5		
2	2		
3	+A1+A2		

	A	B	C
1			5
2			2
3			+C1+C2

Contents of all 3 cells moved to column C

Cell addresses adjust to follow moved entries

(c) Example 3 (all three cells in column A are moved)

	A	B	C
1	5	+A3*4	
2	2		
3	+A1+A2		

	A	B	C
1	5	+C3*4	
2	2		
3			+A1+A2

Cell address adjusts to follow moved entry

Contents of A3 moved to C3

(d) Example 4 (dependent cells)

	A	B	C
1	5	+$A$3*4	
2	2		
3	+$A$1+$A$2		

	A	B	C
1		+$C$3*4	5
2			2
3			+$C$1+$C$2

Absolute addresses treated the same as relative addresses in a move operation

(e) Example 5 (absolute cell addresses)

FIGURE 2.3 The Move Command

addresses and are adjusted as necessary to reflect the move operation. The example combines Figures 2.3b and 2.3c and shows that all of the absolute references were changed to reflect the Move command.

The Move command is a convenient way to improve the appearance of a spreadsheet after it has been developed. It is subtle in its operation, and we suggest you think twice before moving cell entries because of the complexities involved.

The move operation is implemented by using the Windows clipboard and a combination of the Cut and Paste commands from the Edit menu. The contents of the source range are transferred to the clipboard from where they are pasted to the destination range.

HANDS-ON EXERCISE 1:

Creating a Spreadsheet

Objective To build the spreadsheet of Figure 2.1 without regard to its appearance; to create a formula containing relative and absolute references; to use the Copy command within a spreadsheet. Use Figure 2.4 as a guide in doing the exercise.

Step 1: Enter the column headings
➤ Load Lotus as you did in the previous chapter.
➤ Click in cell **A1**. Enter the title of the spreadsheet, **CIS120–Spring 1994,** as in Figure 2.4a.
➤ Press the **down arrow key** twice to move to cell **A3**. Type **Student.**
➤ Press the **right arrow key** to move to cell **B3**. Type **Test 1.**
➤ Press the **right arrow key** to move to cell **C3**. Type **Test 2.** Type **Final** in cell D3 and **Average** in cell **E3.**

Step 2: Save the spreadsheet
➤ Pull down the **File menu.** Click **Save.**
➤ Click drive A or drive C, depending on whether you installed the data disk.
➤ Double click the **LOTDATA** directory to make it the active directory.
➤ Type **MYGRADES** as the name of the spreadsheet as in Figure 2.4a. Press the **enter key.**

Step 3: Enter the student data and literal information
➤ Click in cell **A4** and type **Costa, Frank.**
➤ Move across row four and enter Frank's grades on the two tests and the final. Use Figure 2.4b as a guide. Do *not* enter Frank's average in cell E4 as that will be entered as a formula in step 4.
➤ Do *not* be concerned that you cannot see Frank's entire name because the default width of column A is not yet wide enough to display the entire name.
➤ Enter the names and grades for the other students in rows 5 through 9. Do *not* enter their averages.
➤ Complete the entries in column A by typing **Class Averages** and **Exam Weights** in cells **A11** and **A13,** respectively.
➤ Save the spreadsheet.

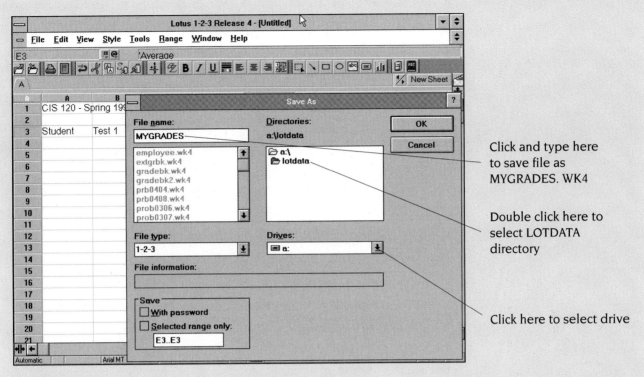

Click and type here
to save file as
MYGRADES. WK4

Double click here to
select LOTDATA
directory

Click here to select drive

(a) Dialog Box for Save Command (step 2)

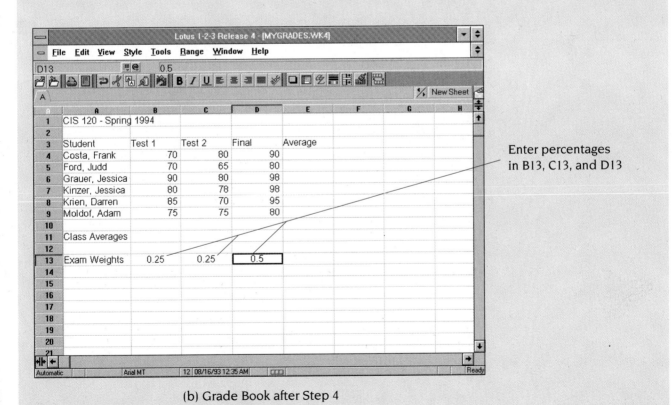

Enter percentages
in B13, C13, and D13

(b) Grade Book after Step 4

FIGURE 2.4   Hands-on Exercise 1

Step 4: Enter the exam weights
- Click in cell **B13** and enter **.25,** the weight for the first exam.
- Press the **right arrow key** to move to cell **C13** and enter **.25,** the weight for the second exam.
- Press the **right arrow key** to move to cell **D13** and enter **.5,** the weight for the final. Do *not* be concerned that the exam weights do not appear as percentages; they will be formatted in the second exercise later in the chapter.
- The spreadsheet should match Figure 2.4b.

Step 5: Compute the weighted average for the first student
- Click in cell **E4** and type the formula **+\$B\$13*B4+\$C\$13*C4+\$D\$13*D4** to compute the weighted average for the first student. Press the **enter key** when you have completed the formula.
- Check that the displayed value in cell E4 is 82.5, which indicates you entered the formula correctly.
- Save the spreadsheet.

CORRECTING MISTAKES

Change the contents of a cell without having to retype the entire contents. Double click the cell whose formula you want to change, then use the **right** and **left arrow keys** (or click where appropriate) to position yourself at the point of correction. You can make the change in either the cell itself or on the edit line. Press the **Ins key** to toggle between insertion and replacement and/or use the **Del key** to delete a character. Press the **Home** and **End keys** to move to the first and last characters, respectively.

Step 6: Copy the weighted average
- Check that cell **E4,** the source range for the Copy command, is still selected.
- Pull down the **Edit menu** as in Figure 2.4c.
- Click **Copy;** you will see the message *Select destination and choose Edit Paste* at the top of the spreadsheet in the left of the title bar.
- Click cell **E5.** Drag the mouse over cells **E5** through **E9** to select the destination range as in Figure 2.4d.
- Pull down the **Edit menu** and click **Paste** to copy the contents of the clipboard to the destination range. You should see the weighted averages for the other students in cells E5 through E9.
- Press **Esc** (or click anywhere in the spreadsheet) to deselect cells E5 through E9.
- Save the spreadsheet.

KEYBOARD SHORTCUTS: CUT, COPY, AND PASTE

Ctrl+X, Ctrl+C, and **Ctrl+V** are shortcuts to cut, copy, and paste, respectively, and apply to Lotus as well as Windows applications in general. The shortcuts are easier to remember when you realize that the operative letters, X, C, and V, are next to each other at the bottom-left side of the keyboard.

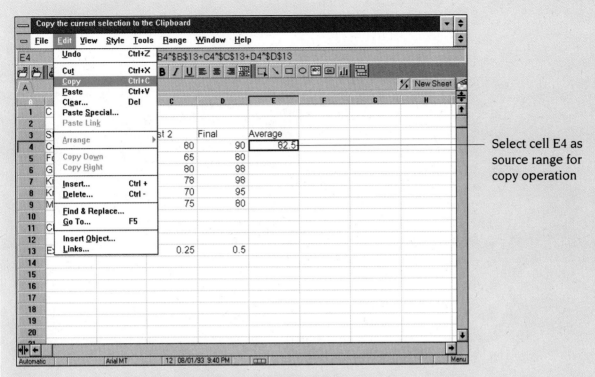

(c) The Copy Command (steps 5 & 6)

Select cell E4 as source range for copy operation

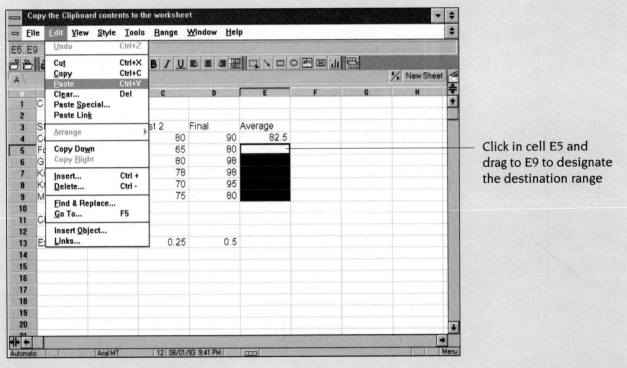

(d) The Destination Range (step 6)

Click in cell E5 and drag to E9 to designate the destination range

FIGURE 2.4 Hands-on Exercise 1 (continued)

Step 7: Compute the class averages

➤ Click in cell **B11** and type the formula **@AVG(B4..B9)** to compute the class average on the first test. Press the **enter key** when you have completed the formula.

➤ Pull down the **Edit menu** and click **Copy.**

➤ Click cell **C11.** Drag the mouse over cells **C11** and **D11,** the destination range for the Copy command.

➤ Pull down the **Edit menu** and click **Paste** to copy the contents of the clipboard to the destination range.

➤ Click anywhere in the spreadsheet to deselect cells C11 through D11.

THE UNDO COMMAND

The *Undo command* reverses the effect of the last operation and is invaluable at any time, but especially when you are learning. Pull down the **Edit menu** and click **Undo** to cancel the effects of a Copy or Move command and restore the spreadsheet to its previous state. If you are unable to execute the Undo command (because it appears as a dimmed command within the Edit menu), pull down the **Tools menu,** click **User Setup,** then click the **Undo check box.**

Step 8: What if? Change the exam weights

➤ Change the entries in cells **B13** and **C13** to **.20** and the entry in cell **D13** to **.60.** The weighted averages for every student change automatically; for example, Costa and Moldof change to 84 and 78, respectively.

➤ The professor decides this does not make a significant difference and goes back to the original weights; reenter **.25, .25,** and **.50** in cells B13, C13, and D13, respectively.

LIMITATIONS OF THE UNDO COMMAND

The Undo command must be executed immediately after a mistake is made; that is, you cannot delete a row, execute one or more additional commands, then expect the Undo command to restore the deleted row. Some commands cannot be undone at all. Once you save a file, for instance, the previous version of that file is erased from the disk and cannot be restored.

Step 9: Save the completed spreadsheet

➤ Pull down the **File menu** and save the spreadsheet a final time.

➤ Exit Lotus if you are not ready to begin the next exercise.

FORMATTING

The professor's grade book is developed in two stages as in Figure 2.5. The exercise just completed created the grade book, but paid no attention to its appearance. It had you enter the data for every student, develop the formulas to compute the average for every student based on exam weights at the bottom of the spreadsheet, and finally, develop the formulas to compute the class averages for each exam.

Figure 2.5a shows the grade book as it exists at the end of the first hands-on exercise. Figure 2.5b shows the grade book at the end of the second exercise after it has been formatted. The differences between the two are due entirely to various formatting commands. Consider:

➤ The exam weights are formatted as percentages in Figure 2.5b as opposed to decimals in Figure 2.5a. The class and student averages are displayed with a single decimal point in Figure 2.5b versus a variable number of places in Figure 2.5a.

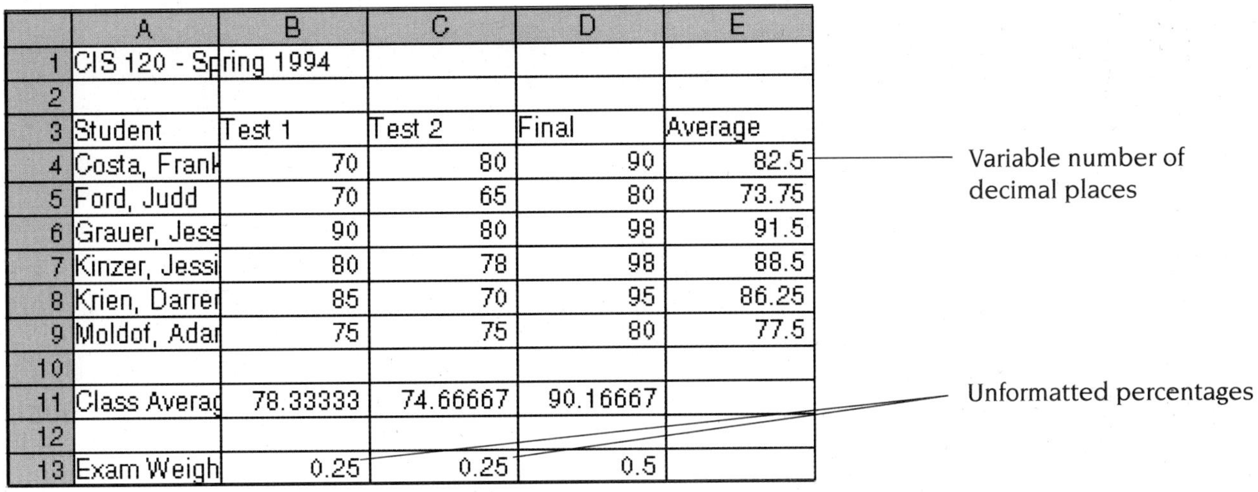

	A	B	C	D	E	
1	CIS 120 - Spring 1994					
2						
3	Student	Test 1	Test 2	Final	Average	
4	Costa, Frank	70	80	90	82.5	—— Variable number of decimal places
5	Ford, Judd	70	65	80	73.75	
6	Grauer, Jess	90	80	98	91.5	
7	Kinzer, Jessi	80	78	98	88.5	
8	Krien, Darrer	85	70	95	86.25	
9	Moldof, Adar	75	75	80	77.5	
10						
11	Class Averag	78.33333	74.66667	90.16667		—— Unformatted percentages
12						
13	Exam Weigh	0.25	0.25	0.5		

(a) At the End of Exercise 1

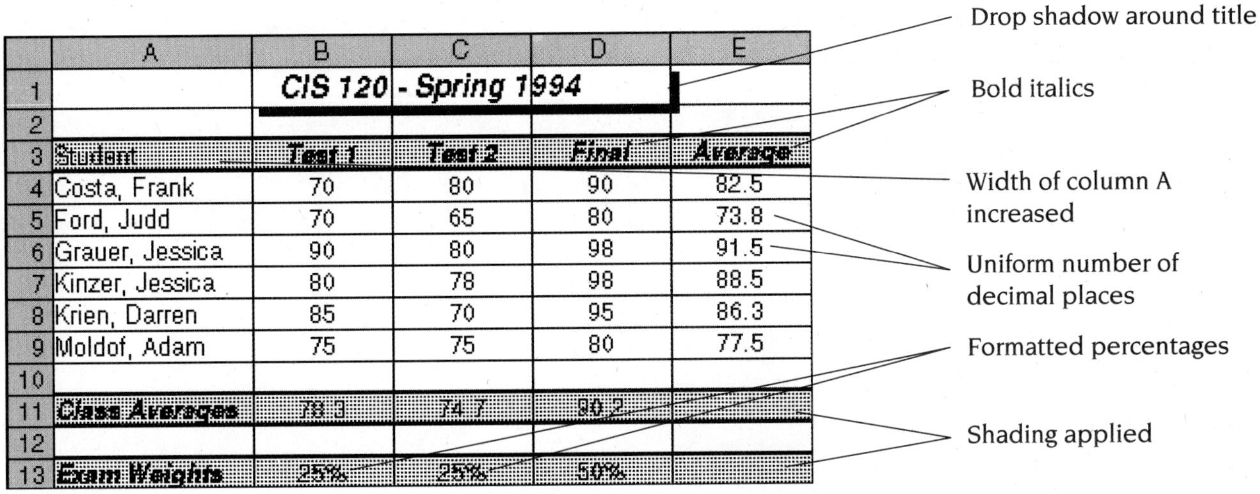

	A	B	C	D	E	
1		*CIS 120 - Spring 1994*			■	—— Drop shadow around title
2						—— Bold italics
3	*Student*	*Test 1*	*Test 2*	*Final*	*Average*	
4	Costa, Frank	70	80	90	82.5	—— Width of column A increased
5	Ford, Judd	70	65	80	73.8	
6	Grauer, Jessica	90	80	98	91.5	—— Uniform number of decimal places
7	Kinzer, Jessica	80	78	98	88.5	
8	Krien, Darren	85	70	95	86.3	
9	Moldof, Adam	75	75	80	77.5	—— Formatted percentages
10						
11	*Class Averages*	78.3	74.7	90.2		—— Shading applied
12						
13	*Exam Weights*	25%	25%	50%		

(b) At the End of Exercise 2

FIGURE 2.5 Developing the Grade Book

➤ Boldface and italics are used for emphasis as are shading and borders.

➤ Exam grades and computed averages are centered under their respective headings.

➤ The spreadsheet title is set in larger type and centered across all five columns.

➤ The width of column A has been increased in Figure 2.5b so that the students' names are completely visible.

Formatting is done within the context of *select-then-do;* that is, select the range to which the formatting is to apply, then execute the appropriate command from within the ***Style menu*** (or click the corresponding SmartIcon). You can, however, reverse the sequence; you can select the format, then specify the range by using the range box within the various formatting commands. The Style menu contains separate commands for Number Formats, Alignment, Fonts and Attributes, and Lines and Colors.

THE ACTIVE CELL VERSUS THE SELECTED CELLS

The active (current) cell is the one into which data is entered when you type an entry. The selected cell(s) is (are) the one(s) that will be affected by any commands executed. The active cell is one of the selected cells, but not all selected cells are active; there is only one active cell at a time.

Number Formats

Numerical entries can be displayed in a variety of ***number formats*** according to the list box in Figure 2.6a. Each format enables you to increase (decrease) the number of decimals by clicking the up (down) arrow within the dialog box. A brief explanation of numeric formats is provided below with additional information available through on-line help. (Click the ? at the right of the title bar or press the F1 key.)

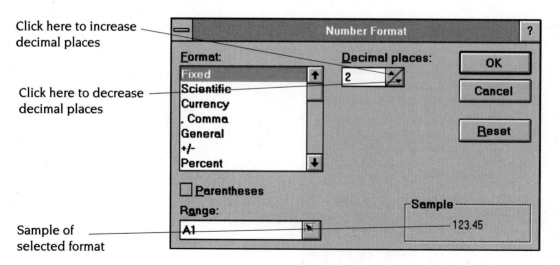

(a) Number Format

FIGURE 2.6 The Style Menu

- **Currency format** displays the currency symbol, commas as appropriate, and up to 15 decimal places. **Comma format** is the same as currency format except the currency symbol is omitted.

- **Fixed format** displays a number with up to 15 decimal places, a minus sign to indicate a negative number, and a leading zero for decimal values. **General format** is similar to fixed format except that trailing (insignificant) zeros are not printed to the right of the decimal point.

- **Percent format** displays numbers as percentages; that is, the number is multiplied by 100 for display purposes only. A percent sign follows the number, and up to 15 decimal places can be specified.

- **Scientific format** displays a number as a decimal fraction followed by a whole number exponent of 10; for example, the number 12345 would appear as 1.2345E+04. The exponent, +04 in the example, is the number of places the decimal point is moved to the right or (if the exponent is negative) left. Very small numbers have negative exponents; for example, the entry .0000012 would be displayed as 1.2E−06. Scientific notation is used only with very large or very small numbers and is generally not used in a business environment.

- **+/− format** is of limited use as it displays a bar of plus or minus signs equal to the integer value of the entry; for example, the number 3.2 would be displayed as a series of three plus signs.

- **Date format** displays a date number in one of several formats according to the way the date was entered, such as 3/16/94 or 16-Mar-94. Dates are further discussed in Chapter 3.

- **Automatic format** is the default numeric format that displays a number according to the way it was entered. Entering $100 or 100%, for example, displays the number in currency and percent format, respectively; entering 100 or 100.1 leaves the number unformatted.

Alignment

Any entry may be horizontally and/or vertically aligned as indicated by the dialog box of Figure 2.6b. The options for horizontal **alignment** include left, center,

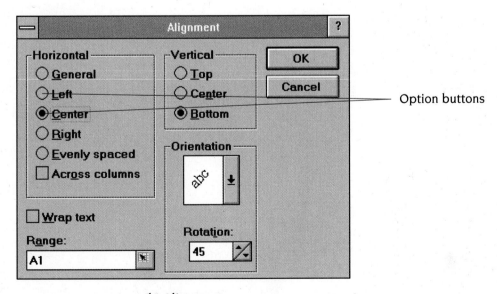

(b) Alignment

FIGURE 2.6 The Style Menu (continued)

right, and full justification. The default (horizontal alignment) is general, which left justifies a label and right justifies a numeric entry. You can also center an entry across a range of selected cells as in the grade book of Figure 2.5b, which centered the title in cell A1 across columns A through E.

Vertical alignment is important only if the row height is changed so that the characters are smaller than the height of the row. Text can be vertically aligned at the top, center, or bottom (the default) of a cell.

It is also possible to wrap the text within a cell to emulate the word wrap capability of a word processor. And finally, you can achieve some very interesting effects by choosing a different orientation. You can, for example, print text vertically within a cell, upside down, or diagonally at any angle such as the 45 degree angle in Figure 2.6b.

Fonts and Attributes

Windows 3.1 includes a new type of font technology known as **TrueType.** True-Type is installed automatically with Windows and is available from any application; that is, you can use the same fonts in Lotus as you do in WordPerfect. All TrueType fonts are scalable, allowing you to select any **point size** from 4 to 127 points (there are 72 points to the inch). And finally, TrueType fonts are truly WYSIWYG (What You See Is What You Get), meaning that the spreadsheet you see on the monitor will match the spreadsheet produced by the printer.

Windows includes a limited number of TrueType fonts: *Arial, Times New Roman, Courier New, Symbol,* and *Wingdings,* which offer sufficient variety to produce some truly impressive spreadsheets. Additional fonts are available from Microsoft and/or other vendors.

Any entry in a spreadsheet may be displayed in any font or point size. All you do is select a range, pull down the Style menu, and choose the **Fonts & Attributes command** to produce the dialog box of Figure 2.6c. The example shows Arial, Bold Italic, and 14 points, and corresponds to the selection for the spreadsheet title in the improved grade book. You can even select a different color, but you will need a color monitor and/or color printer to see the effect.

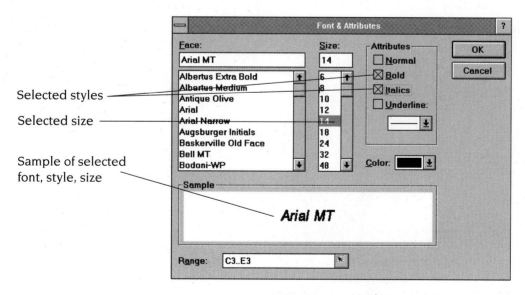

(c) Fonts & Attributes

FIGURE 2.6   The Style Menu (continued)

Lines and Colors

The **Lines & Color command** enables you to create a border and/or shade a cell or cell range for additional emphasis. You can display different entries in color provided you have a color monitor, but you will need a color printer to print in color. You can choose a different style for each line of a border (left, right, top, or bottom) by clicking the appropriate check box to select the side, then making the line selection from the drop-down list box. Shading is achieved by selecting a pattern as shown in Figure 2.6d.

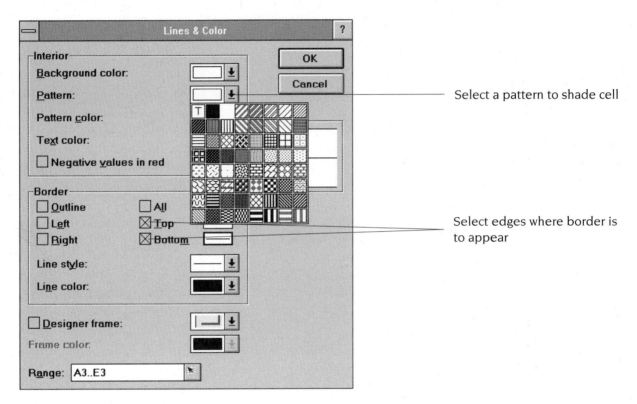

(d) Lines & Color

FIGURE 2.6   The Style Menu (continued)

Column Widths

The column width affects the appearance of a spreadsheet when that width is insufficient to display the entry in the intended format. The student names in Figure 2.5a are not completely visible because column A is too narrow. The contents of the affected cells are not changed; that is, cells A4 through A9 still contain the complete student names, but because the adjacent cells in column B are not empty, the entries appear truncated (cut off) at the cell width.

The situation is different for the spreadsheet title in cell A1. Column A is still too narrow to display the entire title, but because the adjacent cell (cell B1) is empty, the contents of cell A1 are completely visible.

Numbers are treated differently than text if the column width is insufficient to display the number. Lotus displays a series of asterisks (****) to indicate the cell is too narrow to display the number in its current format. To correct the problem, increase the cell width using the **Column Width command** in the Style menu, and/or change the format; for example, display the number with fewer decimal places.

Row Heights

The row height changes automatically as the font size is increased. Row 1 in Figure 2.5b, for example has a greater height than the other rows to accommodate the larger font size in the title of the spreadsheet. The row height can also be changed manually through the **Row Height command** in the Style menu.

CHANGING ROW HEIGHTS AND COLUMN WIDTHS

The easiest way to change the column width is to drag the border between the column labels; to increase the width of column A, for instance, drag the border between column labels A and B to the right. The same technique will change the height of a row; for example, to increase the height of row 1, drag the border between row labels 1 and 2 toward row 2.

SMARTICONS

Until now we have used only the default set of **SmartIcons** which appear at the top of a spreadsheet. There are, however, multiple sets of SmartIcons, and further, each set can be customized to include (remove) additional icons. You can also create your own set of SmartIcons, which is completely customized to the way you work.

All of the options associated with SmartIcons are selected from the dialog box of Figure 2.7, which is produced by clicking on SmartIcons within the Tools menu. You can change the position of the icons within the worksheet by clicking the arrow for the position list box and choosing an alternate location, such as the left, right, or bottom of the document window. You can change the size of the icons by clicking the indicated command button.

To change the icons themselves, click the list box near the top of the window and select an alternate set; for example, the formatting icons as will be done

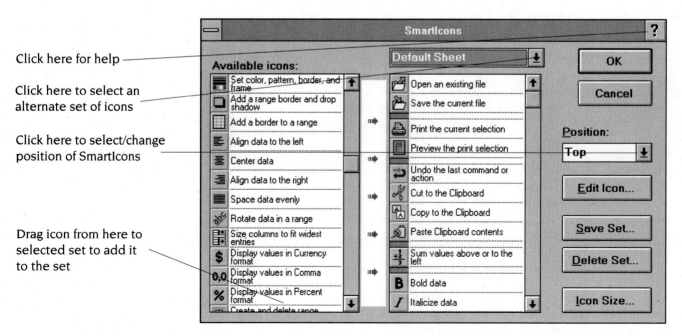

Click here for help

Click here to select an alternate set of icons

Click here to select/change position of SmartIcons

Drag icon from here to selected set to add it to the set

FIGURE 2.7   SmartIcons

in the ensuing hands-on exercise. You can also add icons to the selected set by dragging an icon from the available icons in the list box at the left to the list box in the center. The question mark in the upper-right corner provides immediate access to on-line help with additional information on each of these options.

VARIATIONS IN PRINTING

The final way to control the appearance of a spreadsheet is through printing; for example, you can print a spreadsheet with or without the worksheet frame and/or with or without the cell gridlines. These and other options are controlled by the Page Setup command. You can also view a spreadsheet prior to printing through the Print Preview command. Both commands are executed from the File menu and are illustrated in Figure 2.8.

The Page Setup Command

The *Page Setup command* gives you complete control of the printed page. You can force the output to fit on one page by changing the page size, margins, and/or orientation from *portrait* (8½ by 11) to *landscape* (11 × 8½). You can add the worksheet frame and/or the cell gridlines. You can add a header and/or a footer, the date, time, page number, and other information about the spreadsheet.

The *header* and *footer* are each divided into three sections (left, center, and right) represented by three text boxes within the Page Setup window. Click in the appropriate text box, then enter the desired information; for example, type the word Page in the center section of the footer, then click the page number icon to insert the actual page number. Many of the options may not appear important now, but you will appreciate them as you develop larger and more complicated spreadsheets later in the text.

Remember, too, the conventions associated with a dialog box and the distinction between option buttons and check boxes. Option buttons indicate mutually exclusive choices, one of which *must* be selected; for example, a spreadsheet is printed in either portrait or landscape orientation. Check boxes, on the other hand, allow you to select many (no) options, such as row and column headings *and* cell gridlines.

KEYBOARD SHORTCUTS: THE DIALOG BOX

Press **Tab** (**Shift+Tab**) to move forward (backward) between fields in a dialog box or press the **Alt key** plus the underlined letter to move directly to an option. Use the **space bar** to toggle check boxes on or off and the **up (down) arrow keys** to move between options in a list box. Press **enter** to activate the highlighted command button and **Esc** to exit the dialog box without accepting the changes.

The Print Preview Command

The *Print Preview command* lets you view the completed spreadsheet before printing. It is invaluable and will save you considerable time as you don't have to rely on trial and error to obtain the perfect printout. The command is illustrated in Figure 2.8b, which displays a spreadsheet consistent with the options selected in Figure 2.8a.

The spreadsheet in the figure is printed sideways (landscape) with the worksheet frame and gridlines. The header includes the date and time the spreadsheet was printed and the name of the file on disk. The footer consists of the page number.

Click here to select
landscape (11 × 8½)
orientation

Date

File name

Time

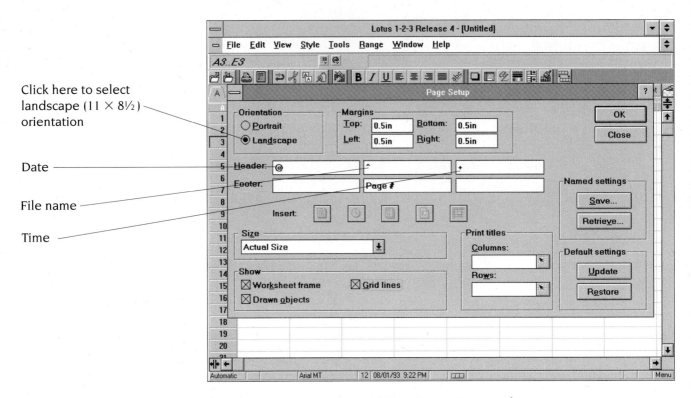

(a) Page Setup Command

Date   File name   Time

Header

Row and column
headings

Landscape orientation

Footer

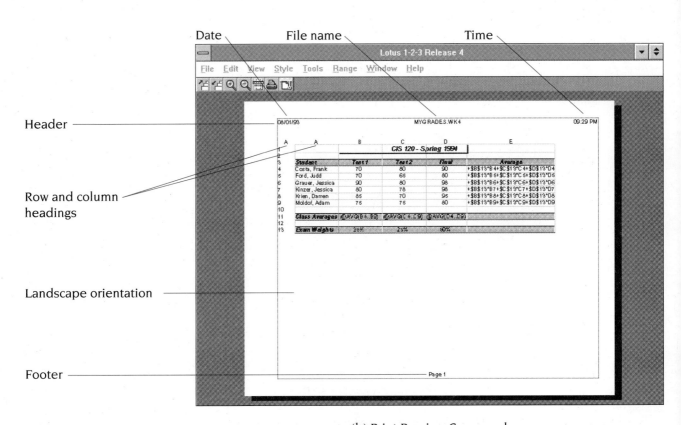

(b) Print Preview Command

FIGURE 2.8 Variations in Printing

CELL CONTENTS

A spreadsheet should always be printed twice, once to show the computed results, and once to show the cell contents. You should, however, **save the spreadsheet** prior to printing the cell contents or else you will lose the formatting in effect.

To print the cell contents, select the entire spreadsheet, then click the **formatting box** at the left of the status bar. Click **text,** then adjust the column widths as necessary to accommodate the cell formulas. Print the spreadsheet in the normal fashion with the worksheet frame and cell gridlines visible.

Pull down the **File menu** and **close** the spreadsheet, but click **No** when asked whether you want to save the changes. The next time you open the spreadsheet the original formatting will be in effect.

HANDS-ON EXERCISE 2:

Formatting a Spreadsheet

Objective To format a spreadsheet to include boldface, italics, shading, and borders; to change the font and/or alignment of a selected entry; to change the width of a column; to print the cell contents as well as the computed values. Use Figure 2.9 as a guide in doing the exercise.

Step 1: SmartIcons
➤ Load Lotus. Pull down the **Tools menu.** Click **SmartIcons.**
➤ Pull down the list box containing the available sets of SmartIcons.
➤ Click **Formatting.** Click **OK.**
➤ The formatting SmartIcons are displayed in the spreadsheet window.

Step 2: The spreadsheet title
➤ Retrieve the **MYGRADES.WK4** spreadsheet from the first exercise.
➤ Click in cell **A1** to select the cell containing the title of the spreadsheet.
➤ Pull down the **Style** menu. Click **Fonts & Attributes.**
➤ Click **Arial** from the font list box. Choose **14** from the size list box.
➤ Click the **Bold** and **Italics** check boxes.
➤ Click the **OK** command button to return to the spreadsheet. Check that cell A1 is still the current cell.
➤ Pull down the **Style menu** a second time.
➤ Click **Alignment.**
➤ Click the **Center command button.** Check the **Across columns** check box.
➤ Click the arrow in the range text box as shown in Figure 2.9a.
➤ Click in cell **A1.** Drag the mouse across cells A1 through E1.
➤ Click **OK** to center the entry in cell A1 over the selected range (cells A1 through E1).
➤ Select cells **B1 through D1.** Click the **Drop Shadow SmartIcon** to produce the effect in Figure 2.9b.

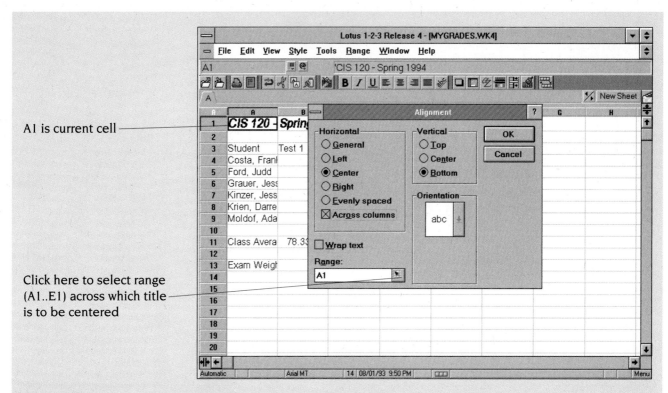

Al is current cell

Click here to select range
(A1..E1) across which title
is to be centered

(a) Centering across Columns (step 2)

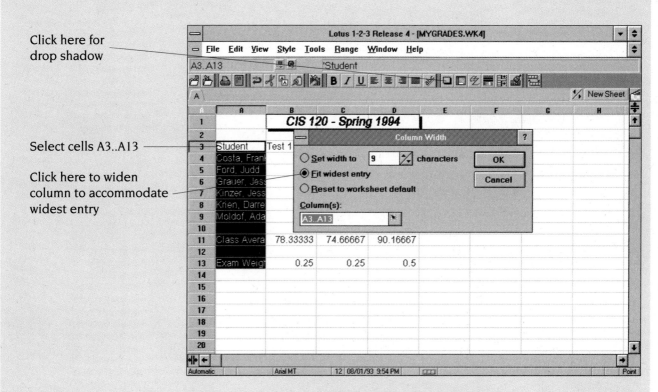

Click here for
drop shadow

Select cells A3..A13

Click here to widen
column to accommodate
widest entry

(b) Changing Column Width (step 3)

FIGURE 2.9   Hands-on Exercise 2

Step 3: Increase the width of column A

➤ Click in cell **A3.** Drag the mouse over cells **A3** through **A13.**

➤ Pull down the **Style menu** and click **Column Width** to produce the window of Figure 2.9b.

➤ Click the **Fit widest entry button.** Click **OK.**

➤ Click the **Save SmartIcon** to save the spreadsheet.

QUIT WITHOUT SAVING

There will be times when you do not want to save the changes to a spreadsheet such as when you have edited it beyond recognition and wish you had never started. The Undo command, useful as it is, reverses only the last operation and is of no use if you need to cancel all changes. Pull down the **File menu** and click the **Close command,** then click **No** in response to the message asking whether to save the changes to the spreadsheet. Pull down the **File menu,** click **Open** to reopen the file, then begin all over.

Step 4: Format the exam weights (Style menu)

➤ Click in cell **B13.** Drag the mouse over cells **B13** through **D13.**

➤ Pull down the **Style menu.**

➤ Click **Number Format.**

➤ Click **Percent** in the open list box.

➤ Click the decimal place text box and enter **0** as the number of decimal places.

➤ Click the **OK** command button. The exam weights are in percent format with zero decimals.

THE STATUS BAR

The status bar is the fastest way to change the format of the selected cells. Click the leftmost box on the status bar to provide a list of numeric formats, then click the desired format. In similar fashion you can click the adjacent areas on the status bar to change the number of decimal places, the typeface, and point size.

Step 5: Format the exam weights (status bar)

➤ Check that cells **B13** through **D13** are still highlighted.

➤ Pull down the **Edit menu.**

➤ Click **Clear** to produce the window in Figure 2.9c.

➤ Click **Styles only,** then click **OK** to remove the formatting from the selected cells.

➤ Check that cells B13 through D13 are still selected.

➤ Click the **formatting box** at the left of the status bar to display the numeric formats as shown in Figure 2.9d. Click **percent.**

Clears entry,
formatting remains

Clears formatting
only, entry remains

Clears entry and
formatting

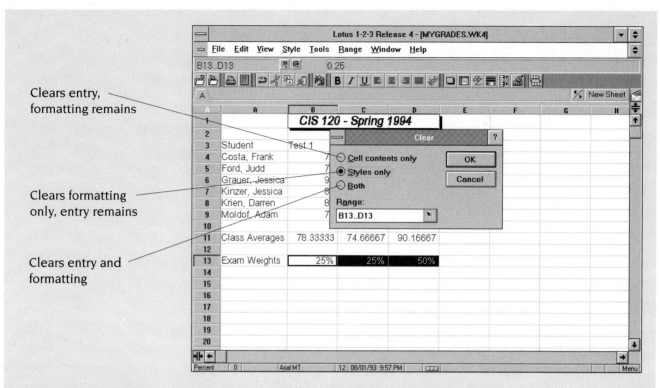

(c) Edit Clear Command (step 5)

Click here to select
numeric format

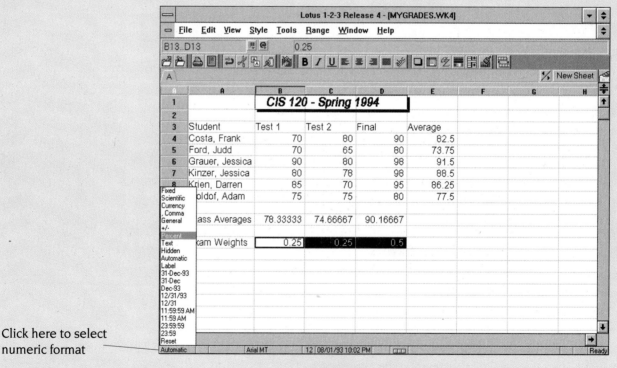

(d) The Status Bar (step 5)

FIGURE 2.9   Hands-on Exercise 2 (continued)

➤ Check that cells B13 through D13 are still selected. Click the second box at the left of the status bar to display the number of decimal points. Click **0**. The exam weights are again in percent format with zero decimals.

➤ Save the spreadsheet.

THE DEL KEY VERSUS THE DELETE COMMAND

The **Del key** is equivalent to the **Edit Clear Cell Contents** command, but is different from the **Edit Delete** command. The **Del key** erases the contents of the selected cells (while retaining the formatting) but does not remove the selected cells from the spreadsheet. This is different from the **Edit Delete** command, which removes the selected row(s) or column(s) from the spreadsheet, causing all other cell addresses to adjust. The keystroke combination **Ctrl+Del** is equivalent to the **Edit Clear Both** command and erases both contents and formatting.

Step 6: Noncontiguous ranges

➤ Select cells **B11** through **D11,** the cells that contain the class averages for the three exams.

➤ Press *and* hold the **Ctrl key** and click cell **E4.** Continue to press the **Ctrl key** and drag the mouse over cells **E4** through **E9.** Release the **Ctrl key.**

➤ You will see two noncontiguous (nonadjacent) ranges highlighted, cells B11..D11 and cells E4..E9 as in Figure 2.9e.

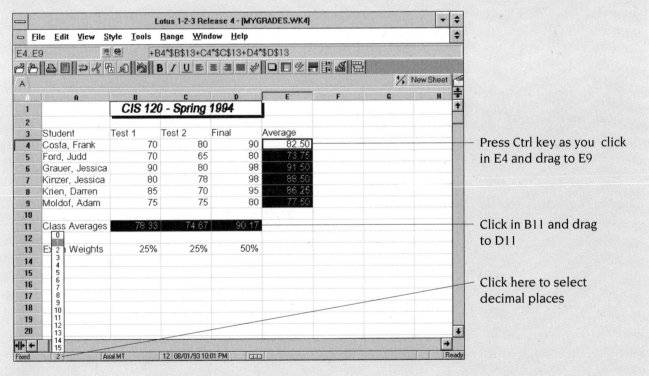

(e) Noncontiguous ranges (step 6)

FIGURE 2.9   Hands-on Exercise 2 (continued)

➤ Click the **formatting box** at the left of the status bar to display the numeric formats. Click **fixed.**

➤ Click the **decimals box** on the status bar as shown in Figure 2.9e. Click **1.**

SELECTING NONCONTIGUOUS RANGES

Dragging the mouse to select a range always produces some type of rectangle; i.e., a single cell, a row or column, or a group of rows and columns. You can, however, select noncontiguous (nonadjacent) ranges (called a collection) by selecting the first range in the normal fashion, then pressing and holding the **Ctrl key** as you drag the mouse over an additional range(s). This is especially useful when the same command is applied to multiple ranges within a spreadsheet.

Step 7: Lines and colors

➤ Drag the mouse over cells **A3** through **E3.**

➤ Press *and* hold the **Ctrl key.** Drag the mouse over the range **A11..E11.**

➤ Continue to press the **Ctrl key.** Drag the mouse over the range **A13..E13.**

➤ Pull down the **Style menu.** Click **Lines & Color** to produce the window of Figure 2.9f.

➤ Check the **Top** and **Bottom** boxes in the Border section.

➤ Pull down the **Pattern list box.** Click an appropriate pattern for light shading.

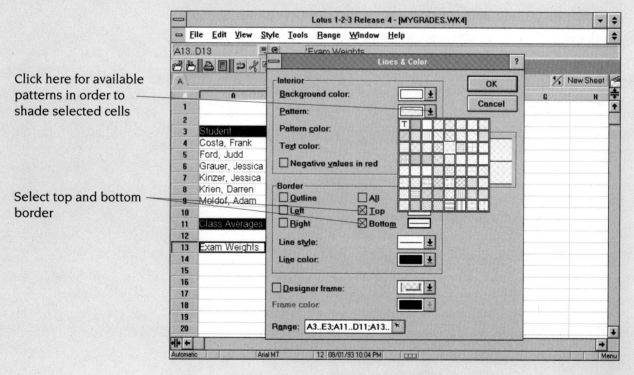

Click here for available patterns in order to shade selected cells

Select top and bottom border

(f) Lines & Color Command (step 7)

FIGURE 2.9   Hands-on Exercise 2 (continued)

➤ Pull down the **Pattern color box.** Click a light shade of grey so that the pattern does not obscure the text. Click the **OK** command button.

➤ Check that all three ranges are still selected (A3..E3, A11..E11, *and* A13..E13).

➤ Click the **boldface SmartIcon.** Click the **italics SmartIcon.**

DESELECTING A RANGE

The effects of a formatting change are often difficult to see when the selected cells are highlighted. You may need to deselect the range by clicking elsewhere in the spreadsheet to see the results of a formatting command.

Step 8: Centering an entry

➤ Select the range **B3** through **E13.**

➤ Pull down the **Style menu.**

➤ Click **Alignment.**

➤ Click **Center** and the **OK** command button, or alternatively click the **centering SmartIcon**. The formatting for the spreadsheet is complete and should match Figure 2.5b shown earlier.

➤ Save the spreadsheet.

Step 9: The Page Setup command

➤ Pull down the **File menu.**

➤ Click **Page Setup** to produce the dialog box in Figure 2.9g.

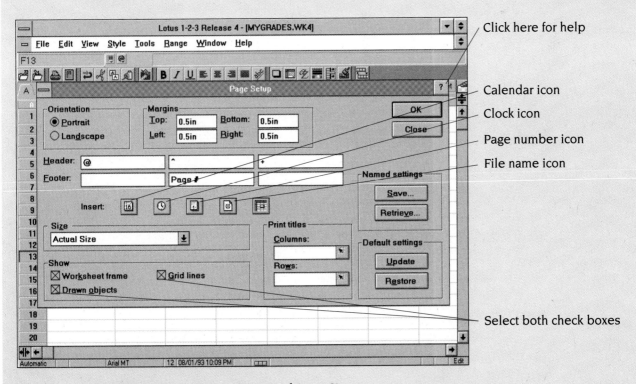

(g) Page Setup Command (step 9)

FIGURE 2.9 Hands-on Exercise 2 (continued)

- ➤ Click the **? icon** for on-line help about the Page Setup command. Click the **maximize button** in the help window, explore on-line help as needed, then press the **Esc key** to return to the spreadsheet.
- ➤ Check the boxes for the **Worksheet frame** and **Grid lines.**
- ➤ Click the **text box** for the left section of the header. Click the **calendar icon** to insert the date in the header; the @ sign will appear in the text box as shown in Figure 2.9g.
- ➤ Click the middle section of the header. Click the **file name icon** to insert the file name (MYGRADES.WK4); a ^ will appear in the text box.
- ➤ Click the right section of the header. Click the **clock icon** to insert the time; a plus sign will appear in the text box.
- ➤ Click the middle section of the footer. Type the word **Page,** press the **space bar,** then click the **page number icon;** a number sign will appear in the text box.
- ➤ Change the margins as indicated in the figure.
- ➤ Click **OK** to return to the spreadsheet.

WHICH VERSION AM I USING?

Use the header and footer within the Page Setup command to date and time stamp a printed spreadsheet so that you know the version you are using. This is especially important within an organization when spreadsheets are passed back and forth from one person to another.

Step 10: The Print Preview command
- ➤ Pull down the **File menu.**
- ➤ Click **Print Preview,** then click **OK** to see the spreadsheet prior to printing as in Figure 2.9h.
- ➤ If you are satisfied with the appearance of the spreadsheet, click the **printer icon.** Click **OK** to begin printing.
- ➤ If you are not satisfied with the appearance of the spreadsheet, click the **page setup icon** to return to the setup dialog box. Make the appropriate changes, then print the spreadsheet.

Step 11: Print the cell contents
- ➤ Save the spreadsheet a final time.
- ➤ Select the entire spreadsheet, cells A1 through E13.
- ➤ Click the **formatting box** in the status bar. Click **text.**
- ➤ Adjust the column widths by clicking the **column widths SmartIcon.**
- ➤ Pull down the **File menu.** Click **Print Preview,** then click **OK** to view the spreadsheet prior to printing. The spreadsheet does not fit on a single page (i.e., column E is not visible).
- ➤ Press the icon to display the page setup dialog box.
- ➤ Click **Landscape** to change the orientation of the printed page.
- ➤ If necessary, check the **Worksheet frame** and **Grid lines** boxes. Click **OK** to close the Page Setup dialog box.

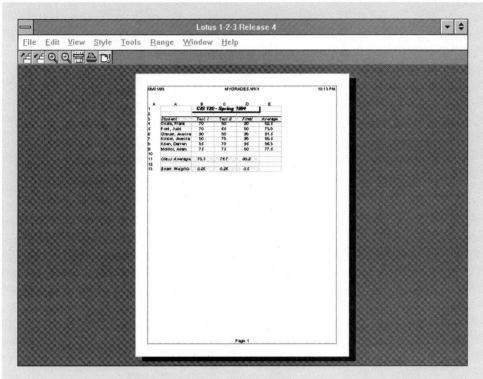

(h) Print Preview Command (step 10)

FIGURE 2.9 Hands-on Exercise 2 (continued)

➤ Click the **Printer SmartIcon** to print the cell contents. Click **OK** to begin the printing operation.

➤ Pull down the **File menu.** Click **Close.** Click **No** when asked whether to save the changes.

A WORD OF CAUTION

The formatting capabilities within Lotus make it all too easy to get caught up in the appearance of a spreadsheet without paying attention to its accuracy. Consider, for example, the grade book of Figure 2.10, which our professor uses in a different course. The grade book is beautifully formatted, *but its calculations are wrong,* and no amount of fancy formatting can compensate for the erroneous results. Consider:

➤ Baker should have received an A rather than a B. His weighted average (the combination of the quiz average and final exam) was 87, and with two bonus points for each completed homework, he should have had a final average of 91.

➤ Charles should have received a B rather than a C. True, he did not do any homework and he did do poorly on the final, but, with the semester quizzes and final exam counting equally, his weighted average should have been 80.

➤ Goodman should have received an A rather than a B. She aced both quizzes (she was excused from the first quiz) as well as the final, and in addition, she received a four-point bonus for home work.

Erroneous grades

	Assignments			Quizzes			Quiz	Final	Wght		Course
Name	#1	#2	#3	#1	#2	#3	Avg	Exam	Avg	Bonus	Grade
Baker		OK	OK	77	89	95	87	87	87	2	B
Charles				84	76	86	82	78	79	0	C
Goodman	OK	OK		Absent	95	94	63	95	85	4	B
Johnson	OK	OK		90	86	70	82	90	88	4	A
Jones		OK	OK	75	85	71	77	86	83	2	B
Irving	OK		OK	65	85	75	75	78	77	2	C
Lang		OK		84	88	83	85	94	91	2	A
London	OK	OK		72	69	75	72	82	79	4	B
Milgrom	OK	OK		100	65	90	85	100	96	4	A
Mills	OK	OK		75	85	80	80	65	70	4	C
Nelson				65	60	61	62	60	61	0	D

Grading Criteria

Bonus for each homework	2
Weight of semester quizzes	50%
Weight of final exam	50%

Wght Avg	Grade
	F
60	D
70	C
80	B
90	A

FIGURE 2.10 Style over Substance

How did these errors occur, and closer to home, will your professor make similar mistakes? Did the professor in our example take the time to validate the spreadsheet, or was he too caught up in the end-of-semester crunch? Our professor is only human, but he would have done well to print the cell contents and audit the mechanics of the spreadsheet.

The errors in our example may be contrived, but consider how they could have occurred in real life:

➤ At the class's urging, the professor decides at the last minute to assign a third homework but neglects to adjust the spreadsheet to include the additional column. (The COUNT function is used in the computation of the homework bonus and is presented in Chapter 3.)

➤ The professor has another last-minute change of heart and decides to count the semester quizzes and final exam evenly. He was careless, however, when he developed the original spreadsheet, because the formulas to compute the weighted average specify constants (as in the spreadsheet of Chapter 1) rather than absolute references to the cells containing the exam weights.

➤ The professor forgot that he had excused Goodman from the first quiz and hence did not adjust the formula to compute Goodman's average on the two quizzes.

Suffice it to say that the accuracy of a spreadsheet is far more important than its appearance and you are well advised to remember this thought as you create and/or use a spreadsheet. Ask yourself if any of the spreadsheets you have created contained an error, and if so, what the financial consequences would have been if those spreadsheets were used for other than an academic exercise.

SUMMARY

All spreadsheet commands operate on a cell or group of cells known as a range. A range is selected by dragging the mouse to highlight the range; the range remains selected until another range is defined or you click another cell in the spreadsheet. Noncontiguous (nonadjacent) ranges may be selected in conjunction with the Ctrl key.

The formulas in a cell or range of cells may be copied or moved anywhere within a spreadsheet. An absolute reference remains constant throughout a copy operation, whereas a relative reference is adjusted for the new location. Absolute and relative references have no meaning in a move operation. The copy and move operations are implemented through the Copy and Paste commands, and the Cut and Paste commands, respectively, in the Edit menu.

Formatting is typically done within the context of select-then-do; that is, select the cell or range of cells, then execute the appropriate command. The Number, Alignment, Fonts & Attributes, and Lines & Color commands are found within the Style menu. The status bar and/or SmartIcons simplify the formatting process.

The Page Setup command provides complete control over the printed page, enabling you to change margins and/or print a spreadsheet with or without the worksheet frame and/or gridlines. The Print Preview command shows the spreadsheet prior to printing.

A spreadsheet should always be printed twice, once with displayed values, and once with cell contents. The latter is an important tool in checking the accuracy of a spreadsheet, which is far more important than its appearance.

Key Words and Concepts

Absolute reference	Fonts & Attributes	Point size
Alignment	command	Portrait orientation
Automatic format	Footer	Print Preview command
Cell contents	General format	Range
Clipboard	Header	Relative reference
Column Width command	Landscape orientation	Row Height command
Comma format	Lines & Color command	Scientific format
Copy command	Mixed reference	SmartIcons
Currency format	Move command	Source range
Cut command	Number format	Style menu
Date format	Page Setup command	Text format
Destination range	Paste command	TrueType
Drop shadow	Percent format	Undo command
Fixed format	+/− format	

Multiple Choice

1. Cell F6 contains the formula @AVG(B6..D6). What will be the contents of cell F7 if the entry in cell F6 is *copied* to cell F7?
   (a) @AVG(B6..D6)
   (b) @AVG(B7..D7)
   (c) @AVG($B$6..$D$6)
   (d) @AVG($B$7..$D$7)

2. Cell F6 contains the formula @AVG(B6..D6). What will be the contents of cell F7 if the entry in cell F6 is *moved* to cell F7?
   (a) @AVG(B6..D6)
   (b) @AVG(B7..D7)
   (c) @AVG($B$6..$D$6)
   (d) @AVG($B$7..$D$7)

3. A formula containing the entry $A$4 is copied to a cell one column over and two rows down. How will the entry appear in its new location?
   (a) Both the row and column will change
   (b) Neither the row nor column will change
   (c) The row will change but the column will remain the same
   (d) The column will change but the row will remain the same

4. Which of the following is true regarding a printed spreadsheet?
   (a) It may be printed with or without the row and column headings
   (b) It may be printed with or without the gridlines
   (c) Both (a) and (b) above
   (d) Neither (a) nor (b)

5. A cell range may consist of:
   (a) One row
   (b) One column
   (c) Both (a) and (b) above
   (d) Neither (a) nor (b)

6. Which command will take a cell, or group of cells, and duplicate them elsewhere in the spreadsheet, without changing the original cell references?
   (a) Copy command, provided relative references were specified
   (b) Copy command, provided absolute references were specified
   (c) Move command, provided relative references were specified
   (d) Move command, provided absolute references were specified

7. Which options are mutually exclusive in the Page Setup menu?
   (a) Portrait and landscape orientation
   (b) Worksheet frame and gridlines
   (c) Headers and footers
   (d) Left and right margins

8. What are the contents in the default header and footer?
   (a) The date and time the spreadsheet is printed
   (b) The worksheet frame and gridlines
   (c) The file name and page number
   (d) None of the above; that is, the header and footer are empty

9. Given that percentage format is in effect, and that the number .056 has been entered into the active cell, how will the contents of the cell appear?
   (a) .056
   (b) 5.6%
   (c) .056%
   (d) 56%

10. What happens if you execute a Copy command, select cell A1, execute a Paste command, select cell A5, and execute the Paste command a second time?

(a) The contents of the original cell are unchanged, and in addition, have been copied to two additional cells, cell A1 and cell A5

(b) The contents of the original cell have been deleted from their initial location, but have been copied to cells A1 and A5

(c) The contents of the original cell have been deleted, but the contents of cells A1 and A5 are unchanged

(d) The situation is not possible; that is, you cannot execute the Paste command twice in a row without an intervening Cut or Copy command.

11. Which of the following is true regarding the printing of cell formulas?

(a) The spreadsheet should be saved prior to printing in order to retain the current formatting and column width settings

(b) The entire spreadsheet should be reformatted as text after which column widths should be adjusted to accommodate the cell formulas

(c) The worksheet frame and cell gridlines should be visible in conjunction with the cell contents

(d) All of the above

12. Which menu contains the commands to preview the spreadsheet before printing, to save the spreadsheet under a new name, and to exit Lotus without saving the spreadsheet at all?

(a) File menu

(b) Edit menu

(c) Save menu

(d) Print menu

13. Which of the following fonts are included in Windows?

(a) Arial and Times New Roman

(b) Courier New

(c) Wingdings and Symbol

(d) All of the above

14. A numerical entry may be:

(a) Displayed in boldface and/or italics

(b) Left, centered, or right aligned in a cell

(c) Displayed in any TrueType font in any available point size

(d) All of the above

15. The default set of SmartIcons contains icons to:

(a) Open and close a spreadsheet

(b) Left, center, or right align an entry

(c) Boldface or italicize an entry

(d) All of the above

ANSWERS

1. b	**4.** c	**7.** a	**10.** a	**13.** d
2. a	**5.** c	**8.** d	**11.** d	**14.** d
3. b	**6.** b	**9.** b	**12.** a	**15.** d

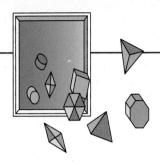

EXPLORING LOTUS

1. Use Figure 2.11a to match each action with its result; a given action may be used more than once.

Action	Result
a. Click on 1	___ Display the class averages with two decimal places
b. Click on 7, then click on 2	___ Save the spreadsheet
c. Click on 7, drag to 9, then click on 3	___ Paste the formula to calculate the class average for test 2 and the final
d. Click on 4, then click on 2	___ Copy the formula to calculate the average for Frank Costa to the clipboard
e. Click on 5, drag to 6, then click on 2	___ Paste the formula to calculate the average for the rest of the students in the class
f. Click on 8, drag to 9, then click on 2	___ Copy the formula to calculate the class average for test 1 to the clipboard

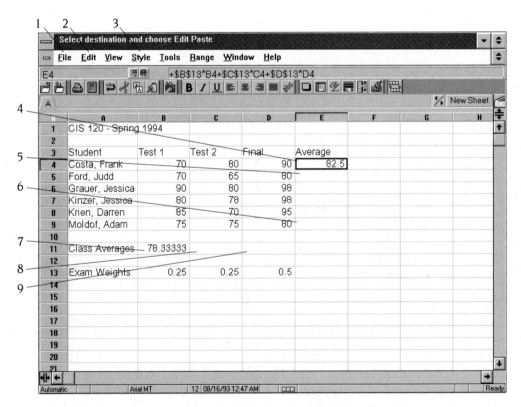

(a) Screen for Problem 1a

FIGURE 2.11 Screen for Problem 1

Use Figure 2.11b to match each action with its result; a given action may be used more than once.

	Action		**Result**

Action

g. Click on 9, drag to 10, then click on 3

h. Click on 1, drag to 2, then click on 3

i. Click on 6, drag to 7, then click on 8

j. Click on 1, click on 4, then click on 5

Result

___ Center the title on the spreadsheet

___ Format the exam weights as percentages

___ Boldface and italicize the spreadsheet title

___ Center the column headings and the numbers for test 1, test 2, the final, and the average for all students in the class

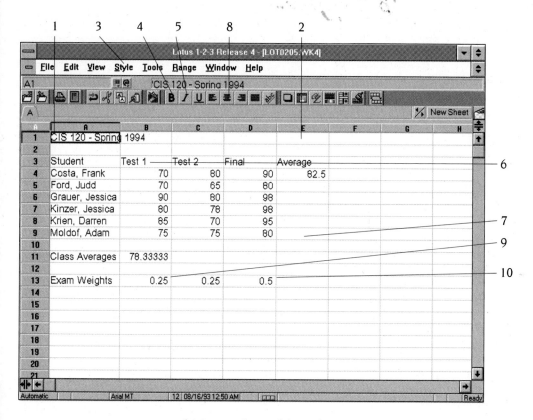

(b) Screen for Problem 1b

FIGURE 2.11 Screen for Problem 1 (continued)

2. Figure 2.12 contains a spreadsheet in which the same number (1.2345) has been entered into every cell. The differences in appearance between the various cell entries are produced by different formats in the individual cells. Indicate the precise formatting for every cell.

	A	B	C	D
1	1	$1	123%	1E+00
2	1.23	$1.23	123.45%	1.23E+00
3	1.2345	$1.2345	123.4500%	1.2345E+00

FIGURE 2.12 Spreadsheet for Problem 2

3. Figure 2.13 contains a spreadsheet depicting simplified payroll calculations for gross pay, withholding tax, social security tax (FICA), and net pay.

   a. What formula should be entered in cell E3 to compute an individual's gross pay? (An individual receives time and a half for overtime.)

   b. What formula should be entered in cell F3 to compute the withholding tax?

   c. What formula should be entered in cell G3 to compute the social security tax?

   d. What formula should be entered in cell H3 to compute the net pay?

   e. What formula should be entered in cell E10 to compute the total gross pay for the company? What formulas should be entered in cells F10 through H10 to compute the remaining totals?

$(B*B_4)+ D_2$

	A	B	C	D	E	F	G	H
1	Employee	Hourly	Regular	Overtime	Gross	Withldg	Soc Sec	Net
2	Name	Wage	Hours	Hours	Pay	Tax	Tax	Pay
3	Adams	$8.00	40	3	$356.00	$99.68	$23.14	$233.18
4	Hall	$6.25	40	0	$250.00	$70.00	$16.25	$163.75
5	Costo	$9.50	25	0	$237.50	$66.50	$15.44	$155.56
6	Lee	$4.50	40	5	$213.75	$59.85	$13.89	$140.01
7	Arnold	$6.25	35	0	$218.75	$61.25	$14.22	$143.28
8	Vedo	$5.50	40	2	$236.50	$66.22	$15.37	$154.91
9								
10			Totals:		$1,512.50	$423.50	$98.31	$990.69
11								
12	Assumptions:							
13	Withholding Tax:		28.00%					
14	Social Security Tax:		6.50%					

FIGURE 2.13   Spreadsheet for Problem 3

4. Figure 2.14 contains two versions of a spreadsheet in which sales, costs, and profits are to be projected over a five-year horizon. The spreadsheets are only partially completed, and the intent in both is to copy the entries from year 2 (cells C2 through C4) to the remainder of the spreadsheet. As you can see, the first spreadsheet uses only relative references and the second uses only absolute references. Both spreadsheets are in error.

   a Show the erroneous entries that will result when column C is copied to columns D, E, and F for both spreadsheets.

   b. What are the correct entries for column C so that the formulas will copy correctly?

5. Figure 2.15 shows how a spreadsheet can be used to prepare a sales invoice. What is your general impression of the spreadsheet? Is it formatted attrac-

	A	B	C	D	E	F
1		Year 1	Year 2	Year 3	Year 4	Year 5
2	Sales	1000	+B2+B2*C7			
3	Cost	800	+B3+B3*C8			
4	Profit	200	+C2-C3			
5						
6	Assumptions					
7	Annual Sales Increase:		10.00%			
8	Annual Cost Increase:		8.00%			

(a) Error 1 (relative cell addresses)

FIGURE 2.14   Spreadsheet for Problem 4

	A	B	C	D	E	F
1		Year 1	Year 2	Year 3	Year 4	Year 5
2	Sales	1000	+$B$2+$B$2*$C$7			
3	Cost	800	+$B$3+$B$3*$C$8			
4	Profit	200	+$C$2-$C$3			
5						
6	Assumptions					
7	Annual Sales Increase:		10.00%			
8	Annual Cost Increase:		8.00%			

(b) Error 2 (absolute cell addresses)

FIGURE 2.14 Spreadsheet for Problem 4 (continued)

tively? Is it accurate? Is the store receiving the correct amount; that is, is the subtotal shown on the invoice correct? Is Cori paying more or less than she should? Is the state getting the correct sales tax?

	A	B	C	D	E
1			**Kidlets Clothes**		
2			**Customer Invoice**		
3					
4		*Customer name:*	Cori Rice		
5		*Address:*	7722 S.W. 142 Street		
6			Miami, Florida 33157		
7		*Phone:*	(305)-254-7111		
8					
9	*Item*		*Quantity*	*Cost*	*Total*
10	Reebok sneakers		1	$45.95	$45.95
11	Summer T-shirts		3	$19.99	$59.97
12	Barrettes		2	$6.00	$12.00
13	Shorts		3	$24.99	$74.97
14	*Subtotal*				$117.92
15	*Sales Tax*				$76.65
16	*Total*				$194.57

FIGURE 2.15 Spreadsheet for Problem 5

6. Figure 2.16 contains a spreadsheet that can be used to calculate the balance due on student loans. Complete the spreadsheet, following the steps outlined below:

   a. Click cell D6 and enter the formula to calculate the balance due on Kim Mallery's loan.

   b. Copy the formula entered in D6 to the range D7..D11 to calculate the balance due for the other student loans.

   c. Click cell B13 and enter the formula to calculate the total due for all student loans.

   d. Copy the formula entered in B13 to the range C13..D13 to calculate the total amount paid and the total balance due.

   e. Select the cells B6..D13 and format the numbers so that they display with dollar signs and commas, and no decimal places (e.g., $2,500).

   f. Select the cells A1..D2 and center the titles across the width of the spreadsheet. With those cells still selected, change the font to 14 point Arial bold.

g. Select cells A5..D5 and create a bottom border to separate the headings from the data.

h. Save and then print the spreadsheet.

	A	B	C	D
1	UNCLE SAM'S LOANS, INC.			
2	College Loans for Good Students			
3				
4				
5	Customer	Amount Due	Amount Paid	Balance Due
6	Mallery, Kim	2500	31.66	
7	Camejo, Oscar	10000	126.67	
8	Rowe, Debbie-Ann	5000	63.33	
9	Bost, Tiffany	3500	44.33	
10	King, Beth Anne	12000	152.01	
11	Lalji, Andrea	6000	76	
12				
13	Totals:			

FIGURE 2.16   Spreadsheet for Problem 6

7. Figure 2.17 contains a spreadsheet that was used to calculate the difference between the Asking Price and Selling Price on various real estate listings that were sold during June, as well as the commission paid to the real estate agency as a result of selling those listings. Complete the spreadsheet, following the steps outlined below:

a. Click cell E5 and enter the formula to calculate the difference between the asking price and the selling price for the property belonging to Mr. Landry.

b. Click cell F5 and enter the formula to calculate the commission paid to the agency as a result of selling the property. (You will need to pay close attention to the difference between relative and absolute cell references so that the calculations will be correct when the formulas are copied to the other rows in the next step.)

c. Select cells E5..F5 and copy the formulas to E6..F11 to calculate the difference and commission for the rest of the properties.

	A	B	C	D	E	F
1	Coaches Realty - Sales for June					
2						
3			Asking	Selling		
4	Customer	Address	Price	Price	Difference	Commission
5	Landry	122 West 75 Terr.	450000	350000		
6	Spurrier	4567 S.W. 95 Street	750000	648500		
7	Shula	123 Alamo Road	350000	275000		
8	Lombardi	9000 Brickell Place	275000	250000		
9	Johnson	5596 Powerline Road	189000	189000		
10	Erickson	8900 N.W. 89 Street	456500	390000		
11	Bowden	75 Maynada Blvd	300000	265000		
12						
13		Totals:				
14						
15	Commission %:	0.035				

FIGURE 2.17   Spreadsheet for Problem 7

d. Click cell C13 and enter the formula to calculate the total asking price, which is the sum of the asking prices for the individual listings in cells C5..C11.

e. Copy the formula in C13 to the range D13..F13 to calculate the other totals.

f. Select the range C5..F13 and format the numbers so that they display with dollar signs and commas, and no decimal places (e.g., $450,000).

g. Click cell B15 and format the number as a percentage.

h. Click cell A1 and center the title across the width of the spreadsheet. With the cell still selected, select cells A3..F4 as well and change the font to 12 point Arial bold italic.

i. Select cells A4..F4 and create a bottom border to separate the headings from the data.

j. Select cells F5..F11 and shade the commissions.

k. Save and then print the spreadsheet.

Case Studies

Make an Impression

You do excellent work but somehow you never get noticed. All of your spreadsheets are completely accurate and meet or exceed the requirements imposed by your supervisor. Something is still lacking, however, and the HELPME.WK4 spreadsheet on the data disk is typical of your work. A colleague took a look and said the problem is in formatting or the lack thereof. Let's see what you can do.

Establishing a Budget

You want to join a sorority and you really would like a car. Convince your parents that you can afford both by developing a detailed budget for your four years at school. Your spreadsheet should include all sources of income (scholarships, loans, summer jobs, work-study, etc.) as well as all expenses (tuition, books, room and board, and entertainment). Make the budget as realistic as possible by building in projected increases over the four-year period.

Your First Million

You have developed the perfect product and are seeking venture capital to go into immediate production. You have a firm order for 100,000 units in the first year at a selling price of $6.00 per unit. Both numbers are expected to increase 20 percent annually. You are able to rent a production facility for $50,000 a year for five years. The variable manufacturing cost is $1.50 per unit and is projected to increase at 10 percent a year. Administration and insurance costs another $25,000 a year and will increase at 5 percent annually. Develop a five-year financial forecast showing profits before and after taxes (assuming a tax rate of 36 percent).

Your spreadsheet should be completely flexible and capable of accommodating a change in any of the initial conditions or projected rates of increase, without having to edit or recopy any of the formulas. This will require you to isolate all of the assumptions (i.e., the initial conditions and rates of increase) in one area of the spreadsheet, and then reference these cells as absolute addresses when building the formulas. It's a challenging assignment, but then again you are going to make a lot of money.

Break-even Analysis

Widgets of America has developed the perfect product and is ready to go into production pending a review of a five-year break-even analysis. The manufacturing cost in the first year is $1.00 per unit and is estimated to increase at 5% annually. The projected selling price is $2.00 per unit and can increase at 10% annually. Overhead expenses are fixed at $100,000 per year over the life of the project. The advertising budget is $50,000 in the first year but will decrease 15% a year as the product gains acceptance. How many units have to be sold each year for the company to break even given the current cost estimates and projected rates of increase?

As in the previous case, your spreadsheet should be completely flexible and capable of accommodating a change in any of the initial conditions or projected rates of increase. Be sure to isolate all of the assumptions (i.e., the initial conditions and rates of increase) in one area of the spreadsheet, and then reference these cells as absolute addresses when building the formulas.

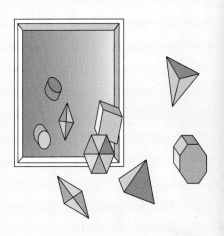

3

Spreadsheets in Decision Making: What if?

CHAPTER OBJECTIVES

After reading this chapter you will be able to:

1. Explain the role of spreadsheets in decision making.
2. List the arguments of the PMT function and describe its use in financial decisions.
3. Use pointing to create a cell formula; explain the advantage of pointing over typing in explicit cell references.
4. Use the AVG, MAX, MIN, and COUNT functions in a spreadsheet; distinguish between these functions and the parallel set of PURE functions.
5. Use the IF function to implement a decision; explain the table lookup function and how it is used in a spreadsheet.
6. Describe the DATE and TODAY functions; explain the use of date arithmetic.
7. Use the Range Sort command to rearrange the rows within a spreadsheet.
8. Differentiate between freezing titles and splitting a spreadsheet into panes; explain how either technique helps in the development of a large spreadsheet.

OVERVIEW

L otus is a truly fascinating program, but it is only a means to an end. A spreadsheet is first and foremost a tool for decision making, and the objective of this chapter is to show you just how valuable that tool can be. We begin by presenting two spreadsheets that we think will be truly useful to you. The first evaluates the purchase of a car and helps you determine just how much car you can afford. The second will be of interest when you establish a career and are looking for a mortgage to buy a home.

The chapter continues to develop your proficiency in Lotus with emphasis on the predefined functions that are built into the program. We consider financial functions such as the PMT function to determine the monthly payment on a loan. We introduce statistical functions (MAX, MIN, and COUNT), date functions

(TODAY and DATE), and the IF and VLOOKUP functions to provide flexibility within a spreadsheet. The chapter also introduces the Freeze Titles and Split Panes commands to facilitate working in large spreadsheets.

The chapter reviews the important concept of relative and absolute cell references that was presented in the previous chapter. It also introduces shortcuts to accomplish tasks you already know, such as pointing to enter formulas more accurately and the use of quick menus.

ANALYSIS OF A CAR LOAN

Figure 3.1 shows how a spreadsheet might be applied to the purchase of a car. In essence you need to know the monthly payment, which depends on the price of the car, the down payment, and the terms of the loan. In other words:

➤ Can you afford the monthly payment on the car of your choice?
➤ What if you settle for a less expensive car and receive a manufacturer's rebate?
➤ What if you work next summer to earn money for a down payment?
➤ What if you extend the life of the loan and receive a more favorable interest rate?

The answers to these and other questions determine whether you can afford a car—and if so, which car you will buy, and how you will pay for it. The decision is made easier by developing the spreadsheet in Figure 3.1, and then by changing the various parameters as indicated.

Figure 3.1a contains the *template,* or "empty" spreadsheet, with row and column headings, the necessary cell formulas, but *without* specific data. The template requires you to enter the price of the car, the manufacturer's rebate and down payment, the interest rate, and length of the loan. The spreadsheet uses these param-

	A	B
1	Price of car	
2	Manufacturer's rebate	
3	Down Payment	
4	Amount to be financed	+B1-(B2+B3)
5	Interest rate	
6	Term (years)	
7	Monthly Payment	@PMT(B4,B5/12,B6*12)

No specific data entered

(a) The Template

	A	B
1	Price of car	14,999
2	Manufacturer's rebate	$0
3	Down Payment	$0
4	Amount to be financed	14,999
5	Interest rate	9%
6	Term (years)	3
7	Monthly Payment	$476.96

Data entered

Payment too high

(b) Initial Parameters

FIGURE 3.1 What if? Analysis on Car Loan

eters to compute the monthly payment. (Implicit in this discussion is the existence of a PMT function within the spreadsheet program, which will be explained shortly.)

The availability of the spreadsheet lets you consider several alternatives, and therein lies its true value. You quickly realize that the purchase of a $14,999 car as shown in Figure 3.1b is prohibitive because the monthly payment is almost $500. Settling for a less expensive car and getting the manufacturer's rebate in Figure 3.1c helps somewhat, but the $413 payment is still too steep. Working next summer to earn an additional $3,000 for the down payment is a necessity (Figure 3.1d), and extending the loan to a fourth year at a lower interest rate makes the purchase possible (Figure 3.1e).

THE SPELL CHECK

Anyone familiar with a word processor takes the spell check for granted, but did you know the same capability exists within a spreadsheet? Pull down the Tools menu, click Spell Check, and let Lotus do the rest.

	A	B	
1	Price of car	13,999	——— Less expensive car
2	Manufacturer's rebate	$1,000	——— Rebate
3	Down Payment	$0	
4	Amount to be financed	$12,999	
5	Interest rate	9%	
6	Term (years)	3	
7	Monthly Payment	$413.36	——— Payment still too high

(c) Less Expensive Car with Manufacturer's Rebate

	A	B	
1	Price of car	13,999	
2	Manufacturer's rebate	$1,000	
3	Down Payment	$3,000	——— Summer job
4	Amount to be financed	$9,999	
5	Interest rate	9%	
6	Term (years)	3	
7	Monthly Payment	$317.97	

(d) Summer Job

	A	B	
1	Price of car	14,999	
2	Manufacturer's rebate	$1,000	
3	Down Payment	$3,000	
4	Amount to be financed	10,999	
5	Interest rate	8%	——— Lower interest rate
6	Term (years)	4	——— More years
7	Monthly Payment	$268.52	

(e) Longer Term and Better Rate

FIGURE 3.1   What if? Analysis on Car Loan (continued)

PMT Function

The **@PMT** function requires three arguments (inputs)—the amount of the loan, the interest rate per period, and the number of periods—in order to compute the associated payment. Consider, for example, the PMT function as it might apply to Figure 3.1b:

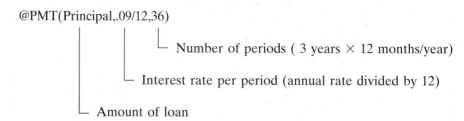

@PMT(Principal,.09/12,36)

      Number of periods (3 years × 12 months/year)

    Interest rate per period (annual rate divided by 12)

  Amount of loan

The arguments in the PMT function of Figure 3.1 are supplied as cell references rather than specific amounts, so that the computed payment is based on the values supplied by the user. In other words, the PMT function is entered as @PMT(B4,B5/12,B6*12) in order to compute the monthly payment according to the terms of a specific loan.

  The analysis associated with Figure 3.1 shows how a spreadsheet is used in the decision-making process. A person defines a problem, then develops a spreadsheet that includes all of the associated parameters. He or she can then plug in specific numbers, changing one or more of the variables until a decision can be reached.

HOME MORTGAGES

The PMT function is incorporated into a more comprehensive example using home mortgages, as shown in Figure 3.2. The spreadsheet lets you vary the amount of the loan and initial interest rate, then displays the associated monthly payment for a 30- and 15-year mortgage, respectively.

  The information provided by the spreadsheet is very different from what you might expect initially, but very informative in helping you decide which mortgage to take. Note, for example, that the difference in monthly payments for a $100,000 mortgage at 7.5% is only $227.80. Yes, this is a significant amount of money, but when viewed as a percentage of the total cost of a home (property taxes, maintenance, and so on), it becomes less significant.

Vary these amounts

	A	B	C	D
1	Amount Borrowed		$100,000	
2	Starting Interest		7.50%	
3				
4			Monthly Payment	
5	Interest	30 Years	15 Years	Difference
6	7.50%	$699.21	$927.01	$227.80
7	8.50%	$768.91	$984.74	$215.83
8	9.50%	$840.85	$1,044.22	$203.37
9	10.50%	$914.74	$1,105.40	$190.66
10	11.50%	$990.29	$1,168.19	$177.90
11	12.50%	$1,067.26	$1,232.52	$165.26

Difference in monthly payment between 30-year
and 15-year loan at various interest rates

FIGURE 3.2 Variable Rate Mortgages

Not convinced? Then consider the additional information presented in the spreadsheets of Figure 3.3. Figure 3.3a indicates the total interest over the life of a $100,000 loan at 7.5% is $151,717 for the 30-year mortgage; that is, you will pay $51,717 more in interest than in principal if you select the longer term. The total interest for the 15-year loan is significantly less.

If, like most people, you move before you pay off the mortgage, you will discover that almost all of the early payments in the 30-year loan go to interest rather than principal. The amortization schedule in Figure 3.3b shows that moving at the end of five years (60 months) pays off less than $6,000 of the 30-year loan versus almost $22,000 with the 15-year loan. (The latter number is not shown; you have to change the term of the loan in cell C5 to see the amortization for the 15-year loan.)

Our objective is not to convince you of the merits of one loan over another, but to show you how useful a spreadsheet can be in the decision-making process. If you do eventually buy a home, and you select a 15-year mortgage, think of us.

	A	B	C	D	E
1	Amount Borrowed		$100,000		
2	Starting Interest		7.50%		
3					
4			30 Years		15 Years
5	Interest	Monthly Payment	Total Interest	Monthly Payment	Total Interest
6	7.50%	$699.21	$151,717	$927.01	$66,862
7	8.50%	$768.91	$176,809	$984.74	$77,253
8	9.50%	$840.85	$202,708	$1,044.22	$87,960
9	10.50%	$914.74	$229,306	$1,105.40	$98,972
10	11.50%	$990.29	$256,505	$1,168.19	$110,274
11	12.50%	$1,067.26	$284,213	$1,232.52	$121,854

Less interest paid on 15-year loan

(a) Total Interest

	A	B	C	D
1	Amortization Schedule			
2				
3	Principal		$100,000	
4	Annual Interest		7.5%	
5	Term (years)		30	
6	Payment		$699.21	
7				
8	Month	Toward Interest	Toward Principal	Balance
9				$100,000
10	1	$625.00	$74.21	$99,925.79
11	2	$624.54	$74.68	$99,851.11
12	3	$624.07	$75.15	$99,775.96
13	4	$623.60	$75.61	$99,700.35
	.	.	.	.
	.	.	.	.
	.	.	.	.
64	55	$595.32	$103.89	$95,146.75
65	56	$594.67	$104.55	$95,042.20
66	57	$594.01	$105.20	$94,937.00
67	58	$593.36	$105.86	$94,831.14
68	59	$592.69	$106.52	$94,724.62
69	60	$592.03	$107.19	$94,617.44

Less than $6,000 paid on principal

5 years (60 months)

(b) Amortization Schedule

FIGURE 3.3 15- vs 30-year Mortgage

Relative versus Absolute Addresses

Figure 3.4 displays the cell formulas for the mortgage analysis. All of the formulas are based on the amount borrowed and the starting interest, in cells C1 and C2, respectively. The user may vary either or both of these parameters, and the spreadsheet will automatically recalculate the monthly payments.

The similarity in the formulas from one row to the next implies that the copy operation will be essential to the development of the spreadsheet. You must, however, remember the distinction between a relative and an absolute reference—that is, a reference that changes during a copy operation (relative) versus one that does not (absolute). Consider, for example, the PMT function as it appears in cell B6:

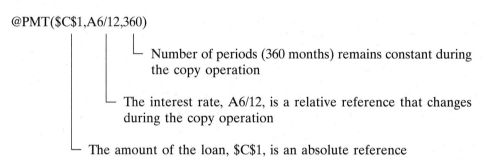

@PMT($C$1,A6/12,360)

Number of periods (360 months) remains constant during the copy operation

The interest rate, A6/12, is a relative reference that changes during the copy operation

The amount of the loan, $C$1, is an absolute reference

The entry A6/12 (which is part of the formula in cell B6) is interpreted to mean "divide the contents of the cell one column to the left by 12." Thus, when the PMT function in cell B6 is copied to cell B7, it (the copied formula) is adjusted to maintain this relationship and will contain the entry A7/12. The copy command does not duplicate a *relative address* exactly, but adjusts it from row to row to maintain the relative relationship. The cell address for the amount of the loan should not change, however, and is specified as an *absolute address*.

Absolute address (does not adjust during copy operation)

Relative address (adjusts during copy operation)

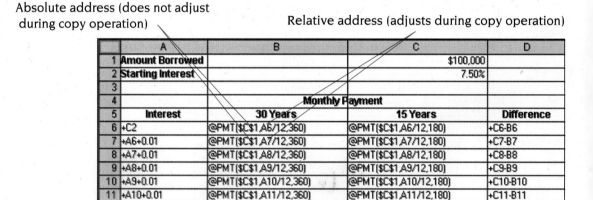

	A	B	C	D
1	Amount Borrowed		$100,000	
2	Starting Interest		7.50%	
3				
4		Monthly Payment		
5	Interest	30 Years	15 Years	Difference
6	+C2	@PMT($C$1,A6/12,360)	@PMT($C$1,A6/12,180)	+C6-B6
7	+A6+0.01	@PMT($C$1,A7/12,360)	@PMT($C$1,A7/12,180)	+C7-B7
8	+A7+0.01	@PMT($C$1,A8/12,360)	@PMT($C$1,A8/12,180)	+C8-B8
9	+A8+0.01	@PMT($C$1,A9/12,360)	@PMT($C$1,A9/12,180)	+C9-B9
10	+A9+0.01	@PMT($C$1,A10/12,360)	@PMT($C$1,A10/12,180)	+C10-B10
11	+A10+0.01	@PMT($C$1,A11/12,360)	@PMT($C$1,A11/12,180)	+C11-B11

FIGURE 3.4   Cell Formulas

ISOLATE ASSUMPTIONS

The formulas in a spreadsheet should be based on cell references rather than specific values—for example, C1 or $C1$1 rather than $100,000—and further the cells containing these values should be clearly labeled and set apart from the rest of the spreadsheet. It is then a simple matter to vary the inputs (assumptions) to the spreadsheet and immediately see the effect.

POINTING

Accuracy is paramount in any spreadsheet. **Pointing** provides a more accurate way to develop the formulas within a spreadsheet as you use the mouse or cursor keys to reference a cell, rather than type the cell address explicitly. In other words, you point to a cell rather than type its address explicitly, because it is all too easy to make a mistake in typing, such as typing A40 when you really mean A41.

Pointing is much easier than it sounds, and you get to practice in the hands-on exercise. In essence, you:

➤ Select (click) the cell to contain the formula.
➤ Type a plus sign or left parenthesis to begin entering a formula, or type the @ sign if you intend to enter a function. The status bar indicates that you are in the **Value mode** as the formula or function is being entered.
➤ Click the cell you wish to reference (or use the cursor keys to move to the cell); the cell reference will be highlighted within the active cell, followed by a flashing vertical line; the status bar indicates the **Point mode.**
➤ Type an arithmetic operator or the next character required by the formula or function.
➤ Continue pointing to additional cells in this fashion until you complete the formula.
➤ Press the enter key to return to the Ready mode.

As with everything else, the more you practice, the easier it is. The exercise that follows gives you ample opportunity to practice everything that you have learned.

HANDS-ON EXERCISE 1:

Mortgage Analysis

Objective To develop the spreadsheet for the mortgage analysis; to use pointing to enter a formula. Use Figure 3.5 as a guide.

Step 1: Enter the descriptive labels
➤ Do not worry about formatting at this time as all formatting will be done at the end of the exercise.
➤ Click in cell **A1.** Type **Amount Borrowed.**
➤ Press the **down arrow key** to move to cell A2. Type **Starting Interest.**
➤ Type **Monthly Payment** in cell A4.
➤ Type the remaining labels in cells A5 through D5 as shown Figure 3.5a.
➤ Save the spreadsheet under the name **MORTGAGE.WK4**

Step 2: The Spell Check
➤ Click in cell **A1** to begin the spell check at the beginning of the spreadsheet.
➤ Pull down the **Tools menu.**
➤ Click **Spell Check.** Click **Entire file,** then click **OK** to begin the spell check, which functions in similar fashion to that of any word processor.
➤ Make corrections as necessary; for example, Figure 3.5a indicates that "monthly" is misspelled. Click **Correct spelling,** then click **Replace,** or enter the correction in the **Replace with** text box.
➤ Continue checking until you see the message indicating that the spell check is complete. Click **OK** to return to the spreadsheet.

Select A1 to begin spell check ———

Misspelled word found ———

Select correct spelling ———

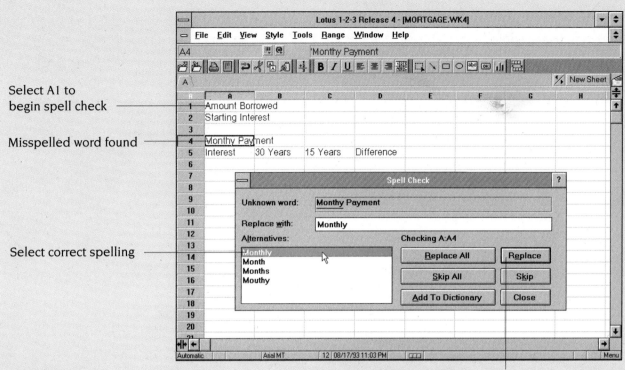

Click here to replace with correctly spelled word

(a) The Spell Check (step 2)

FIGURE 3.5 Hands-on Exercise 1

Step 3: Enter the initial conditions
➤ Click in cell **C1.** Type **$100,000.**
➤ Click in cell **C2.** Type **7.5%.**
➤ Save the spreadsheet.

Step 4: Copy the column of interest rates
➤ Click in cell **A6.** Type **+C2** to reference the interest rate in cell A6.
➤ Click in cell **A7.** Type the formula **+A6+.01** to increment the interest rate by one percent. Press **enter.**
➤ Make sure that cell A7 is still selected as in Figure 3.5b and that the mouse pointer is over the selected cell. Click the **right mouse button** to produce a quick menu. Click **Copy.**
➤ Click in cell **A8,** then drag the mouse over cells A8 through A11. Pull down the **Edit menu.** Click **Paste;** the formula in cell A7 has been copied to cells A8 through A11.
➤ Use the status bar to format cells A6 through A11 as percentages with two decimal points.

QUICK MENUS

A *quick menu* contains context sensitive commands for the selected item. Point to any cell, or to any row or column label, then click the **right mouse button** to display a Quick Menu with commands from the Edit and Style menus.

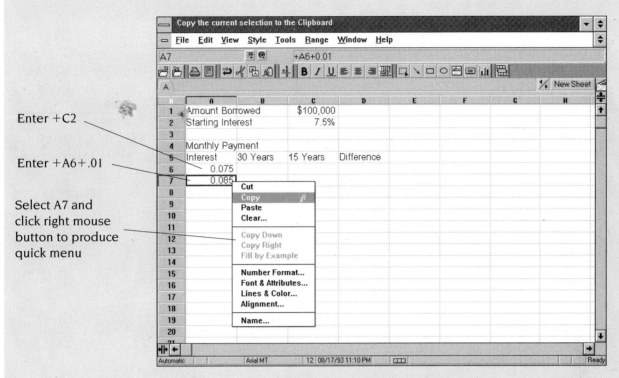

Enter +C2

Enter +A6+.01

Select A7 and
click right mouse
button to produce
quick menu

(b) The Copy Command (step 4)

FIGURE 3.5 Hands-on Exercise 1 (continued)

Step 5: Determine the 30-year payments

➤ Click in cell **B6.**

➤ Type the formula **@PMT($C$1,A6/12,360).**

➤ Press the **enter key.** Click the **formatting selector** at the left of the status bar
and select **currency format.** Cell B6 should display $699.21.

➤ Make sure that cell B6 is still selected. Pull down the **Edit menu.** Click **Copy.**

➤ Click in cell **B7,** then drag the mouse over cells B7 through B11. Pull down
the **Edit menu.** Click **Paste;** if you have done this step correctly, cell B11 will
display $1,067.26.

➤ If you see a series of asterisks instead of numbers, it means that the cell (column) is too narrow to display the computed results in the selected format.
Pull down the **Style menu,** click **Column Width,** then click the **Fit widest entry**
command button.

➤ Save the spreadsheet.

COPYING TO AN ADJACENT RANGE

The **Copy Right** and/or **Copy Down** commands save a step within the copy
and paste sequence provided you are copying the contents of a single cell
to an adjacent range. Either command requires you to select the source
and destination ranges at the same time. Select the cell you want to copy
and the cells that will contain the copied data, such as cells A7 through
A11, given that you want to copy the contents of cell A7 to cells A8
through A11. Pull down the **Edit menu** and click **Copy Down,** and the
contents of cell A7 will be copied to cells A8 through A11.

Step 6: Determine the 15-year payments (pointing)

➤ Click in cell **C6.**

➤ Type the partial formula, **@PMT(**

➤ Press the **up arrow key** until you reach cell **C1.** The status bar indicates the Point mode as in Figure 3.5c, and the reference to cell C1 is highlighted within the partially completed formula.

➤ Press the **F4 key** to convert C1 to an absolute address ($C$1), then type a **comma** to return to cell C6 to continue entering the function via pointing.

➤ Press the **left arrow key** twice to move to cell **A6;** the Point mode is again active.

➤ Type **/12** to divide the interest rate in cell A6 by 12; the status bar returns to the Value mode.

➤ Type **,180** (there is a comma before the 180) to enter the third argument in the payment function.

➤ Type a **)** to complete the formula. Press the **enter key.**

➤ Click the **formatting selector** at the left of the status bar and select **currency format.** Cell C6 should display $927.01.

Press up arrow until you reach C1, then press F4 to
convert it to an absolute address; type a comma to
continue building the formula

Select C6 and type @PMT(

(c) Pointing (step 6)

Formatting selector

Indicates Point mode

FIGURE 3.5 Hands-on Exercise 1 (continued)

THE F4 KEY

The F4 key cycles through relative, absolute, and mixed addresses. Click on any reference within the formula bar; for example, click on A1 in the formula +A1+A2. Press the F4 key once and it changes to an absolute reference. Press the F4 key a second time and it becomes a mixed reference, A$1; press it again and it is a different mixed reference, $A1. Press the F4 key a fourth time and it returns to the original relative address, A1.

Step 7: Copy the 15-year payments
➤ Check that cell **C6** is still selected.
➤ Pull down the **Edit menu.** Click **Copy.**
➤ Click in cell **C7,** then drag the mouse over cells C7 through C11. Pull down the **Edit menu.** Click **Paste.** The contents of cell C6 have been copied to cells C7 through C11.
➤ Adjust the width of column C if you see asterisks in any of its cells.
➤ Save the spreadsheet.

THE OPTIMAL (WIDEST ENTRY) COLUMN WIDTH

The appearance of asterisks within a cell indicates that the cell (column width) is insufficient to display the computed results in the selected format. Double click the right border of the column label to change the column width to accommodate the widest entry in that column. For example, to increase the width of column B, double click the border between the column labels for columns B and C.

Step 8: Compute the monthly difference (more practice with pointing)
➤ Click in cell **D6.**
➤ Type + to begin the formula.
➤ Press the **left arrow key** (or click in cell **C6**).
➤ Press the **minus sign,** then press the **left arrow key** twice (or click in cell **B6**).
➤ Press **enter** to complete the formula. Cell D6 should display $227.80 after formatting.
➤ Copy the contents of cell D6 cells D7 through D11. If you have done the step correctly, cell D11 will display $165.26 as shown in Figure 3.5d.
➤ Save the spreadsheet.

Step 9: The finishing touches
➤ Add formatting as necessary using Figure 3.5d as a guide.
➤ Click cell **A4.** Drag the mouse over cells A4 through D4. Pull down the **Style menu.** Click **Alignment.** Click **Center.** Check **Across columns.** Click **OK.**
➤ Add boldface and/or italics to the text and/or numbers as you see fit.
➤ Type **Financial Consultant** in cell A13. Enter **your name** in cell C13.
➤ Save the spreadsheet.
➤ Print the spreadsheet to show the displayed values.

10142.08

Printer SmartIcon

Entry is in A4, but is centered over A4..D4

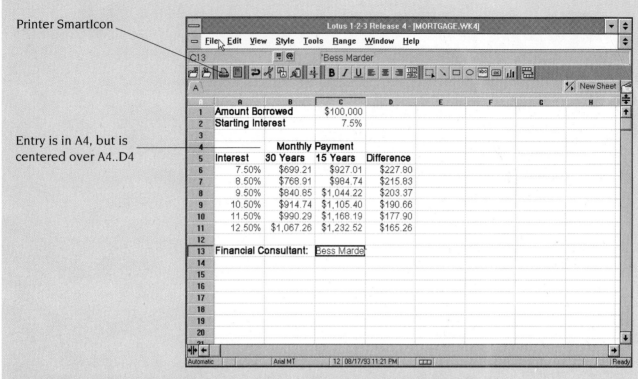

(d) The Finishing Touches

FIGURE 3.5   Hands-on Exercise 1 (continued)

Step 10: Print the cell contents

➤ Save the spreadsheet a final time.

➤ Select the entire spreadsheet, cells A1 through E13.

➤ Click the **formatting box** in the status bar. Click **text.** Adjust column widths as necessary.

➤ Pull down the **File menu.** Click **Print Preview,** then click **OK** to view the spreadsheet prior to printing.

➤ Press the icon to display the Page Setup dialog box.

➤ Click **Landscape** to change the orientation of the printed page.

➤ If necessary, check the **Worksheet frame** and **Grid lines** boxes. Click **OK** to close the Page Setup dialog box.

➤ Click the **Printer SmartIcon** to print the cell contents. Click **OK** to begin the printing operation.

➤ Pull down the **File menu.** Click **Close.** Click **No** when asked whether to save the spreadsheet.

THE FUNCTION SELECTOR

Click the *function selector* represented by the @ sign on the edit line to display a quick list of functions, then click the **List All command button** to view the complete set of available functions. The functions are grouped by categories: financial, statistical, date, and so on. To customize the quick list, click the **List All command button**, click the **Menu command button,** select the desired function, click **Add,** then click **OK.** Use on-line help to search for additional information.

Top labels (with leader lines): IF function   Table lookup function   Date function

	A	B	C	D	E	F	G	H	I	J
1			Professor's Grade Book							13-May-94
2										
3	Name	Soc Sec Num	Test 1	Test 2	Test 3	Test 4	Test Avg	Home Work	Final Avg	Grade
4	Adams, John	111-22-3333	80	71	70	84	77.8	Poor	77.8	C
5	Barber, Maryann	444-55-6666	96	98	97	90	94.2	OK	97.2	A
6	Boone, Dan	777-88-9999	78	81	70	78	77.0	OK	80.0	B
7	Borow, Jeff	123-45-6789	65	65	65	60	63.0	OK	66.0	D
8	Brown, James	999-99-9999	92	95	79	80	85.2	OK	88.2	B
9	Carson, Kit	888-88-8888	90	90	90	70	82.0	OK	85.0	B
10	Coulter, Sara	100-00-0000	60	50	40	79	61.6	OK	64.6	D
11	Fegin, Richard	222-22-2222	75	70	65	95	80.0	OK	83.0	B
12	Ford, Judd	200-00-0000	90	90	80	90	88.0	Poor	88.0	B
13	Glassman, Kris	444-44-4444	82	78	62	77	75.2	OK	78.2	C
14	Goodman, Neil	555-55-5555	92	88	65	78	80.2	OK	83.2	B
15	Milgrom, Marion	666-66-6666	94	92	86	84	88.0	OK	91.0	A
16	Moldof, Adam	300-00-0000	92	78	65	84	80.6	OK	83.6	B
17	Smith, Adam	777-77-7777	60	50	65	80	67.0	Poor	67.0	D
18										
19	Average		82	78	71	81	HW Bonus	3	Grading Criteria	
20	High		96	98	97	95			Minimum Req'd	
21	Low		60	50	40	60				F
22	Range		36	48	57	35			60	D
23									70	C
24	Exam Weights		20%	20%	20%	40%			80	B
25									90	A

Bottom label (with leader lines): Statistical functions

FIGURE 3.6 Extended Gradebook

THE GRADE BOOK REVISITED

Figure 3.6 contains our final look at the professor's grade book, which has been expanded to include more students, an additional test, a potential homework bonus, and the automatic determination of a student's letter grade. The spreadsheet was built using several additional capabilities, each of which is explained shortly. Consider:

Statistical functions: The AVG, MAX, and MIN functions are used to compute statistics for the class as a whole. The range of grades is computed by subtracting the minimum value from the maximum value.

IF function: The IF function conditionally adds a homework bonus to the student's test average and potentially raises the final average prior to determining the grade. The bonus is awarded to those students whose homework is "OK". Students whose homework grade is poor receive neither a bonus nor are they penalized.

Table lookup function: The expanded grade book converts a student's final average to a letter grade, in accordance with the table shown in the lower-right portion of the spreadsheet. A student needs an average of 60 or higher to earn a D, 70 or higher for a C, and so on.

Date function: The current date appears in the upper-right corner of the spreadsheet. **Date arithmetic** (that is, the elapsed time between two dates) is also possible, although it is not illustrated explicitly in the figure.

Sorting: The students are listed alphabetically, but could just as easily have been listed in a different sequence according to any criteria required by the professor.

The professor does, in fact, sort the students according to their final average prior to assigning the final grade in order to determine the curve for the class.

Large spreadsheets: The expanded grade book is larger than the applications considered so far, and requires additional commands for viewing on the monitor and/or printing.

Statistical Functions

The **@AVG, @MAX,** and **@MIN** functions return the average, highest, and lowest values, respectively, from an argument list. The list may include individual cell addresses, ranges, numeric values, functions, or mathematical expressions. Empty cells within the argument list are ignored, but cells containing nonnumeric entries (labels) are counted as zero. Accordingly, there is a parallel set of "pure" functions that ignore nonnumeric entries in their computation. Both types of functions are illustrated in the simple spreadsheet of Figure 3.7.

	A
1	70
2	80
3	90
4	
5	text

(a) The Spreadsheet

Function	Value
@AVG(A1..A3)	80
@AVG(A1..A3,200)	110
@AVG(A1..A4)	80
@AVG(A1..A3,A5)	60
@MAX(A1..A3)	90
@MAX(A1..A3,200)	200
@MAX(A1..A4)	90
@MAX(A1..A3,A5)	90
@MIN(A1..A3)	70
@MIN(A1..A3,200)	70
@MIN(A1..A4)	70
@MIN(A1..A3,A5)	0
@COUNT(A1..A3)	3
@COUNT(A1..A3,200)	4
@COUNT(A1..A4)	3
@COUNT(A1..A3,A5)	4

(b) Traditional Functions

Function	Value
@PUREAVG(A1..A3)	80
@PUREAVG(A1..A3,200)	110
@PUREAVG(A1..A4)	80
@PUREAVG(A1..A3,A5)	80
@PUREMAX(A1..A3)	90
@PUREMAX(A1..A3,200)	200
@PUREMAX(A1..A4)	90
@PUREMAX(A1..A3,A5)	90
@PUREMIN(A1..A3)	70
@PUREMIN(A1..A3,200)	70
@PUREMIN(A1..A4)	70
@PUREMIN(A1..A3,A5)	70
@PURECOUNT(A1..A3)	3
@PURECOUNT(A1..A3,200)	4
@PURECOUNT(A1..A4)	3
@PURECOUNT(A1..A3,A5)	3

(c) Pure Functions

FIGURE 3.7 Statistical Functions with a Text Entry

The function @AVG(A1..A3) computes the average of cells A1 through A3 by adding the values in the indicated range (70, 80, and 90), then dividing the result by three, to obtain an average of 80. Additional arguments in the form of values and/or cell addresses can be specified within the parentheses; for example, the function @AVG(A1..A3,200), computes the average of cells A1, A2, and A3, and the number 200.

Empty cells are *not* included in the computation; that is, the function @AVG(A1..A4) ignores the contents of cell A4 and returns an average of 80 (240/3), the identical result as the function @AVG(A1..A3). Nonnumeric cells (labels) are included, however, and counted as zero; for example, @AVG(A1..A3,A5) includes cells A1, A2, A3, and A5, and returns a value of 60 (240/4).

The **@PUREAVG** function ignores cells with nonnumeric entries as opposed to the AVG function, which treats them as zero. Examples of the PUREAVG function, parallel to those of the AVG function, are shown in Figure 3.7c. Note the different values returned by the AVG and PUREAVG functions with respect to cell A5: @AVG(A1..A3,A5) is 60, whereas the @PUREAVG(A1..A3,A5) is 80.

The MIN and MAX functions ignore empty cells, but treat nonnumeric cells as zero. Thus the function @MIN(A1..A4) returns a value of 70 because cell A4 is excluded, but @MIN(A1..A3,A5) returns a value of zero since the text entry in cell A5 is treated as zero. Note, however, that **@PUREMIN**(A1..A3,A5) returns a value of 70 as it ignores the entry in cell A5.

The **@COUNT** and **@PURECOUNT** functions tally the number of *nonempty* cells in the argument list with the same distinction as that of the other statistical functions; that is, COUNT includes cells with nonnumeric entries (labels), whereas PURECOUNT does not. In the examples of Figure 3.7, @COUNT(A1..A3) and @PURECOUNT(A1..A3) both return a value of 3, as do the functions @COUNT(A1..A4) and @PURECOUNT(A1..A4), because cell A4 is empty and thus excluded. Note, however, that @COUNT(A1..A3,A5) returns a value of 4 because it includes the nonnumeric entry in cell A5, whereas the corresponding @PURECOUNT function returns 3.

FIND AND REPLACE

Anyone familiar with a word processor knows the advantages of the **Find and Replace** command. The identical capability is available within Lotus; just pull down the **Edit menu** and click on **Find and Replace.** You can restrict the search to a specific range within the spreadsheet, and/or limit the search to labels, formulas, or both labels and formulas.

Arithmetic Expressions versus Functions

Many spreadsheet calculations, such as an average or a sum, can be performed in two ways—via a formula, such as (B1+B2+B3)/3, or through the equivalent function @AVG(B1..B3). *The use of functions is generally preferable* as will be shown in Figure 3.8.

The two spreadsheets in Figure 3.8a may appear equivalent, but the SUM function in spreadsheet one is inherently superior to that of the arithmetic expression in spreadsheet two. As the example is presently constructed, the entries in cell A5 of both spreadsheets return a value of 100. Now consider what happens if a new row is inserted between existing rows 2 and 3, with the entry in the new cell equal to 25. The SUM function adjusts automatically to include the new value (returning a sum of 125 in the first spreadsheet) because the SUM function was defined originally for the cell range *A1 through A4*. The new row is inserted within these cells, so that the ending cell in the range is changed from A4 to A5.

No such accommodation is made in spreadsheet two because the arithmetic expression was defined to include four *specific* cells, rather than a range of cells. The addition of the new row does, however, modify the cell references (since the values in cells A3 and A4 are now in cells A4 and A5), but no provision is made to include the new row in the adjusted expression.

Similar reasoning holds for deleting a row as shown in Figure 3.8c, which returns to the *original* spreadsheets, then deletes row two. The **@SUM** function in spreadsheet one adjusts automatically to @SUM(A1..A3) and returns the value 80. The formula in spreadsheet two, however, returns an error because it is still attempting to add four numbers, one of which no longer exists. In summary, a function expands and contracts to adjust for insertions or deletions, and should be used wherever possible.

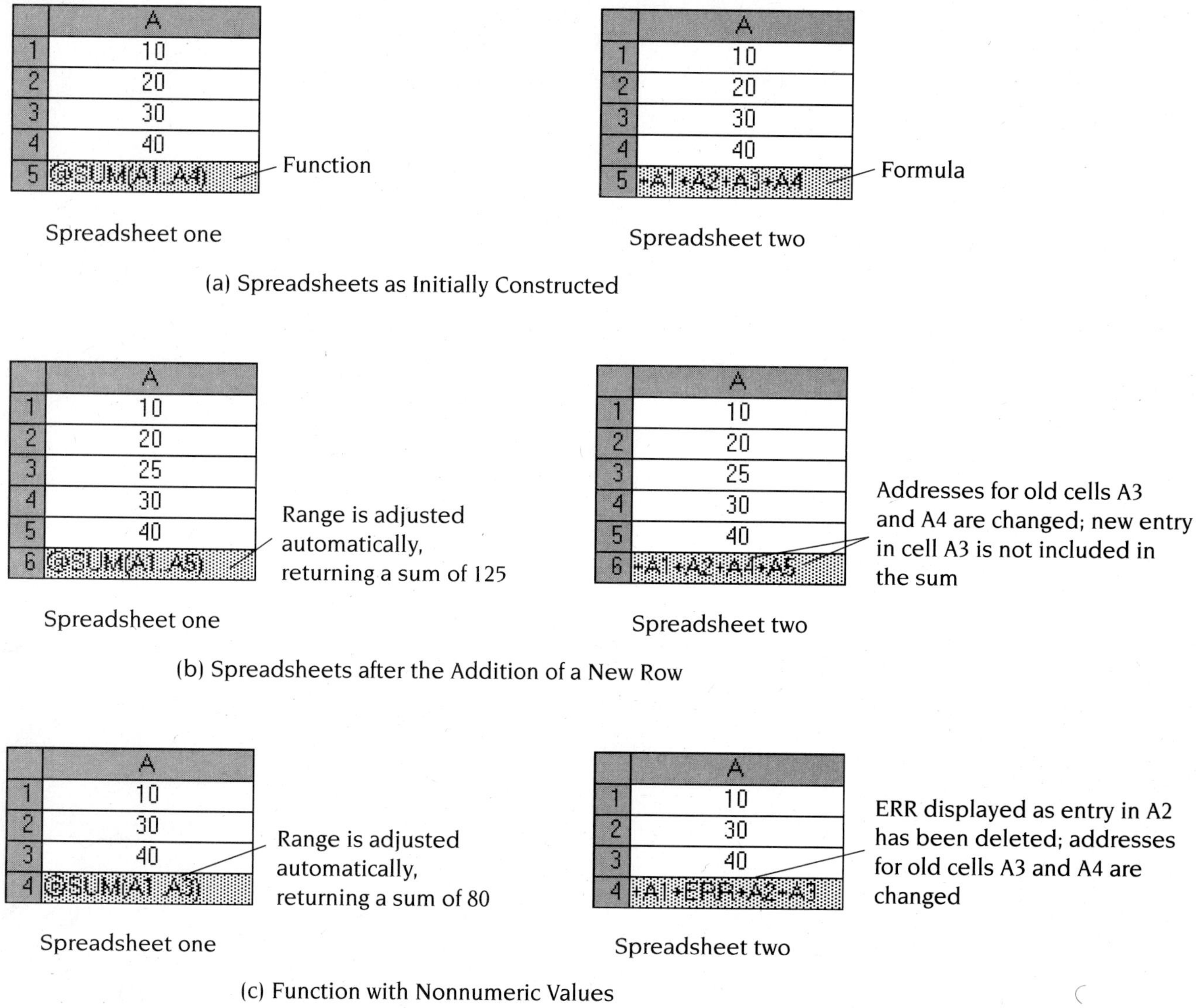

Function — Spreadsheet one

Formula — Spreadsheet two

(a) Spreadsheets as Initially Constructed

Range is adjusted automatically, returning a sum of 125 — Spreadsheet one

Addresses for old cells A3 and A4 are changed; new entry in cell A3 is not included in the sum — Spreadsheet two

(b) Spreadsheets after the Addition of a New Row

Range is adjusted automatically, returning a sum of 80 — Spreadsheet one

ERR displayed as entry in A2 has been deleted; addresses for old cells A3 and A4 are changed — Spreadsheet two

(c) Function with Nonnumeric Values

FIGURE 3.8 Arithmetic Expressions versus Functions

IF function

The **@IF** function enables decision making to be implemented within a spreadsheet, such as a conditional bonus for students whose homework is satisfactory. Students with inferior homework do not get this break.

The IF function has three arguments: a condition that is evaluated as true or false, a value if the condition is true, and a value if the condition is false. Consider:

@IF(condition,value-if-true,value-if-false)

└ Displayed value for a false condition

└ Displayed value for a true condition

└ Condition is either true or false

The IF function returns either the second or third argument, depending on the result of the condition; if the condition is true, the function returns the second argument, whereas if the condition is false, the function returns the third argument.

The condition uses one of the six *relational operators* in Figure 3.9a. The IF function is illustrated using the spreadsheet in Figure 3.9b, which produced the examples in Figure 3.9c. In every instance the condition is evaluated, then the second or third argument is displayed, depending on whether the condition is true or false. The arguments may be numeric (1000 or 2000), a cell reference to display the contents of the specific cell (B1 or B2), a formula (B1+10 or B1−10), a function @(MAX(B1..B2) or @MIN(B1..B2)), or a literal ("Go" or "Hold").

Operator	Description
=	Equal to
<>	Not equal to
<	Less than
>	Greater than
<=	Less than or equal to
>=	Greater than or equal to

(a) Relational Operators

	A	B	C
1	10	15	April
2	10	30	May

(b) The Spreadsheet

IF Function	Evaluation
@IF(A1=A2,1000,2000)	1000
@IF(A1<>A2,1000,2000)	2000
@IF(A1<>A2,B1,B2)	30
@IF(A1<B1,@MAX(B1..B2),@MIN(B1..B2))	30
@IF(A1<A2,B1+10,B1-10)	5
@IF(A1=A2,C1,C2)	April
@IF(@SUM(A1..A2)>20,"Go","Hold")	Hold

(c) Examples

FIGURE 3.9 The IF Function

The IF function is used in the grade book of Figure 3.6 to award a bonus for homework. Students whose homework is "OK" receive the bonus, whereas other students do not. The IF function to implement this logic for the first student is entered in cell H4 as follows:

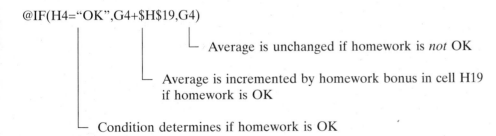

@IF(H4="OK",G4+$H$19,G4)

        └ Average is unchanged if homework is *not* OK

      └ Average is incremented by homework bonus in cell H19 if homework is OK

   └ Condition determines if homework is OK

The IF function compares the value in cell H4 (the homework grade) to the literal "OK". If the condition is true (the homework is OK), the bonus in cell H19 is added to the student's test average in cell G4. If, however, the condition is false (the homework is not OK), the average is unchanged.

The bonus is specified as a cell address rather than a specific value so that the number of bonus points can be easily changed. The professor can make a single change to the spreadsheet by increasing (decreasing) the bonus in cell H19 and see immediately the effect on every student without having to edit or retype any other formula. An absolute (rather than a relative) reference is used to reference the homework bonus, so that when the IF function is copied to the other rows in the column, the address will remain constant. A relative reference, however, was used for the student's homework and semester averages in cells H4 and G4, because these addresses change from one student to the next.

Table Lookup Function

Consider for a moment how the professor assigns letter grades to students at the end of the semester. He or she computes a test average for each student, and conditionally awards the bonus for homework. The professor then determines a letter grade according to a predetermined scale; for example, 90 or above is an A, 80 to 89 is a B, and so on.

The *table lookup* function duplicates this process within a spreadsheet, by assigning an entry to a cell based on a numeric value contained in another cell. In other words, just as the professor knows where on the grading scale a student's numerical average will fall, the table lookup function determines where within a specified table a numeric value (a student's average) is found, and retrieves the corresponding entry (the letter grade).

The table lookup function contains three arguments: the numeric value to look up, the range of cells containing the table, and the *offset* (column) within the table that contains the result. These concepts are illustrated in Figure 3.10, which was taken from the expanded grade book in Figure 3.6. The table in Figure 3.10 extends over two columns (I and J) and five rows (21 through 25); that is, the table is located in the range I21..J25. The *break points* (that is, the lowest numeric value for each grade) are contained in column I (the first column in the table), with the corresponding letter grades in column J.

Cell J4 contains @VLOOKUP(I4,$I$21..$J$25,1)

	A	. . .	G	H	I	J
1		Professor's Grade Book				13-May-94
2						
3	Name	. . .	Test Avg	Home Work	Final Avg	Grade
4	Adams, John	. . .	77.8	Poor	77.8	C
18						
19	Average				Grading Criteria	
20	High				(Minimum Req'd)	
21	Low					F
22	Range				60	D
23					70	C
24	Exam Weights				80	B
25					90	A

Cells I21 through I25 contain the break points in ascending order

Grades are in Column J

FIGURE 3.10 Table Lookup Function

The **@VLOOKUP** function in cell J4 determines the letter grade (for John Adams) based on the computed average in cell I4. Consider:

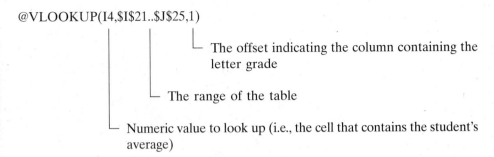

@VLOOKUP(I4,$I$21..$J$25,1)

        └ The offset indicating the column containing the letter grade

      └ The range of the table

    └ Numeric value to look up (i.e., the cell that contains the student's average)

The first argument is the value to look up, which in this example is Adams' computed average, found in cell I4. A relative reference is used so that the address will adjust when the formula is copied to the other rows in the spreadsheet.

The second argument is the range of the table, found in cells I21 through J25 as explained earlier. Absolute references are specified so that the addresses will not change when the function is copied to determine the letter grades for the other students. The first column in the table (column I in this example) contains the break points, which must be in ascending order.

The third argument is the offset indicating the column where the letter grades are found. (The first column in the table has an offset of zero, the second column an offset of one, and so on.) To determine the letter grade for Adams (whose computed average is 77.8), the table lookup function searches cells I21 through I25 for the first value greater than 77.8 (the computed average in cell I4). When that break point (80 in the example) is found, the entry in column 2 of the *previous* row is returned as the grade. In other words, to determine Adams' grade, the table lookup function searches the column of break points for the first value greater than 77.8; this turns out to be 80 and is found in cell I24. The lookup function then retrieves the corresponding letter grade from cell J23, which is in the second column one row above the break point.

Date Functions and Date Arithmetic

Lotus provides several functions that enable you to work with dates, two of which are illustrated in Figure 3.11. The **@TODAY()** function displays the current date (the date on which a spreadsheet is created or retrieved), whereas the **@DATE(yy,mm,dd)** function returns a specific date, such as May 13, 1994. The TODAY() function will display May 13, 1994 only on that specific date; the @DATE(94,5,13) function will display May 13, 1994 regardless of the date.

WHAT DAY IS IT?

Use the **@DATEINFO** function to determine the day of the week for any given date—for example, @DATEINFO(@DATE(94,11,24),1) to learn the day of the week for November 24, 1994. The number 1 following the date indicates the attribute to be returned by the DATEINFO function, in this case the day of the week. (A total of 13 attributes are available.) Use on-line help to search on date functions for additional information.

In actuality, both functions store the date as a serial number corresponding to the number of days in this century. January 1, 1900, is stored as the number 1; January 2, 1900, as the number 2; etc. May 13, 1994, corresponds to the number 34467 as can be seen in Figure 3.11a. You can, however, format dates to display the month, day, and year as shown in the figure. You can also enter a date directly in the desired format—for example, 5/13/94—*without* having to use the @DATE function at all.

The fact that dates are stored as serial numbers enables you to compute the number of days between two dates by simple subtraction. Age, for example, can be computed by subtracting the date of birth from the current date, and dividing the result by 365. Realize, however, that while the subtraction provides the exact number of elapsed days, the subsequent division is only approximate, in that leap years (with 366 days) are not accounted for. Note, too, the IF function in Figure 3.11a, which examines the computed age, then displays an appropriate message indicating whether the individual is legal or still under the age of 21. Additional examples of date arithmetic are provided in Figure 3.11b, which adds a constant number to the date of purchase in order to obtain the due date.

Displays current date (date spreadsheet is retrieved)

Always displays 10/31/73 (may be formatted as 31-Oct-73)

Date displayed as serial number

May also be entered as 10/31/73

	A	B	C	D
1		Cell Formulas	Date Format	Numeric Format
2	Today's Date	@TODAY	13-May-94	34467
3	Birthdate	@DATE(73,10,31)	31-Oct-73	26968
4				
5	Elapsed Time (days)	+B1-B2		7499
6	Age (years)	+B3/365		20.5
7				
8		@IF(D6>=21,"LEGAL!", "Minor")		Minor

(a) Date Functions and Date Arithmetic
(current date: May 13, 1994)

Formula entered: +C4+$C$10

	A	B	C	D
1		Accounts Receivable		
2				
3	Customer	Account Number	Date of Purchase	Date Due
4	Rice, Doug	R2345655886744	15-Dec-93	14-Jan-94
5	Dembrow, Harriet	D3498768696003	22-Jan-94	21-Feb-94
6	Center, Sol	C1298750986995	31-Jan-94	02-Mar-94
7	Morris, Gail	M8769856553321	03-Feb-94	05-Mar-94
8	Black, Chuck	B0987522333445	26-Feb-94	28-Mar-94
9				
10		Number of days til due:	30	

(b) Date Arithmetic

FIGURE 3.11 Date Functions and Date Arithmetic

VIEWING LARGE SPREADSHEETS

A large spreadsheet, such as the extended grade book, can seldom be seen on the monitor in its entirety; only a portion of the spreadsheet is in view at any given time. Scrolling takes place automatically in Lotus as it does in any other Windows application. In addition, Lotus offers the ability to freeze titles and/or split a worksheet into panes. Each of these is discussed in turn.

KEYBOARD SHORTCUTS: MOVING WITHIN A SPREADSHEET

Press **Ctrl+Home** and **End+Home** to move to the beginning and end of a spreadsheet, that is, to move to cell A1 and to the cell in the lower-right corner, respectively. The latter combination, **End+Home,** is *different* from the Ctrl+End combination that works in other Windows applications.

Scrolling

The specific rows and columns that are displayed are determined by an operation called **scrolling,** which shows different parts of a spreadsheet at different times. Scrolling enables you to see any portion of the spreadsheet at the expense of not seeing another portion. The spreadsheet in Figure 3.12a, for example, displays column J containing the students' grades, but not column A, which contains the students' names. In similar fashion, you can see rows 21 through 25 that display the grading criteria, but you cannot see the column headings.

Scrolling comes about automatically as the active cell changes and may take place in both horizontal and vertical directions. Clicking the right arrow on the horizontal scroll bar (or pressing the right arrow key), when the active cell is already in the rightmost column of the screen, causes the entire screen to move

Can't see columns A and B or rows 1–4

	C	D	E	F	G	H	I	J
5	96	98	97	90	94.2	OK	97.2	A
6	78	81	70	78	77.0	OK	80.0	B
7	65	65	65	60	63.0	OK	66.0	D
8	92	95	79	80	85.2	OK	88.2	B
9	90	90	90	70	82.0	OK	85.0	B
10	60	50	40	79	61.6	OK	64.6	D
11	75	70	65	95	80.0	OK	83.0	B
12	90	90	80	90	88.0	Poor	88.0	B
13	82	78	62	77	75.2	OK	78.2	C
14	92	88	65	78	80.2	OK	83.2	B
15	94	92	86	84	88.0	OK	91.0	A
16	92	78	65	84	80.6	OK	83.6	B
17	60	50	65	80	67.0	Poor	67.0	D
18								
19	82	78	71	81	*HW Bonus*	3	*Grading Criteria*	
20	96	98	97	95			*Minimum Req'd*	
21	60	50	40	60				F
22	36	48	57	35			60	D
23							70	C
24	20%	20%	20%	40%			80	B
25							90	A

(a) Scrolling

FIGURE 3.12 Large Spreadsheets

one column to the right. In similar fashion, clicking the down arrow in the vertical scroll bar (or pressing the down arrow key), when the active cell is in the bottom row of the screen, causes the entire screen to move one row down.

Freezing Titles

Scrolling brings distant portions of a large spreadsheet into view, but moves the text headings for existing rows and/or columns off the screen. You can, however, retain the row and/or column headings by *freezing titles* as shown in Figure 3.12b. The grades and grading criteria are visible as in the previous figure, but so too are the students' names and column headings.

Look closely at this figure and you will see that columns B through D (social security number, test 1, and test 2) are missing as are rows 4, 5, and 6 (the first three students). Scrolling still takes place as you move beyond the rightmost column or below the bottom row, but you will always see column A and rows 1, 2, and 3 displayed on the monitor.

The Freeze (Clear) Titles command is found in the View menu. It offers the advantage of providing permanent labels for the rows and columns displayed in the monitor regardless of the scrolling in effect.

Column A remains on screen (but cannot be accessed)

Rows 1–3 remain on screen (but cannot be accessed)

(b) Freezing Panes

FIGURE 3.12 Large Spreadsheets (continued)

Splitting Panes

Freezing titles is limited in that you cannot work in the frozen area of the spreadsheet even though it is visible on the monitor. You couldn't, for example, correct a misspelled name in the screen of Figure 3.12b because the name is in the frozen area. Nor could you modify entries in columns that are not visible unless you reposition yourself through scrolling, after which you would have to scroll again to see the effect on the final grade.

Dividing the spreadsheet into panes solves the problem as shown in Figure 3.12c. Assume, for example, that you made a mistake in entering test scores on the first exam, and that you want to see the effects of the corrected scores immediately as they are made. In other words, you want to make changes in column C, and see the results in column J. You need, therefore, the ability to view two areas of the spreadsheet and, further, to be able to change cells in either view.

The View Split command does precisely this by dividing the spreadsheet into (horizontal or vertical) panes with the entire spreadsheet available in either pane. You could, for example, change Adams' grade on test 1 in the pane on the left, then see the result immediately in the pane on the right. You can work in either pane by clicking in the pane you want, or by pressing the F6 function key to switch back and forth.

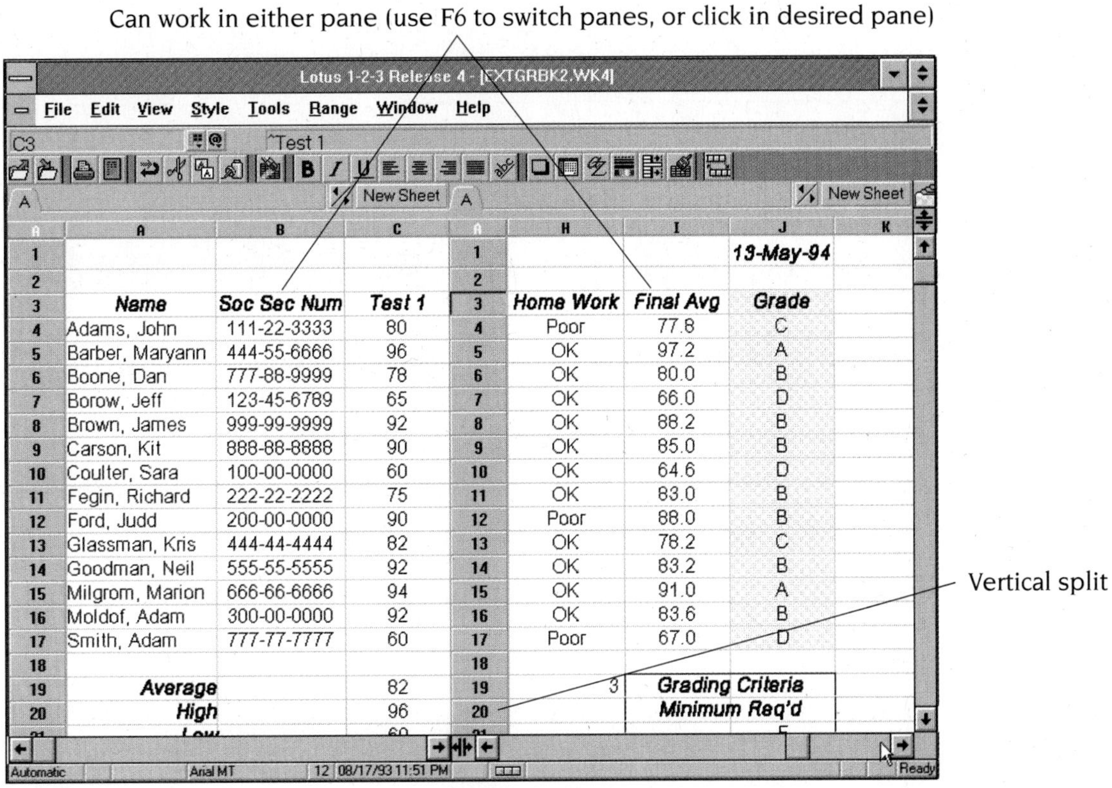

Can work in either pane (use F6 to switch panes, or click in desired pane)

(c) Splitting Panes

FIGURE 3.12 Large Spreadsheets (continued)

HANDS-ON EXERCISE 2:

Extended Grade Book

Objective To develop the expanded grade book; to use the IF and VLOOKUP functions; to introduce the Range Sort command; to illustrate a quick menu. Use Figure 3.13 as a guide.

Step 1: Retrieve the extended grade book
➤ Pull down the **File menu.** Click **Open.**
➤ Retrieve the **EXTGRBK** spreadsheet from the data disk.

➤ Pull down the **File menu.** Click **Save As.**

➤ Save the spreadsheet as **EXTGRBK2** so that you can return to the original spreadsheet if necessary.

Step 2: Fill by Example command

➤ Click in cell **C3,** the cell containing the label Test 1, then drag over cells C3 through F3. The selected cells are highlighted as in Figure 3.13a.

➤ Pull down the **Range command.**

➤ Click **Fill by Example.** Cells D3, E3, and F3 now contain the labels Test 2, Test 3, and Test 4, respectively.

FILL BY EXAMPLE

The **Range Fill By Example** command is one of the nicest features in Lotus as it automatically creates a series of values based on the initial value you supply. Click in the first cell that will contain the series and enter the starting value, such as January (or Jan). Remain in this cell and drag the mouse over the remaining cells in the range—for example, the next 11 cells in that row. Pull down the Range menu and click *Fill by Example;* Lotus will complete the series by anticipating the entries you want (February, March, and so on, for this example). You can enter the days of the week or any literal followed by a number, such as Quarter 1. Use on-line help to learn more by searching on the key words Filling Ranges.

Select C3..F3

(a) Fill by Example (step 2)

FIGURE 3.13 Hands-on Exercise 2

Step 3: Freeze Titles

➤ The number of columns displayed on your monitor depends on the resolution of your monitor; unless you are running extended VGA (1,024 × 768), you will not be able to see the entire spreadsheet.

➤ Click in cell **B4.**

➤ Pull down the **View menu.**

➤ Click **Freeze Titles.** Click **Both** as shown in Figure 3.13b. Click **OK.**

➤ Press the **right arrow key** repeatedly to move one column at a time until column J is visible.

➤ Look at the column headings and note that one or more columns are missing from the display; for example, columns B through D are not shown in Figure 3.13c.

➤ Press the **down arrow key** (or click the **scroll bar**) repeatedly to see that rows one, two, and three remain on the screen.

Select B4 to freeze Column A, rows 1–3

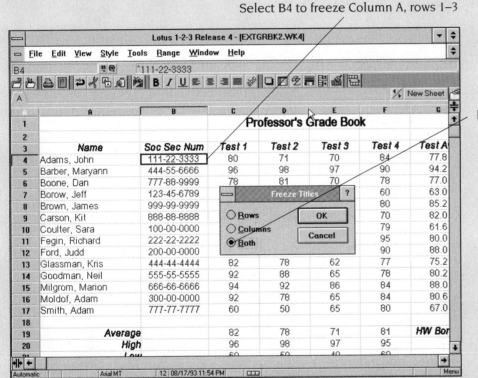

Freeze rows and columns

(b) Freeze Titles Command (step 3)

FIGURE 3.13   Hands-on Exercise 2 (continued)

Step 4: Enter the IF and VLOOKUP functions

➤ Click in cell **I4.**

➤ Use pointing to enter the IF function:

— Type the partial formula **@IF(**

— Click in cell **H4** or press the **left arrow key** to reach cell H4. Type **="OK".** Type a **comma** after the closing quotation mark.

— Click in cell **G4** or press the **left arrow key** to move to cell G4. Type a **plus sign.**

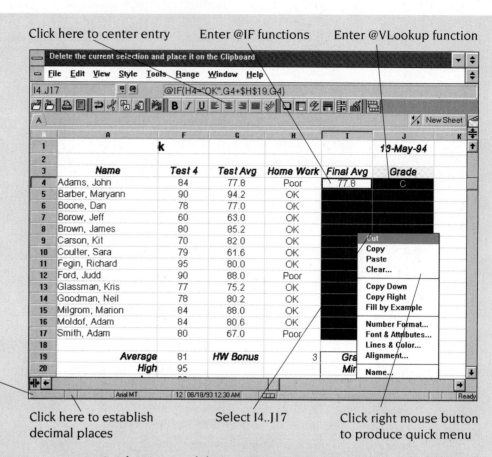

Click here to center entry   Enter @IF functions   Enter @VLookup function

Click here to apply
numeric format

Click here to establish
decimal places

Select I4..J17

Click right mouse button
to produce quick menu

(c) Quick Menus and the Copy Down Command (steps 4 & 5)

FIGURE 3.13   Hands-on Exercise 2 (continued)

— Click in cell **H19** (scrolling if necessary) or use the arrow keys to reach cell H19. Press the **F4 key** to convert the reference to $H$19. Type a **comma.**

— Click in cell **G4** or press the **left arrow key** to reach cell G4. Type a **right parenthesis,** then press the **enter key** to complete the IF function, which should appear as **@IF(H4="OK",G4+$H$19,G4).**

— Use the status bar to format the final average in cell I4 to a fixed number with one decimal point, then use the appropriate SmartIcon to center the entry.

➤ Click in cell **J4.**

➤ Use pointing to enter the table lookup function to determine the student's grade. The function is **@VLOOKUP(I4,$I$21..$J$25,1).** Remember to press the **F4 key** after selecting the range I21..J25 to specify an absolute reference.

➤ Use the appropriate SmartIcon to center the grade in cell J4.

Step 5: Copy the IF and VLOOKUP functions

➤ Click in cell **I4,** then drag the mouse over cells **I4 through J17,** as in Figure 3.13c.

➤ Click the **right mouse button** to produce the quick menu shown in the figure. Click **Copy Down.** If you have done everything correctly, Adam Smith will have a grade of D based on a final average of 67.0.

➤ Save the spreadsheet.

Step 6: The Split command

➤ The Freeze Titles and Split commands may be active simultaneously, but for simplicity we will clear titles to see the Split command in isolation.

➤ Pull down the **View menu.** Click **Clear Titles.**

➤ Click in any cell in row 15.

➤ Pull down the **View menu.** Click **Split.**

➤ Click the **Horizontal button.** Click the **Synchronize** check box, then click **OK** to produce a screen similar to Figure 3.13d.

➤ Click in the bottom window. Scroll as necessary to change the weights of the tests; for example, decrease the weight of the third test to 10% and increase the weight of the fourth test to 50%. The effects of this change are immediately visible in the top window.

➤ Reset the exam weights back to their original values: 20% for the third test and 40% for the fourth test. As previously, the effects of this change are immediately visible in the top window.

SPLITTING PANES

The fastest way to split a worksheet into horizontal (vertical) panes and/or change the size of existing panes is to point the splitter icon on the horizontal (vertical) scroll bar; the mouse pointer changes to a black two-headed vertical arrow, at which point you drag the mouse pointer to the row (column) at which you want to divide the window. Press the **F6 key** to switch between panes, or simply click in the pane you wish to work.

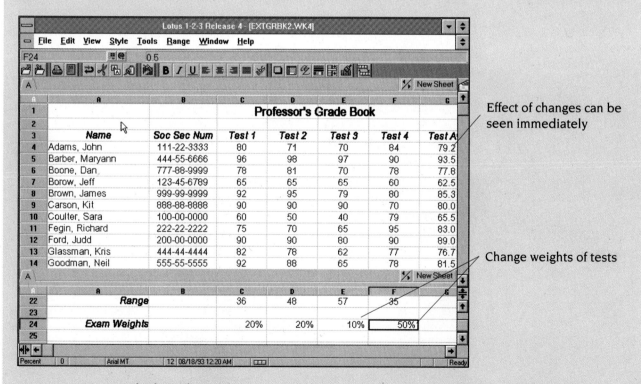

Effect of changes can be seen immediately

Change weights of tests

(d) The Split Windows Command (step 6)

FIGURE 3.13 Hands-on Exercise 2 (continued)

Step 7: Sorting

➤ Pull down the **View menu.** Click **Clear Split.**

➤ Press **Ctrl+Home** to move to cell A1.

➤ Click cell **A4.**

➤ Drag the mouse over the range **A4 through J17** to select the sort range.

➤ Pull down the **Range menu.**

➤ Click **Sort** to produce the dialog box in Figure 3.13e.

➤ Click the **range selector icon** in the Sort by list box to return to the spreadsheet; the mouse pointer changes shape to indicate you are selecting a range.

➤ Use the scroll bar to scroll to the right edge of the spreadsheet. Click cell **I4** to select the sort key.

➤ Click the button for a **Descending sort.**

➤ Click **OK** to perform the sort. The students should be rearranged in descending order according to their final average; Maryann Barber is at the top of the class with an average of 97.2.

➤ Click outside the selected range to deselect it.

➤ Save the spreadsheet.

Step 8: Printing

➤ Pull down the **File menu.**

➤ Click **Page Setup** to establish the appropriate parameters to print the spreadsheet.

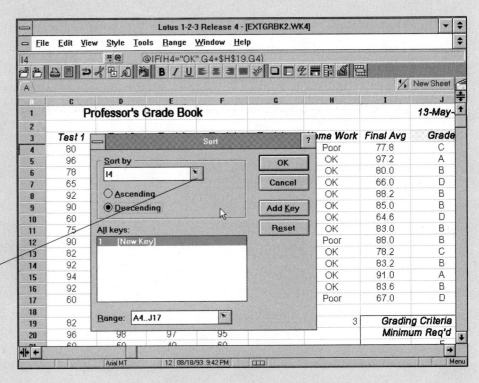

Click here to scroll and select sort key (I4)

(e) The Sort Command (step 7)

FIGURE 3.13 Hands-on Exercise 2 (continued)

- ➤ Select **Landscape.** Click in the Size drop-down list box and select **Fit all to page.** Click **OK.**
- ➤ Pull down the **File menu.** Click **Print Preview.** Click the **Current worksheet button,** then click **OK** to view the spreadsheet as in Figure 3.13f.
- ➤ Click the **printer icon** to print the spreadsheet. Click **OK.**
- ➤ Save the spreadsheet and exit Lotus.

Row and column headings and worksheet grid are both selected

Click here to print spreadsheet

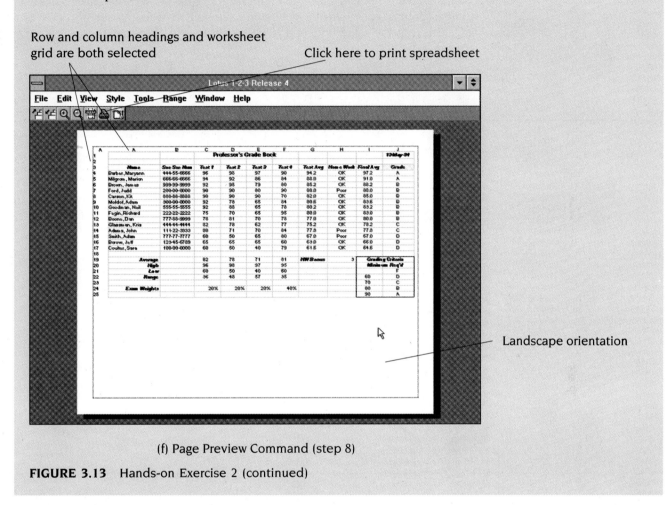

Landscape orientation

(f) Page Preview Command (step 8)

FIGURE 3.13   Hands-on Exercise 2 (continued)

SUMMARY

The PMT function requires three arguments—the amount of the loan, the interest rate per period, and the number of periods—from which it computes the associated payment.

Pointing is a more accurate way to enter a cell reference into a formula as it uses the mouse or cursor keys to reference the cell directly. Quick menus are accessed by clicking the right (alternate) mouse button.

The AVG, MAX, and MIN functions return the average, highest, and lowest values from an argument list; the COUNT function indicates the number of nonempty cells. Empty cells are ignored, but cells containing nonnumeric entries are counted as zero. The corresponding PURE functions ignore nonnumeric entries.

The IF function has three arguments: a logical test, which is evaluated as true or false, a value if the test is true, and a value if the test is false. The VLOOKUP (table lookup) function also has three arguments: the numeric value to look up, the range of cells containing the table, and the column number within the table that contains the result.

The TODAY() function returns the current date; the DATE(yy,mm,dd) function returns a specific date. Both functions store the date as a serial number corresponding to the number of days in this century, thus enabling date arithmetic.

Scrolling enables you to view any portion of a large spreadsheet but moves the headings for existing rows and/or columns off the screen. The Freeze Titles command keeps the row and/or column headings on the screen while scrolling in a large spreadsheet. Splitting panes enables you to view distant portions of a spreadsheet at the same time and to make changes in either area.

Key Words and Concepts

@AVG	@TODAY()	Portrait
@COUNT	@VLOOKUP	Quick menu
@DATE(yy,mm,dd)	Absolute address	Range Sort command
@DATEINFO	Break point	Relational operator
@IF	Date arithmetic	Relative address
@MAX	Fill by Example	Scrolling
@MIN	Find and Replace	Sorting
@PMT	Freezing titles	Splitting panes
@PUREAVG	Function selector	Table lookup
@PURECOUNT	Landscape	Template
@PUREMAX	Offset	Value mode
@PUREMIN	Point mode	
@SUM	Pointing	

Multiple Choice

1. Which command displays two distant portions of a spreadsheet on the screen at the same time, and allows you to make changes in either area?
   (a) Freeze Titles command
   (b) Split Panes command
   (c) Both (a) and (b)
   (d) Neither (a) nor (b)

2. If the results of a formula contain more characters than can be displayed according to the present format and cell width,
   (a) The extra characters will be truncated under all circumstances
   (b) All of the characters will be displayed if the cell to the right is empty
   (c) A series of asterisks will be displayed
   (d) A series of pound signs will be displayed

3. Which cell—A1, A2, or A3—will contain the amount of the loan, given the function @PMT(A1,A2,A3)?
   (a) A1

(b) A2

(c) A3

(d) Impossible to determine

4. Which of the following will compute the average of the values in cells D2, D3, and D4?

(a) The function @AVG(D2..D4)

(b) The function @AVG(D2,D4)

(c) Both (a) and (b)

(d) Neither (a) nor (b)

5. The function @IF(A1>A2,+A1+A2,+A1*A2) returns

(a) The product of cells A1 and A2 if cell A1 is greater than A2

(b) The sum of cells A1 and A2 if cell A1 is less than A2

(c) Both (a) and (b)

(d) Neither (a) nor (b)

6. Which of the following is the preferred way to sum the values in cells A1 to A4?

(a) @SUM(A1..A4)

(b) +A1+A2+A3+A4

(c) Either (a) or (b) is equally good

(d) Neither (a) nor (b) is correct

7. Which of the following will return the highest and lowest arguments from a list?

(a) HIGH/LOW

(b) LARGEST/SMALLEST

(c) MAX/MIN

(d) MAXIMUM/MINIMUM

8. Which of the following is a *required* technique to develop the spreadsheet for the mortgage analysis?

(a) Pointing

(b) Quick menus

(c) Both (a) and (b)

(d) Neither (a) nor (b)

9. Given that cells B6, C6, and D6 contain the numbers 10, 20, and 30, respectively, what value will be returned by the function @IF(B6>10,C6*2,D6*3)?

(a) 10

(b) 40

(c) 60

(d) 90

10. Which formula will compute the age of a person born on March 16, 1977?

(a) @TODAY()−DATE(77,3,16)

(b) @TODAY()−DATE(77,3,16)/365

(c) (@TODAY()−DATE(77,3,16))/365

(d) @AGE(77,3,16)

11. What is the best way to enter January 21, 1994 into a spreadsheet, given that you create the spreadsheet on that date, and further, given that you always want to display that specific date?

    (a) @TODAY()

    (b) 1/21/94

    (c) Both (a) and (b) are equally acceptable

    (d) Neither (a) nor (b)

12. Which function will return the number of *numeric entries* in the range A2..A6?

    (a) @COUNT(A2..A6)

    (b) @PURECOUNT(A2..A6)

    (c) @COUNT(A2,A6)

    (d) @PURECOUNT(A2,A6)

13. What happens if you select a range, then press the right (alternate) mouse button?

    (a) The range will be deselected

    (b) Nothing; the button has no effect

    (c) The Edit and Style menus will be displayed in their entirety

    (d) A quick menu will be displayed

14. The spreadsheet displayed in the monitor shows columns A and B, skips columns D, E, and F, then displays columns G, H, I, J, and K. What is the most likely explanation for the missing columns?

    (a) The columns were previously deleted

    (b) The columns are empty and thus are automatically hidden from view

    (c) Either (a) or (b) is a satisfactory explanation

    (d) Neither (a) nor (b) is a likely reason

15. Given the function @VLOOKUP(C6,D12..F18,2)

    (a) The entries in cells D12 through D18 are in ascending order

    (b) The entries in cells D12 through D18 are in descending order

    (c) The entries in cells F12 through F18 are in ascending order

    (d) The entries in cells F12 through F18 are in descending order

ANSWERS

1. b	**6.** a	**11.** b
2. c	**7.** c	**12.** b
3. a	**8.** d	**13.** d
4. a	**9.** d	**14.** d
5. d	**10.** c	**15.** a

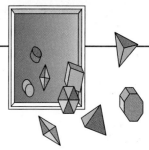

1. Use Figure 3.14 to match each action with its result; a given action may be used more than once, or not at all.

FIGURE 3.14 Screen for Problem 1

a. Click at 1

b. Click at 2, then at 3

c. Click at 4, then at 5

d. Click right button at 6

e. Click at 6, drag to 7, then click at 8

f. Click at 9

g. Double click at 10

h. Click at 11

i. Click at 12, enter @AVG(, click at 13, drag to 14, enter), and press return

j. Click at 4, enter @AVG(, click at 13, drag to 15, enter), and press return

___ Freeze column A and rows 1–3

___ Copy the test average for John Adams to the clipboard

___ Display a quick menu

___ Check spelling

___ Widen column A to accommodate the widest entry

___ Use the Fill by Example feature to enter Test 2, Test 3, and Test 4 headings

___ Save the spreadsheet

___ Enter the formula to obtain the test average for John Adams

___ Print the spreadsheet

___ Enter the formula to obtain the class average for Test 1

2. Consider the two spreadsheets shown in Figure 3.15 and the entries, @AVG(A1..A4) versus (A1+A2+A3+A4)/4, both of which calculate the average of cells A1 through A4. Assume that a new row is inserted in the spreadsheet between existing rows 2 and 3, with the entry in the new cell equal to 100.

   a. What value will be returned by the AVG function in spreadsheet 1 after the new row has been inserted?

   b. What value will be returned by the formula in spreadsheet 2 after the new row has been inserted?

   c. In which cell will the AVG function itself be located after the new row has been inserted?

   Return to the original problem, but this time delete row 2.

   d. What value will be returned by the AVG function in spreadsheet 1 after the row has been deleted?

   e. What will be returned by the formula in spreadsheet 2 after the row has been deleted?

	A
1	10
2	20
3	30
4	40
5	@AVG(A1..A4)

(a) Spreadsheet 1

	A
1	10
2	20
3	30
4	40
5	(A1+A2+A3+A4)/4

(b) Spreadsheet 2

FIGURE 3.15   Spreadsheets for Problem 2

3. Answer the following with respect to Figure 3.16. (Cell B5 is empty.) What value will be returned by the spreadsheet functions?

   a. @IF(A1=0,A2,A3)

   b. @SUM(A1..A5)

   c. @MAX(A1..A5,B1..B5)

   d. @MIN(A1..A3,5,A5)

   e. @AVG(B1..B4)

   f. @AVG(B1..B5)

   g. @PUREAVG(B1..B4)

   h. @PUREAVG(B1..B5)

   i. @MIN(10,MAX(A2..A4))

   j. @MAX(10,MIN(A2..A4))

   k. @PURECOUNT(A1..A5)

   l. @PURECOUNT(B1..B5)

   m. @COUNT(A1..A5)

   n. @COUNT(B1..B5)

   o. @VLOOKUP(15,A1..B5,1)

	A	B
1	10	60
2	20	70
3	30	80
4	40	90
5	50	

FIGURE 3.16   Spreadsheet for Problem 3

4. Refer to the spreadsheet in Figure 3.3a, which shows the total interest paid over the life of a loan. The numbers in the spreadsheet may be surprising; for example, the total interest on a 30-year loan at 9.5% comes to more than twice the principal. The results are considerably better for the 15-year mortgage.

   a. What formula (function) should be entered into cell C6 to compute the total interest for a 30-year loan?

   b. What formula (function) should be entered into cell E6 to compute the total interest for a 15-year loan?

   c. Implement the spreadsheet in Lotus. Add your name somewhere in the spreadsheet, then print the spreadsheet as well as the cell formulas. Prepare a cover page and submit both printouts to your instructor.

5. Refer to the spreadsheet in Figure 3.3b, which used the PMT function to compute the amortization schedule for a loan.

   a. What formula (function) should be entered into cell C6?

   b. What formula (function) should be entered into cell D9?

   c. What formula should be entered into cell B10? (The amount of each payment that goes toward interest is the interest rate per period times the unpaid balance of the loan.)

   d. What formula should be entered into cell C10? (The amount of each payment that goes toward the principal is the payment amount minus the amount which goes toward interest.)

   e. What formula should be entered into cell D10?

   f. Implement the spreadsheet in Lotus, but supply your own parameters for the principal, interest, and length of the loan. Add your name somewhere in the spreadsheet, then print the spreadsheet as well as the cell formulas. Prepare a cover page and submit both printouts to your instructor.

6. Figure 3.17 contains a spreadsheet used to determine information about Certificates of Deposit purchased at First National Bank of Miami. Retrieve PROB0306.WK4 from the data disk, then complete the spreadsheet following the steps below:

   ➤ Enter the function to display the current date in B1.
   ➤ Enter the formula to calculate the Maturity Date in cell E9. (To determine the Maturity Date, add the duration of the certificate to the date purchased.) Copy the formula to the remaining entries in the column.

	A	B	C	D	E	F
1	Date:					
2						
3	Certificates of Deposit					
4	First National Bank of Miami					
5						
6						# of Days
7			Date		Maturity	Remaining
8	Customer	Amount of CD	Purchased	Duration	Date	Til Mature
9	Harris	500000	12/01/93	180		
10	Bodden	50000	01/30/94	180		
11	Dorsey	25000	02/03/94	60		
12	Rosell	10000	03/30/94	60		
13	Klinger	10000	04/01/94	60		

FIGURE 3.17 Spreadsheet for Problem 6

> ➤ Move to cell F9 and enter the formula to calculate the number of days remaining until the certificate matures, or if the certificate has already matured, the word *Matured* should appear in the cell. The determination of whether or not the CD has matured can be made by comparing the Maturity date to the current date; if the Maturity date is greater than the current date, the CD has not yet matured.

> ➤ Format all of the dates so that they are displayed in the dd-mmm-yy format (e.g., 15-May-94 rather than 5/15/94).

> ➤ Format the Amount of CD with dollar signs and commas, but no decimal places.

> ➤ Center the entries in A3 and A4 over the width of the spreadsheet. Change the font to 14 point Arial bold italic.

> ➤ Boldface the column headings.

> ➤ Save and print the spreadsheet.

7. Figure 3.18 contains a spreadsheet used to determine information about software purchases for HOT SPOT Software Sales. Figure 3.18a shows the spreadsheet as it exists on disk, while Figure 3.18b shows the completed spreadsheet. Retrieve PROB0307.WK4 from the data disk and complete it so that it is identical to the spreadsheet in Figure 3.18b. In doing so, you will need the following facts:

> ➤ The total sale is determined by multiplying the current price by the number of units sold.

> ➤ A discount is given if the total sale is equal to or greater than the discount threshold. (The discount percentage is determined by multiplying the total sale by the discount percentage, and the exact percentage to be used is indicated in the assumption area at the bottom of the spreadsheet.) If the total sale is less than the discount threshold, no discount is given.

> ➤ The discounted total is determined by subtracting the Amount of Discount from the total sale.

	A	B	C	D	E	F	G	H	I
1	HOT SPOT Software Sales								
2	Miami, Florida								
3									
4	Customer		Current	Units	Total	Amount of	Discounted	Sales	Amount
5	Name	Program	Price	Sold	Sale	Discount	Total	Tax	Due
6	Macy's	Windows	59.99	2					
7	Kings Bay Athletics	Word for Windows	295	5					
8	Bloomingdale's	After Dark	29.95	10					
9	Service Merchandise	Excel	495	3					
10	Lord & Taylor	Lotus for Windows	595	3					
11	Burdine's	WordPerfect	245	2					
12	Sports Authority	Word for Windows	295	3					
13	The Gap	Excel	495	7					
14	Home Depot	Windows	59.99	12					
15	Brookstone	Lotus for Windows	595	8					
16	Coconuts	WordPerfect	245	10					
17	Express	Windows	59.99	3					
18									
19									
20	Discount Threshold:		1000				Number of Customers:		
21	Discount Percentage:		0.15				Highest Current Price:		
22	Sales Tax:		0.065				Fewest Units Sold:		
23							Average Discount:		
24							Total Amount Due:		

FIGURE 3.18a Spreadsheet for Problem 7

Customer Name	Program	Current Price	Units Sold	Total Sale	Amount of Discount	Discounted Total	Sales Tax	Amount Due
				HOT SPOT Software Sales				
				Miami, Florida				
Macy's	Windows	$60	2	$119.98	$0.00	$119.98	$7.80	$127.78
Kings Bay Athletics	Word for Windows	$295	5	$1,475.00	$221.25	$1,253.75	$81.49	$1,335.24
Bloomingdale's	After Dark	$30	10	$299.50	$0.00	$299.50	$19.47	$318.97
Service Merchandise	Excel	$495	3	$1,485.00	$222.75	$1,262.25	$82.05	$1,344.30
Lord & Taylor	Lotus for Windows	$595	3	$1,785.00	$267.75	$1,517.25	$98.62	$1,615.87
Burdine's	WordPerfect	$245	2	$490.00	$0.00	$490.00	$31.85	$521.85
Sports Authority	Word for Windows	$295	3	$885.00	$0.00	$885.00	$57.53	$942.53
The Gap	Excel	$495	7	$3,465.00	$519.75	$2,945.25	$191.44	$3,136.69
Home Depot	Windows	$60	12	$719.88	$0.00	$719.88	$46.79	$766.67
Brookstone	Lotus for Windows	$595	8	$4,760.00	$714.00	$4,046.00	$262.99	$4,308.99
Coconuts	WordPerfect	$245	10	$2,450.00	$367.50	$2,082.50	$135.36	$2,217.86
Express	Windows	$60	3	$179.97	$0.00	$179.97	$11.70	$191.67

Discount Threshold:		$1,000				Number of Customers:		12
Discount Percentage:		15%				Highest Current Price:		$595
Sales Tax:		6.5%				Fewest Units Sold:		2
						Average Discount:		$192.75
						Total Amount Due:		$16,828.42

FIGURE 3.18b   Spreadsheet for Problem 7

➤ The sales tax is determined by multiplying the discounted total by the sales tax percentage (as indicated in the assumption area).

➤ The amount due is determined by adding the sales tax to the discounted total.

➤ The number of customers, highest current price, fewest units sold, average discount, and total amount due are determined by entering the appropriate functions in the indicated cells.

Would it be a good idea to lower the discount threshold to $500 and lower the discount percentage to 10%? Why or why not? Why should the discount threshold, discount percentage, and sales tax percentage be isolated from the main body of the spreadsheet? What advantages does this give you in working with the spreadsheet?

8. Figure 3.19 suggests how the spreadsheet application can be extended to the preparation of sales invoices. The figure assumes the existence of a template, which the user retrieves for each new order. All entries in the shaded area are made after the template is retrieved, depending on the particular order.

   a. What formula should you enter into cell D9 to compute the amount due for the first item?

   b. What entry should you use in cell D14 to compute the subtotal? Your answer should accommodate the potential insertion of additional rows (after row 12) should the customer order more than four items.

   c. What entry should you use in cell C15 to determine the discount percentage (based on the table shown in the lower-left portion of the spreadsheet?)

   d. What entry should you use in cell D15 to compute the discount?

   e. What formula should you use to compute the sales tax? (Customers with a tax status of "Exempt" pay no tax; all other customers pay the tax rate shown in cell A24 for the discounted order.)

f. What formula should you use in cell D17 for the total due?

g. Implement the spreadsheet in the figure, add your name as the customer, and submit the assignment to your instructor.

	A	B	C	D
1	*INVOICE*			16-Mar-94
2				
3	Customer:	Mr. John Doe		
4		10000 Sample Road		
5		Coral Springs, FL 33065		
6	Tax Status:	Exempt		
7				
8	Quantity	Item	Unit Price	Amount
9	15	Widgets (small)	$14.00	$210.00
10	6	Widgets (medium)	$20.00	$120.00
11	2	Widgets (large)	$25.00	$50.00
12	14	Widgets (extra large)	$30.00	$420.00
13				
14		Subtotal		$800.00
15		Discount	10%	$80.00
16		Sales Tax		$0.00
17		Total		$720.00
18				
19				
20				
21				
22				
23	Sales Tax (non-exempt)		Order	Discount
24	6%		$200	2%
25			$400	5%
26			$750	10%

FIGURE 3.19 Spreadsheet for Problem 8

9. Use Figure 3.1 at the beginning of the chapter as the basis for this exercise.

a. Retrieve the spreadsheet **PROB0309.WK4** from the data disk.

b. Enter the parameters for your specific car in cells B1, B2, and B3 as in Figure 3.1. Enter the terms of the loan in cells B5 and B6 to determine the projected monthly payment.

c. The monthly payment is only one expense; a realistic estimate requires insurance, gas, and maintenance. Enter these labels in cells A8, A9, and A10, then put the projected expenses in cells B8, B9, and B10.

d. Add the label, **Total,** in cell A11, and the formula to compute this amount in cell B11.

e. The spreadsheet can make the decision for you. Click in cell A13 and enter the label, *The Decision. . :* Enter an IF function into cell B13 that will display Yes if the *total* expenses are $500 or less, and No otherwise.

f. Insert two rows at the top of the spreadsheet to accommodate the title of the spreadsheet. Click in cell A1 and type the title of the spreadsheet, *Can I Afford It?*, followed by your name.

g. Format the title in boldface, italics, and/or a larger typeface. Leave row two blank to offset the title from the remainder of the spreadsheet.

h. Save the updated spreadsheet.

i. Print the entire spreadsheet two ways, once with computed values and once with cell formulas. Submit both spreadsheets to your instructor.

10. Inserting an object: This exercises requires the availability of the appropriate clip art to enhance a spreadsheet as shown in Figure 3.20. We used an image from Lotus Freelance for Windows, copied it to the clipboard, then pasted it into the spreadsheet. (Alternatively, you might try the HOTROD.WPG file available with WordPerfect 6.0.) Regardless of the image you use, once the object has been copied to the spreadsheet, you can select it, then move and/or size the image just as you would in any Windows application.

	A	B	C
1	Price of car	16,999	
2	Manufacturer's rebate	$1,000	
3	Down Payment	$3,500	
4	Amount to be financed	12,499	
5	Interest rate	8%	
6	Term (years)	4	
7	Monthly Payment	$305.14	
8	Gas (month)	$40.00	
9	Insurance (month)	$125.00	
10	Maintenance	$25.00	
11	Total	$495.14	
12			
13	The Decision...	Yes!	

FIGURE 3.20   Spreadsheet for Problem 10

Use the **PROB0309.WK4** spreadsheet from the data disk or the updated spreadsheet developed in the previous exercise.

Case Studies

Startup Airlines

You have been hired as the spreadsheet expert for a small start-up airline that needs to calculate the fuel requirements and associated cost for its available flights. The airline currently has two types of aircraft, a Boeing-727 and a DC-9, which consume 10,000 and 8,000 gallons of fuel, respectively, for each hour in the air. The fuel needed for any given flight depends on the aircraft and number of flying hours; for example, a five-hour flight in a DC-9 can be expected to use 40,000 gallons. The plane must carry an additional 10% of the required fuel in order to maintain a holding pattern (4,000 gallons in this example) and an additional 20% as reserve (8,000 gallons in this example). Use the data in AIRLINES.WK4 to compute the fuel necessary for the listed flights as well as the estimated cost based on a fuel price of $1.00 per gallon. Your spreadsheet should be completely flexible and amenable to change; that is, the hourly fuel requirements, price per gallon, holding and reserve percentages are all subject to change at a moment's notice.

Compensation Analysis

A corporation typically uses several different measures of compensation in an effort to pay its employees fairly. Most organizations closely monitor an employee's salary history, keeping both the present and previous salary in order to compute various statistics, including:

➤ The percent salary increase, which is computed by taking the difference between the present and previous salary, and dividing by the previous salary.

➤ The months between increase, which is the elapsed time between the date the present salary took effect and the date of the previous salary. (Assume 30 days per month for ease of calculation.)

➤ The annualized rate of increase, which is the percent salary increase divided by the months between increase; for example, a 5% raise after 6 months is equivalent to an annualized increase of 10%; a 5% raise after two years is equivalent to an annual increase of 2.5%.

Use the data in SALARIES.WK4 to compute salary statistics for the employees who have had a salary increase; employees who have not received an increase should have a suitable indication in the cell. Compute the average, minimum, and maximum value for each measure of compensation for those employees who have received an increase.

The Automobile Dealership

The purchase of a car usually entails extensive bargaining between the dealer and the consumer. The dealer has an asking price but typically settles for less. The commission paid to a salesperson depends on how close the selling price is to the asking price. Exotic Motors has the following compensation policy for its sales staff:

➤ A 3% commission on the actual selling price for cars sold at 95% or more of the asking price.

➤ A 2% commission on the actual selling price for cars sold at 90% or more (but less than 95%) of the asking price.

➤ A 1% commission on the actual selling price for cars sold at less than 90% of the asking price. The dealer will not go below 85% of his asking price.

The dealer's asking price is based on the dealer's cost plus a 20% markup; thus, the asking price on a car which cost the dealer $20,000 would be $24,000. Develop a spreadsheet to be used by the dealer that shows his profit (the selling price minus the salesperson's commission) on every sale. The spreadsheet should be completely flexible and allow the dealer to vary the markup or commission percentages without having to edit or recopy any of the formulas. Use the data in CARS.WK4 to test your spreadsheet.

The Birthday Problem

How much would you bet *against* two people in your class having the same birthday? Don't be too hasty, for the odds of two classmates sharing the same birthday (month and day) are much higher than you would expect; for example, there is a 50% chance in a class of 23 students that two people will have been born on the same day. The probability jumps to 70% in a class of 30, and to 90% in a class of 41.

You need a basic knowledge of probability to prove these statements, but the solution is readily amenable to a spreadsheet. In essence, you calculate the probability of individuals *not* having the same birthday, then subtract this number from one, to obtain the probability of the event coming true. In a group of two people, for example, the probability of *not* being born on the same day is 365/366; that is, the second person can be born on any of 365 days and still have a different birthday. The probability of two people having the same birthday becomes 1−365/366.

The probability for *different* birthdays in a group of three is (365/366)*(364/366); the probability of *not* having different birthdays—that is, of two people having the same birthday—is one minus this number. In similar fashion, the probability for different birthdays in a group of four is (365/366)*(364/366)*(363/366), and so on. Develop a spreadsheet that shows the probability of two people being born on the same day in classes of up to 50 students.

The Financial Consultant

A friend of yours is in the process of buying a home and has asked you to compare the payments and total interest on a 15- and 30-year loan. You want to do as professional a job as possible and have decided to analyze the loans in Lotus, then incorporate the results into a memo written in a word processor. As of now the principal is $150,000, but it is more than likely that your friend will change his mind several times, and so you want to use the OLE capability within Windows to dynamically link the spreadsheet to the word processing document. Your memo should include a letterhead that takes advantage of the formatting capabilities within the word processor; a graphic logo would be a nice touch.

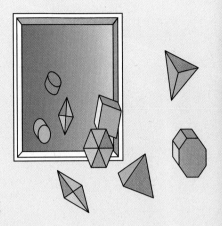

4

Graphs and Charts: Delivering a Message

CHAPTER OBJECTIVES

After reading this chapter you will be able to:

1. Distinguish between different types of charts, stating the advantages and disadvantages of each.
2. Create and/or modify a chart within a spreadsheet; explain how many charts can be derived from the same spreadsheet.
3. Enhance a chart by using arrows and text.
4. Explain how one chart can plot multiple data series; differentiate between data series that are specified in rows versus data series in columns.
5. Describe how a chart can be statistically accurate, yet totally misleading.
6. Create a compound document consisting of a word processing memo, a spreadsheet, and a chart.

OVERVIEW

Business has always known that the graphic representation of data is an attractive, easy-to-understand way to convey information. Indeed, business graphics has become one of the most exciting Windows applications, enabling charts (graphs) to be easily created from a spreadsheet, with just a few simple keystrokes or mouse clicks.

The chapter begins by emphasizing the importance of determining the message to be conveyed by a chart. It describes the different types of charts that are available within Lotus and how to choose among them, then explains how to embed a chart within a spreadsheet. It also describes how to enhance that chart with arrows and additional text.

The second half of the chapter explains how one chart can plot multiple sets of data, and how several charts can be based on the same spreadsheet. It describes how to create a compound document, in which a chart and its associated spreadsheet are dynamically linked to a memo produced by a word processor. All told, we think you will find this to be one of the most enjoyable chapters in the text.

CHART TYPES

The spreadsheet in Figure 4.1 is used throughout the chapter as the basis for various charts that we will create. Let us assume that you have been given the assignment of analyzing the data in the spreadsheet and developing a series of charts to convey that information. Your manager believes that the sales data can be understood more easily from charts than from the strict numerical presentation of a spreadsheet.

	A	B	C	D	E	F
1		*Superior Software*	*Monthly Sales*			
2						
3		*Miami*	*Denver*	*New York*	*Boston*	*Total*
4	*Word Processing*	$50,000	$67,500	$9,500	$141,000	$268,000
5	*Spreadsheets*	$44,000	$18,000	$11,500	$105,000	$178,500
6	*Database*	$12,000	$7,500	$6,000	$30,000	$55,500
7	*Total*	$106,000	$93,000	$27,000	$276,000	$502,000

FIGURE 4.1   Superior Software

The sales data in the spreadsheet can be presented several ways—for example, by geographic area, by product category, or by a combination of the two. Ask yourself, which type of chart is best suited to answer the following questions?

➤ What percentage of the total revenue comes from each city? from each product category?
➤ What was the dollar revenue produced by each city? by each product category?
➤ What is the rank of each city with respect to sales? to product category?
➤ How much revenue did each product category contribute in each city?

In every instance realize that a chart exists only to deliver a message, and that you cannot create an effective chart unless you are sure of what that message is. The next several pages discuss the different types of business charts, each of which is best suited to a particular type of message.

THE POUND AND THE YEN

Today's global economy makes it necessary to use currency symbols from other countries, such as the British pound and the Japanese yen. To change the currency symbol, pull down the **Tools menu,** click **User Setup,** then click the International command button. Click in the text box for the Currency symbol, then use the **numeric keypad** to enter **Alt+156** or **Alt+157** for the £ or ¥, respectively. Click OK to exit from the International dialog box, then click OK a second time to exit from User Setup.

Pie Charts

A *pie chart* is the most effective way to display proportional relationships; it is the type of chart that should be selected whenever words like *percentage* or *market share* appear in the message to be delivered. The pie, or complete circle, denotes the total amount; each slice of the pie corresponds to the appropriate percentage of the total.

The pie chart in Figure 4.2a divides the pie representing total sales into four slices, one for each city, with the size of each slice proportional to the percentage of total sales in that city. To create a pie chart, Lotus computes the total sales ($502,000 in our example), then calculates the percentage contributed by each geo-

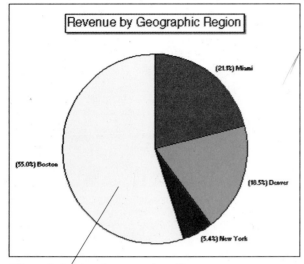

Slice of pie sized proportionally
to its percent of the total

(a) Simple Pie Chart

Title emphasizes problems in New York

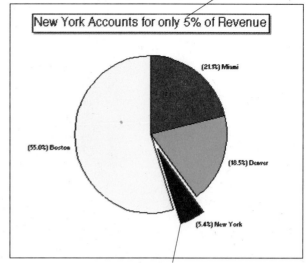

Slice of pie separated for emphasis

(b) Exploded Pie Chart

Title emphasizes Boston's contribution

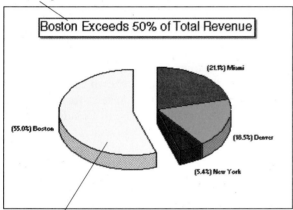

Slice exploded for emphasis

(c) Exploded Three-dimensional Pie Chart

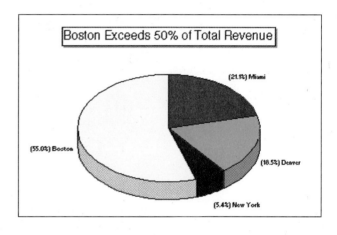

(d) Nonexploded Three-dimensional Pie Chart

FIGURE 4.2 Pie Charts

graphic area, and draws each slice of the pie in proportion to its computed percentage. Boston's sales of $276,000 account for 55 percent of the total, and so this slice of the pie is allotted 55 percent of the area of the circle. ***An exploded pie chart,*** as shown in Figure 4.2b, separates one or more slices of the pie for emphasis.

One way to achieve emphasis in a chart is to choose a title that reflects the message you are trying to deliver. The title in Figure 4.2a, for example, *Revenue by Geographic Region,* is neutral and leaves the reader to develop his or her own conclusion about the relative contribution of each area. By contrast, the title in Figure 4.2b, *New York Accounts for only 5% of Revenue,* is more suggestive and emphasizes the problems in this office. Alternatively, the chart could be retitled to *Boston Exceeds 50% of Total Revenue* if the intent were to emphasize the contribution of this city.

Three dimensional pie charts may be created in exploded or non-exploded format as shown in Figures 4.2c and 4.2d. Lotus also enables you to add arrows and text for emphasis.

A pie chart is easiest to read when the number of slices is limited (not more than six or seven), and when small percentages (percentages less than five) do not appear. The latter may be avoided by grouping several separate, but small, categories into a single class with the **category label** of Other.

EXPLODED PIE CHARTS

You can click and drag wedges in and out of a pie chart and thus convert an ordinary pie chart to an exploded pie chart; for best results pull the wedge out only slightly from the main body of the pie.

Bar Charts

A **bar chart** is used when there is a need to show actual numbers rather than percentages. The bar chart in Figure 4.3a plots the identical data as the earlier pie chart, but displays it differently. The values for the descriptive category (Miami, Denver, New York, and Boston) are shown along the **X** (horizontal) **axis** with values of the quantitative variable (monthly sales) plotted on the **Y** (vertical) **axis**. The height of each column is proportional to the value of the quantitative variable.

A bar chart can also be given a horizontal orientation as shown in Figure 4.3b. Some individuals prefer the horizontal chart over its vertical counterpart because the longer horizontal bars accentuate the difference between the cities. Horizontal bar charts are also preferable to display long descriptive names that crowd the X axis of a vertically aligned chart. Note, too, how the title of the chart, *Boston Leads All Cities,* is phrased to lead the reader and further emphasize the message.

A three-dimensional effect creates added interest as shown in Figures 4.3c and 4.3d. The latter figures plot a different set of numbers, the sales for each application, rather than the sales for each city. Arrows and text can be added to any chart to enhance the message.

As with a pie chart, bar charts are easiest to read when the number of categories is relatively small, say, seven or fewer; otherwise the bars run together and labeling becomes impossible.

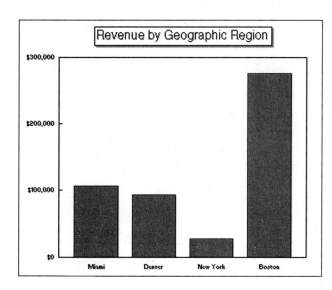

(a) Bar Chart

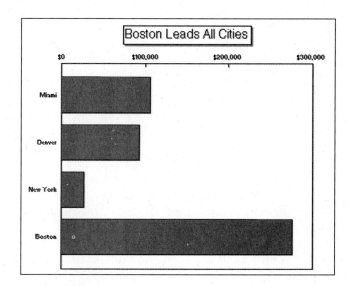

(b) Horizontal Bar Chart

FIGURE 4.3 Bar Charts

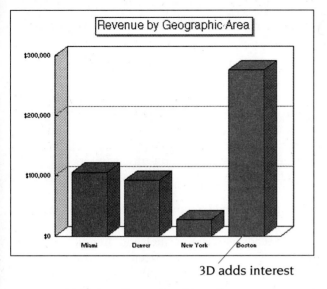

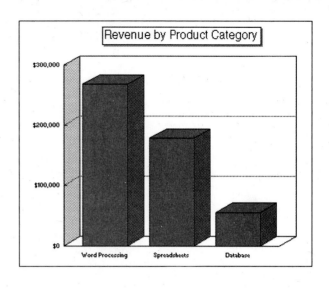

3D adds interest

(c) Three-dimensional Bar Chart   (d) Alternate Bar Chart

FIGURE 4.3   Bar Charts (continued)

CREATING A CHART

A chart is created from a spreadsheet and embedded within that spreadsheet as shown in Figure 4.4. The chart is linked directly to the spreadsheet so that changes in the data are automatically reflected in the chart. Several charts may be based on the same spreadsheet, and as previously stated, if you

Currently selected chart   SmartIcons reflect chart commands

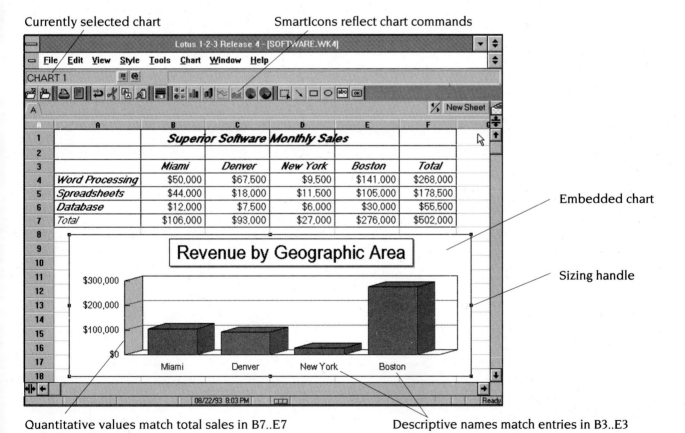

Embedded chart

Sizing handle

Quantitative values match total sales in B7..E7   Descriptive names match entries in B3..E3

FIGURE 4.4   An Embedded Chart

change the spreadsheet, the **embedded chart** (or charts) derived from that spreadsheet will also change.

Study the chart in Figure 4.4 to see how it corresponds to the spreadsheet. The descriptive names on the X axis match the entries in cells B3 through E3. The quantitative values on the Y axis match the total sales in cells B7 through E7. The **sizing handles** surrounding the chart indicate that the chart is currently selected and that the next command will affect the chart. If, for example, you were to press the Del key, you would erase the chart from the spreadsheet. The reference to CHART1 on the edit line also indicates the chart is currently selected, and the SmartIcons have changed to reflect commands associated with the chart. The icons will change back to the default set of icons when you select a cell within the spreadsheet.

Once the chart is selected, it can be sized or moved in the same way as any Windows object. To size the chart, just drag any of the handles in the desired direction. To move the chart within the spreadsheet, simply click and drag the chart to its new location. Click anywhere outside the chart to deselect it and return to the Ready mode in the spreadsheet. Click on the border of the chart to select the entire chart and produce the sizing handles.

Creating a chart is simple. Just select the data on which the chart is based, such as cells B3 through E3 and B7 through E7 in Figure 4.4, pull down the Tools menu and click Chart, then click in the spreadsheet at the location where you want the chart to appear. Lotus creates a chart according to its default settings, but you can modify the chart in any number of ways through commands in the Chart menu and/or the SmartIcons.

Figure 4.5a displays the bar chart as it is initially created, whereas Figure 4.5b displays the modified chart. Several items bear mention:

➤ The chart type has been changed from the default bar chart to a three-dimensional bar chart.
➤ The title, *Revenue by Geographic Area,* has been entered and the titles *Y Axis* and *X Axis* have been deleted; the legend *Data A* has been deleted.
➤ The scale has been changed on the Y axis and light grid lines have been added
➤ A drop shadow has been added to highlight the entire graph.

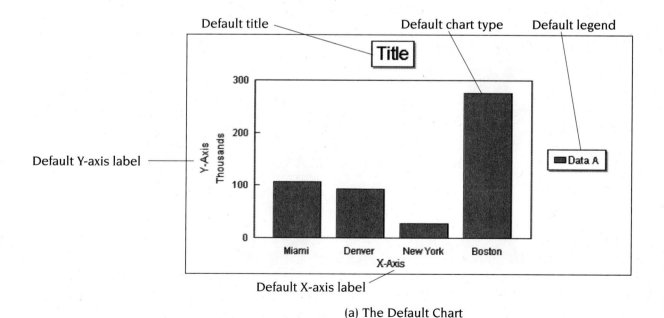

(a) The Default Chart

FIGURE 4.5 Creating a Chart

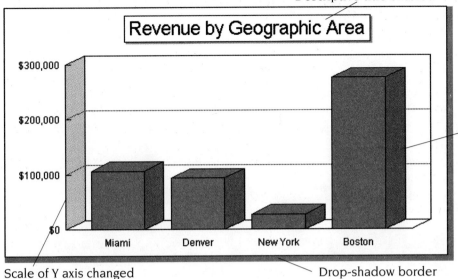

Descriptive title entered

Revenue by Geographic Area

Chart type changed to 3D bar chart

Scale of Y axis changed

Drop-shadow border

(b) The Completed Chart

FIGURE 4.5   Creating a Chart (continued)

The exercise that follows takes you through the steps to go from the spreadsheet in Figure 4.4, to the default chart in Figure 4.5a, to the completed chart in Figure 4.5b.

KEEP IT SIMPLE

Keep it simple—both your message and the means of conveying that message. Lotus makes it almost too easy to change fonts, styles, type sizes, and colors, but such changes will often detract, rather than enhance, a chart. More is not necessarily better, and just because the features are there, does not mean you have to use them. Just remember that any chart must ultimately succeed on the basis of content and clarity in communicating that content.

HANDS-ON EXERCISE 1:

Charts

Objective To create and modify a chart in Lotus; to embed a chart within a spreadsheet; to print the chart with and without the spreadsheet.

Step 1: Open the Superior Software spreadsheet
➤ Load Lotus.
➤ Pull down the **File menu** and click **Open** (or click the **open folder icon**).
➤ Retrieve the **SOFTWARE.WK4** spreadsheet from the data disk.
➤ Save the spreadsheet as **MYCHART.WK4** so that you can return to the original spreadsheet if necessary.

Step 2: Define the data range
➤ Click in cell **B3.**
➤ Drag the mouse over cells **B3 through E3,** which contain the labels for the X axis (the names of the cities).
➤ Press and hold the **Ctrl key** as you drag the mouse over cells **B7 through E7** to select the data series (the cells containing the sales data for the individual cities).
➤ Check that both ranges **B3..E3** and **B7..E7** are selected as shown in Figure 4.6a.

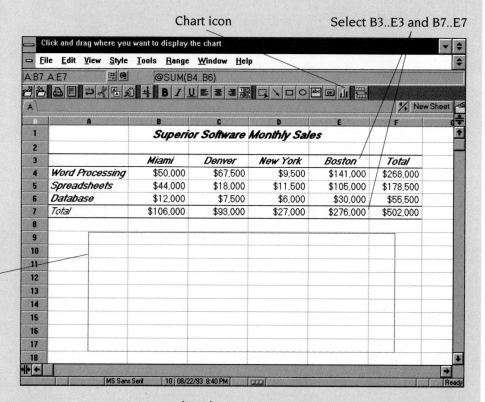

(a) Define the Data Range (step 2)

FIGURE 4.6   Hands-on Exercise I

Step 3: Create the default chart
➤ Pull down the **Tools menu** and click **Chart** (or click the **chart icon** in the default set of SmartIcons).
➤ The mouse pointer changes to a tiny cross attached to an image of the chart icon.
➤ Click **below** cell A7, then drag the mouse to define the area in the spreadsheet to hold the chart.
➤ Release the mouse to produce the default chart shown in Figure 4.6b.

Step 4: Modify the default chart
➤ Click on the border surrounding the **legend,** which reads Data A; the legend is now selected and surrounded by sizing handles. Press the **Del key** to delete the legend box, which is unnecessary with a bar chart that plots only a single variable.
➤ Click on the text that reads **Y-axis** (representing the title of the Y axis). Press the **Del key** to delete the selected entry. Delete the text **X-Axis** in similar fashion so that your chart matches the one in Figure 4.6c.

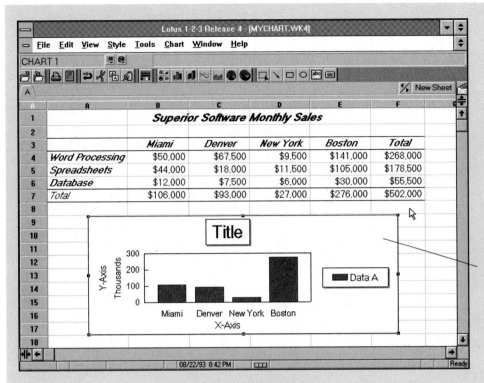

Default chart appears
when you release
the mouse button

(b) The Default Chart (step 3)

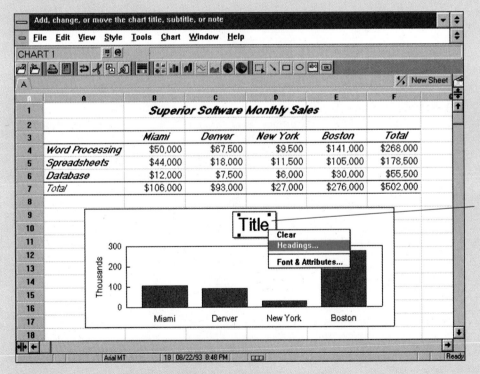

Click here and then click
the right mouse button to
produce quick menu.

(c) Modify the Chart (step 4)

FIGURE 4.6   Hands-on Exercise 1 (continued)

- Click the text that reads **Title,** then press the **right mouse button** to pull down the quick menu as shown in Figure 4.6c.
- Click **Headings.** Type the name of the chart, **Revenue by Geographic Area.** Click **OK.**
- Save the spreadsheet.

ENTER TITLES AUTOMATICALLY

The title of a chart can be taken directly from the contents of a cell within the spreadsheet. Click the title box within a chart, pull down the Chart menu, click Headings, click the cell check box, then enter the cell address (containing the title) in the text box for line 1. Click OK to return to the chart; the title will match the contents of the specified cell, and will reflect any subsequent changes in the contents of that cell.

Step 5: Change the spreadsheet
- Click in cell **B4.** Change the entry to **$300,000.** Press the **enter key.**
- The totals in cells F4 and B7 change automatically to reflect the increased sales for word processing in the Miami office.
- The bar for Miami changes in the chart and is now larger than the bar for Boston.
- Pull down the **Edit menu.** Click **Undo** to return to the initial value of $50,000.
- The spreadsheet and chart are restored to their original values.

DESIGNER FRAMES

Click the **right mouse button** anywhere along the border of the chart to select the border and simultaneously produce a quick menu. Click **Lines & Color,** then check **Designer Frame** in the ensuing dialog box. Click the drop-down list box to choose an appropriate frame, then click **OK** to highlight the chart within the spreadsheet with the designer frame of your choice.

Step 6: The pie chart
- Click anywhere in the bar chart to select the chart.
- Pull down the **Chart menu.** Click **Type** to produce the dialog box in Figure 4.6d.
- Click the **Pie button,** then click **OK.** The bar chart is converted to a pie chart as shown in Figure 4.6e.
- Pull down the **Chart menu.** Click **Data Labels** to produce the dialog box in Figure 4.6e.
- Experiment with the various check boxes to change the appearance of the pie chart; for example, check **Contents of X data range** to display the city names next to the percentages.

Click here to pull down Chart menu

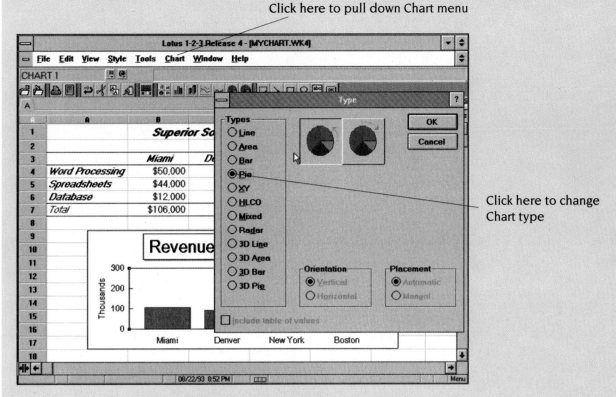

Click here to change Chart type

(d) Changing the Chart Type (step 6)

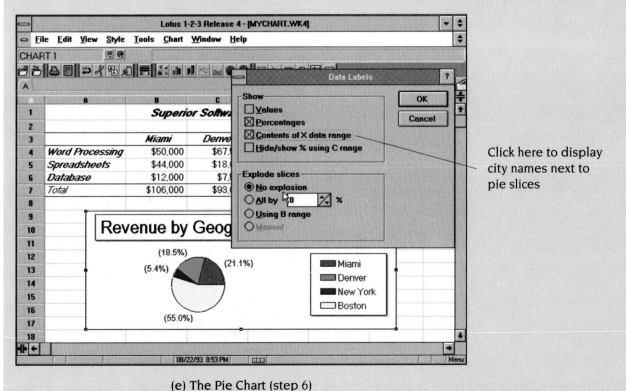

Click here to display city names next to pie slices

(e) The Pie Chart (step 6)

FIGURE 4.6 Hands-on Exercise 1 (continued)

SMARTICONS

The SmartIcons change automatically according to the selected object to reflect commands associated with that object; that is, any time a chart is selected, the icons that may be needed to modify the chart are displayed. The fastest way to change the chart type is to click the appropriate Smart-Icon; for example, click the pie or three-dimensional pie to convert a bar chart to a pie chart.

Step 7: 3D bar chart
➤ Click anywhere in the pie chart to select the chart.
➤ Click the **3D Bar icon** to change to a three-dimensional bar graph.
➤ Click any number in the scale for the Y axis to select the entire scale as shown in Figure 4.6f.
➤ Pull down the **Chart menu.** Click **Axis.** Click **Y-Axis** to produce the dialog box in Figure 4.6f.
➤ Click **Options.** Change both Axis units and Units title to **Manual** (in order to remove the word Thousands from the Y-axis scale). Click **OK** to exit the Options box. Click **OK** a second time to exit the Y-axis box.
➤ Check that the numbers on the Y axis are still selected. Pull down the **Style**

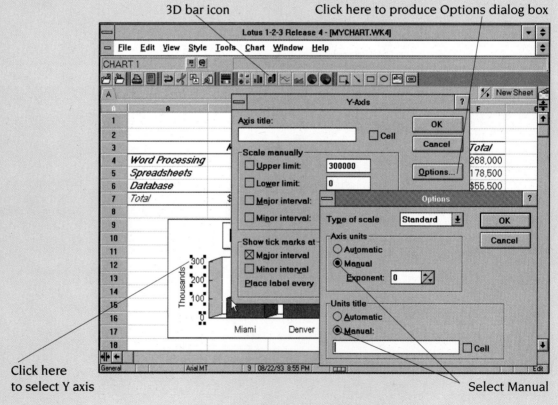

(f) 3D Bar Chart (step 7)

FIGURE 4.6 Hands-on Exercise I (continued)

menu. Click **Number format,** then change the formatting to currency with no decimals. Click **OK.**
- ➤ Pull down the **Chart menu.** Click **Grids.** Click the drop-down box for the Y axis. Click **major interval,** then click **OK** to complete the chart as shown in Figure 4.6g.
- ➤ Save the spreadsheet with the completed chart.

QUICK MENUS

Press the **right mouse button** when the chart (or specific element within the chart) is selected to display the appropriate quick menu. The menu is context sensitive and displays the applicable commands from the various pull-down menus.

Step 8: Print the spreadsheet and the embedded chart
- ➤ Pull down the **File menu** and click the **Print** command (or click the **Printer icon**).
- ➤ Click **Current Worksheet** to select the spreadsheet *and* the embedded chart.
- ➤ Click the **Preview command button** to preview the selection as in Figure 4.6g.
- ➤ Click the **Page Setup icon** to change one or more parameters:
  — Change the top margin to two inches.
  — Add a header as indicated.

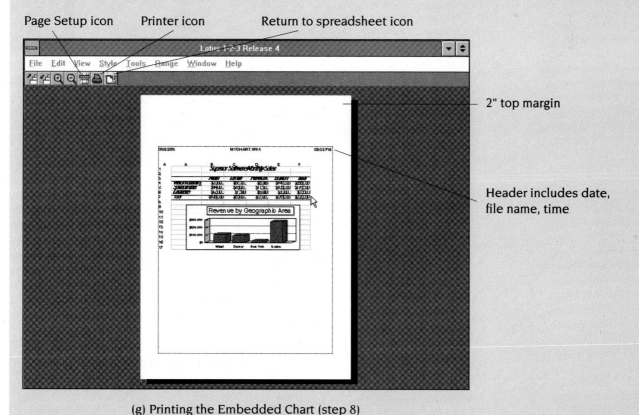

(g) Printing the Embedded Chart (step 8)

FIGURE 4.6 Hands-on Exercise 1 (continued)

➤ Click **OK** to exit the Page Setup dialog box.
➤ Click **OK** to print the spreadsheet with the embedded chart.

Step 9: Print the chart by itself
➤ Click anywhere in the chart.
➤ Pull down the **File menu** and click the **Print** command (or click the **Printer icon**).
➤ Click the option button to print the **selected chart;** if you do not see this option, it is because you forgot to select the chart prior to pulling down the File menu.
➤ Click the **Page Setup command button.**
➤ Change to **Landscape** printing. Change the Size to **Fill Page.** Click **OK.**
➤ Click **Preview** to see the spreadsheet as shown in Figure 4.6h.
➤ Click the **Print command button.**
➤ Click **OK** to print the embedded chart.

Step 10: Return to the spreadsheet
➤ Save the spreadsheet a final time.
➤ Pull down the **File menu** and click **Exit** to quit Lotus.

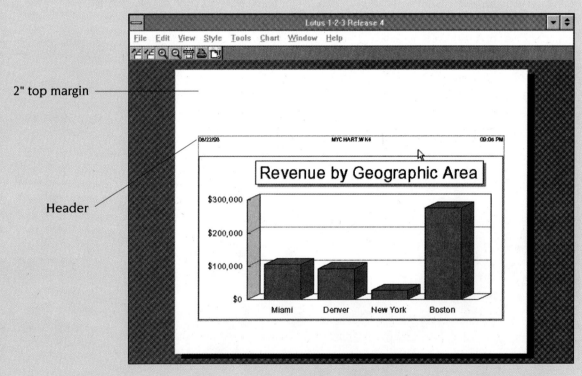

(h) Landscape Printing (step 9)

FIGURE 4.6   Hands-on Exercise 1 (continued)

MULTIPLE DATA SERIES

The charts presented so far displayed only a single *data series,* such as the total sales by location or the total sales by product category. Although such charts are useful, it is often necessary to view *multiple data series* on the same chart—perhaps the sales of each product category in each location.

Figure 4.7a displays the sales in each location according to product category. We see the rankings within each city, and further, that word processing is the lead-

Word processing is leading application

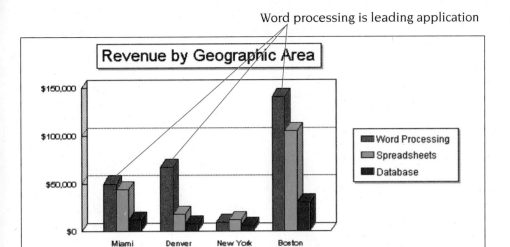

(a) Side-by-side Bar Chart

Boston is leading city

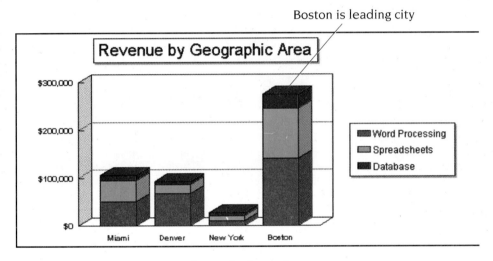

(b) Stacked Bar Chart

FIGURE 4.7 Bar Charts

ing application in three of the four cities. Figure 4.7b plots the identical data but in stacked bars rather than multiple bars.

The choice between the two types of charts depends on your message. If, for example, you want your audience to see the individual sales in each product category, the side-by-side (multi) bar chart is more appropriate. If, on the other hand, you want to emphasize the total sales for each city, the ***stacked bar chart*** is preferable. Note, too, the different scale on the Y axis in the two charts. The ***multibar chart*** in Figure 4.7a shows the sales of each product category and so the Y axis goes only to $150,000. The stacked bars in Figure 4.7b, however, reflect the total sales for each city and thus the scale goes to $300,000.

The biggest difference is that the stacked bar chart explicitly totals the sales for each city, whereas the multibar chart does not. The advantage of the stacked bar chart is that the city totals are clearly shown and can be easily compared, and further the relative contributions of each product category within each city are apparent. The disadvantage is that the segments within each bar do not start at the same point, making it difficult to determine the actual sales for the individual product categories or to compare the product categories between cities.

Realize, too, that for a stacked bar chart to make sense, its numbers must be additive. This is true in Figure 4.7b, where the stacked bars consist of three components, each of which is measured in dollars, and which can be logically added together to produce a total. You shouldn't, however, automatically convert a side-by-side multibar chart to its stacked bar equivalent. It would not make sense, for example, to convert a bar chart that plots unit sales and dollar sales side by side, to a stacked bar chart which adds the two, because units and dollars represent different physical concepts, and are not additive.

Rows versus Columns

Figure 4.8 illustrates a critical concept associated with multiple data series—whether the data series are in rows or columns. Figure 4.8a displays the spreadsheet we have been using throughout the chapter with multiple data series selected. Figure 4.8b shows the resultant chart when the data series are in rows (B4..E4, B5..E5, and B6..E6), whereas Figure 4.8c assumes the data series are in columns (B4..B6, C4..C6, D4..D6, and E4..E6).

Multiple data series in columns
(B4..B6, C4..C6, D4..D6, E4..E6)

	A	B	C	D	E	F
1		*Superior Software Monthly Sales*				
2						
3		*Miami*	*Denver*	*New York*	*Boston*	*Total*
4	*Word Processing*	$50,000	$67,500	$9,500	$141,000	$268,000
5	*Spreadsheets*	$44,000	$18,000	$11,500	$105,000	$178,500
6	*Database*	$12,000	$7,500	$6,000	$30,000	$55,500
7	*Total*	$106,000	$93,000	$27,000	$276,000	$502,000

Multiple data series in rows
(B4..E4, B5..E5, B6..E6)

(a) The Spreadsheet

FIGURE 4.8 Multiple Data Series

Both charts plot a total of twelve data points (three product categories for each of four locations) but group the data differently. Figure 4.8b displays the data by city; the sales of three product categories are shown for each of four cities. Figure 4.8c is the reverse; it groups the data by product category. The choice between the two depends on your message and whether you want to emphasize revenue by city or by product category. It sounds complicated, but it's not, and Lotus will create either chart for you according to your specifications.

➤ If you specify that the data is in rows (Figure 4.8b), Lotus will:
  — Use the first row (cells B3 through E3) in the selected range for the category names on the X axis
  — Use the first column (cells A4 through A6) for the *legends*
➤ If you specify the data is in columns (Figure 4.8c), Lotus will:
  — Use the first column (cells A4 through A6) in the selected range for the category names on the X axis
  — Use the first row (cells B3 through E3) for the legends

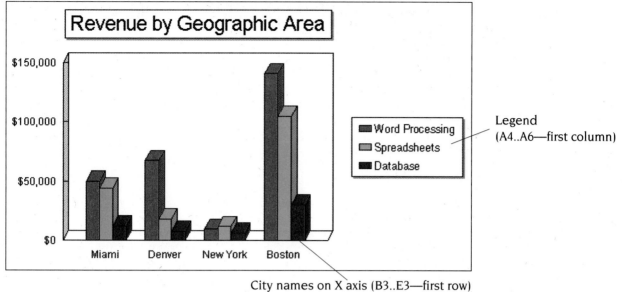

Legend
(A4..A6—first column)

City names on X axis (B3..E3—first row)

(b) Data in Rows

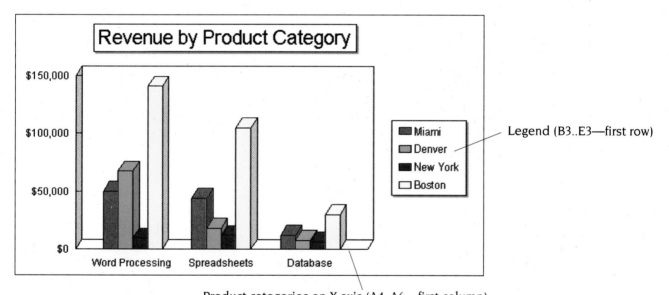

Legend (B3..E3—first row)

Product categories on X axis (A4..A6—first column)

(c) Data in Columns

FIGURE 4.8   Multiple Data Series (continued)

Stated another way, the data series in Figure 4.8b are in rows. Thus there are three data series (not counting the category names in row 3), one for each product category. The first data series plots the word processing sales in Miami, Denver, New York, and Boston; the second series plots the spreadsheet sales for each city, and the third series plots the database sales for each city.

The data series in Figure 4.8c are in columns. This time there are four data series (not counting the category names in column A), one for each city. The first series plots the Miami sales for word processing, spreadsheets, and database; the second series the Denver sales for each software category, and so on.

DEFAULT SELECTIONS

Lotus makes a default determination as to whether the data is in rows or columns by assuming that you want fewer data series than categories. Thus, if the selected cells contain more rows than columns, it will assume that the data series are in columns. If, on the other hand, there are more columns than rows (or an equal number of rows and columns), it will assume the data series are in rows.

HANDS-ON EXERCISE 2:

Multiple Data Series

Objective To plot multiple data series in the same chart; to differentiate between data series in rows and columns; to create and save multiple charts associated with the same spreadsheet.

Step 1: Open the spreadsheet
➤ Pull down the **File menu** and click **Open** (or click the **open folder SmartIcon**).
➤ Retrieve the **SOFTWARE.WK4** spreadsheet from the data disk.
➤ Save the spreadsheet as **MYCHART2.WK4** so that you can return to the original spreadsheet if necessary.

Step 2: Create a bar chart
➤ Click in cell **A3.** Drag the mouse over cells **A3 through E6.** Release the mouse button.
➤ Be sure that cells **A3..E6** are selected.
➤ Pull down the **Tools menu** and click **Chart** (or click the **Chart SmartIcon**).
➤ The mouse pointer changes to a tiny cross attached to an image of the chart icon.
➤ Click **below** cell A7, then drag the mouse to define the area in the spreadsheet to hold the chart.
➤ Release the mouse to produce the default chart shown in Figure 4.9a.
➤ Save the spreadsheet with the embedded chart.

MOVE AND/OR SIZE THE EMBEDDED CHART

To move the embedded chart elsewhere within a spreadsheet, click just *inside* the border of the chart, then drag it to the new location. To size the chart, select it, then drag any of the eight sizing handles in the desired direction. You can also move any individual element within the chart by selecting the element then dragging it to a new location within the chart border.

Step 3: Customize the default chart
➤ Use commands from the previous exercise to modify the default chart in Figure 4.9a so that it matches the 3D bar chart in Figure 4.9b:
➤ Change the chart type to a three-dimensional bar chart.

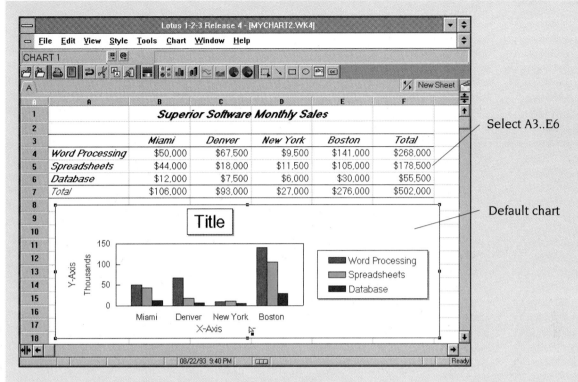

Select A3..E6

Default chart

(a) The Default Chart (step 2)

Copy chart to clipboard

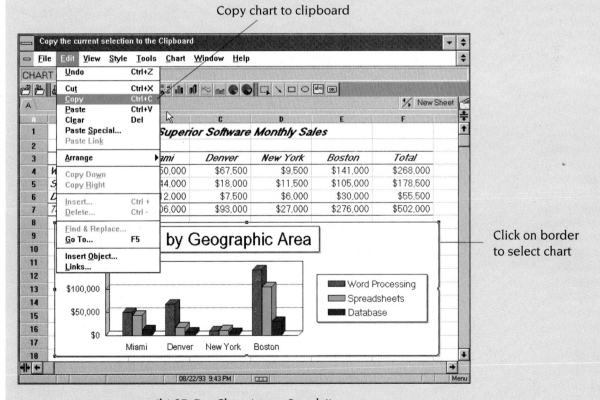

Click on border
to select chart

(b) 3D Bar Chart (steps 3 and 4)

FIGURE 4.9 Hands-on Exercise 2

➤ Add the title, **Revenue by Geographic Area.**
➤ Delete the labels X-Axis and Y-Axis.
➤ Change and format the scale on the Y Axis.
➤ Add a grid for the major intervals on the Y Axis.
➤ Add a designer frame to the chart.

Step 4: Copy the chart
➤ If necessary, click on the border of the chart to select it.
➤ Pull down the **Edit menu** and click **Copy** as shown in Figure 4.9b or click the appropriate SmartIcon.
➤ Scroll down several rows until the chart is no longer visible.
➤ Click in the desired cell—for example, cell A23.
➤ Pull down the **Edit menu** and click **Paste** or click the appropriate SmartIcon.
➤ The 3D bar chart has been copied to a second location as shown in Figure 4.9c.

NAME THE CHART

Charts can be named, then subsequently referenced by name for easy access. (See the following tip on the Edit Go To command.) Select the chart you wish to name, pull down the Chart menu, click Name, type the name of the chart, then click the Rename command button. Chart names can be up to 15 characters long and should consist entirely of numbers and/or letters; spaces are not allowed.

Copied chart is currently selected chart

Change the data series to columns

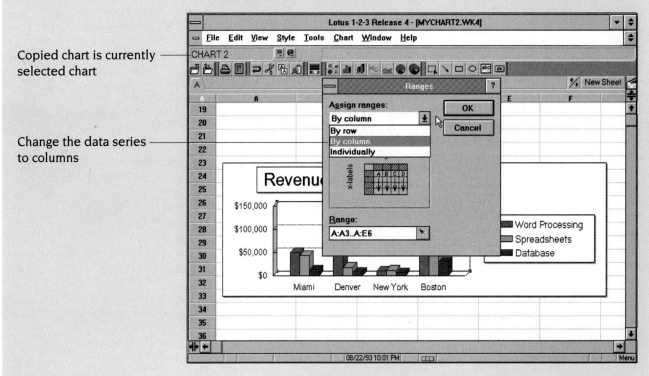

(c) The Chart Ranges Command (step 5)

FIGURE 4.9 Hands-on Exercise 2 (continued)

Step 5: Change the data series

➤ If necessary, click on the border of the chart to select it.

➤ Pull down the **Chart menu.** Click **Ranges** to produce the dialog box in Figure 4.9c.

➤ Click the drop-down list box for **Assign ranges.**

➤ Click **By column** as shown. Click **OK.** The chart changes to the one in Figure 4.9d with the software categories shown along the X axis.

➤ **Double click** the title of the chart to produce the dialog box in Figure 4.9d. Change the title to **Revenue by Product Category.** Click **OK** or press the **enter key** to return to the spreadsheet.

➤ Save the spreadsheet.

THE EDIT GO TO COMMAND

The **Edit Go To command** (or equivalent F5 key) is the easiest way to select a chart. Press the **F5** key to produce a dialog box, then click the down arrow in the Type of item list box and click Chart. Click the chart you want (the charts have default names of Chart 1, Chart 2, and so on), then click OK. Use the Chart Name command (see previous tip) to substitute a meaningful name for each chart, such as 3DREGION instead of Chart 1.

Change title to reflect change in orientation

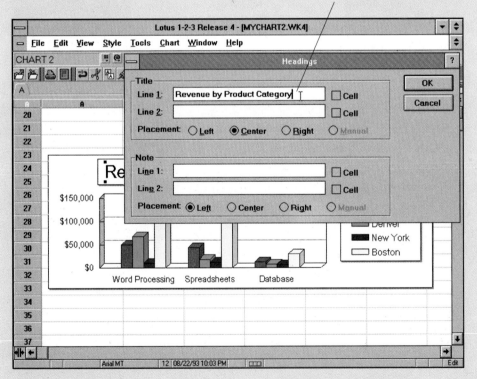

(d) Changing the Title (step 5)

FIGURE 4.9   Hands-on Exercise 2 (continued)

Step 6: The Print Preview command

➤ Pull down the **File menu** and click the **Print** command (or click the **Printer icon**).

➤ Click **Current Worksheet** to select the spreadsheet *and* the embedded charts.

➤ Click the **Preview command button** to preview the selection as in Figure 4.9e. If you have done the exercise correctly, you will see the sales data at the top of the spreadsheet followed by the two charts, which plot the data by geographic area and product category, respectively.

➤ Press the **Printer icon.** Click **OK** to print the spreadsheet or press the **Esc key** to return to the spreadsheet.

Click here to print spreadsheet and embedded charts

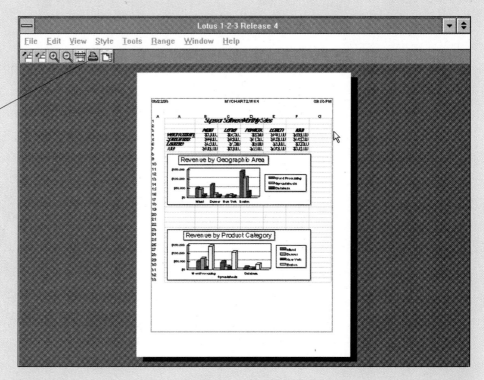

(e) The Print Preview Command (step 6)

FIGURE 4.9 Hands-on Exercise 2 (continued)

PRINTING A CHART

To print an embedded chart *without* the associated spreadsheet, select the chart, then pull down the File menu, click Print, then click the option button to print the selected chart. Use the Page Setup command to specify landscape orientation and to size the chart so that it fills the page but maintains its original proportions.

Step 7: The stacked bar chart

➤ Select the chart that plots revenue by product category.

➤ Pull down the **Chart menu** and click the **Type command** (or click the appropriate SmartIcon).

➤ Click the picture of the **stacked bar** in the dialog box of Figure 4.9f. Click **OK** to convert the chart to a stacked bar chart as shown in Figure 4.9g.

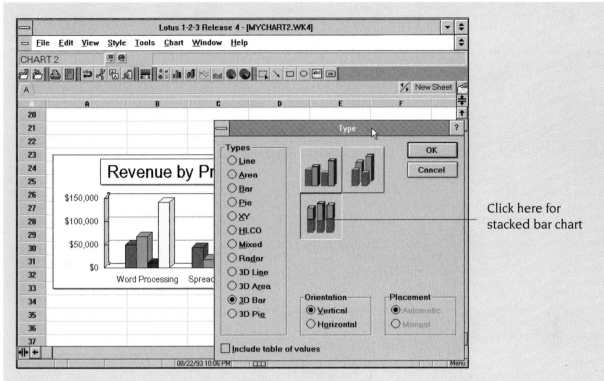

Click here for
stacked bar chart

(f) Changing the Chart Type (step 7)

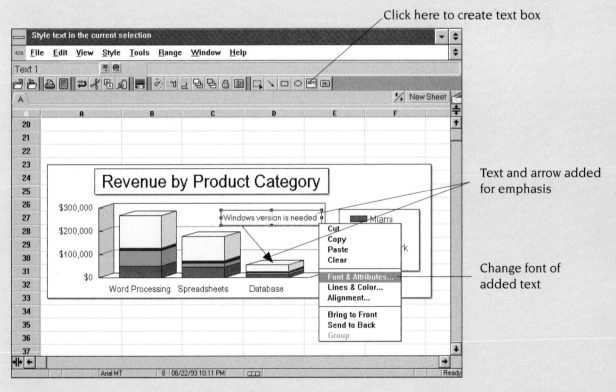

Click here to create text box

Text and arrow added
for emphasis

Change font of
added text

(g) Enhancing a Chart (step 8)

FIGURE 4.9 Hands-on Exercise 2 (continued)

Step 8: Enhance the chart
- Click the **arrow SmartIcon.**
- Click in the chart at the approximate place where the arrow is to begin, then drag the mouse to complete the arrow. Do not be concerned about precise size or location because you can always move and/or size the arrow by dragging the sizing handles.
- Click the **abc SmartIcon** to create a text box as shown in Figure 4.9g.
- Click in the chart at the approximate place where the text box is to begin, then drag the mouse to complete the box. Do not be concerned about the precise size or location because you can always move and/or size the text box by dragging the sizing handles.
- **Double click** in the text box to enter text; type **Windows version is needed** as shown in the figure. Click outside the box to complete the entry. Once the text has been entered, you can change its attributes (font and size) by clicking on the box with the **right mouse button** to produce the quick menu shown in the figure.
- Save the spreadsheet.

REMOVE THE BORDER

The border that surrounds the text created by the ABC text tool can be removed by selecting the text box, then clicking the right mouse button to produce a quick menu. Click the Lines & Color command, click the arrow in the drop-down list box for Line style, click None, then click OK. The border is gone.

Step 9: Exit Lotus
- Double click the **control-menu box** or pull down the **File menu** and click **Exit** to quit Lotus. Congratulations on a job well done.

ASK LOTUS

The arrows and/or text that were added to enhance a chart will print only if you print the spreadsheet and the embedded chart together; they do not appear when the chart is selected by itself prior to executing the Print command. This may be corrected in a future release of Lotus, but the problem existed in the initial version.

OBJECT LINKING AND EMBEDDING

One of the primary advantages of Windows is the ability to produce a *compound document,* that is, a document containing data from multiple applications. The memo in Figure 4.10 was created with a word processor (e.g., WordPerfect), but it contains elements that were created with another application. The spreadsheet and associated chart were created using Lotus.

Pasting is the simplest way to create a compound document and is done with the Cut, Copy, and Paste commands present in all Windows applications. You cut or copy data onto the clipboard, then paste it into a different application to produce the compound document. The disadvantage to the simple paste operation is that it is *static;* that is, if the data is subsequently changed in the original document, the change is *not* reflected in the document into which the data was copied.

Object Linking and Embedding (OLE) offer a superior way to share data between documents in that linking is dynamic; change the data (i.e., the object) in one document and it automatically changes in the other. The ***source document*** is the place where the object originates. The ***destination document*** is the file into which the object is placed, such as the word processing memo. The source document is created by the ***server application,*** perhaps Lotus. The destination document is created by the ***client application,*** possibly WordPerfect.

To: Mr. White
                Chairman, Superior Software

From: Julie Rubin
                Vice President, Marketing

Subject: May Sales Data

The chart below reflects our most recent sales data and clearly indicates that Boston is outperforming our other offices. I believe that Ms. Bost, the office supervisor, is directly responsible for this success and that she should be awarded accordingly. In addition, we should think about transferring Ms. Bost to New York, as that office is in desperate need of new leadership.

I look forward to hearing from you.

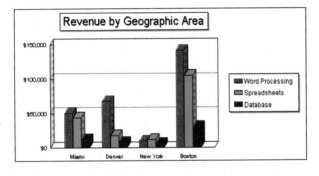

FIGURE 4.10   A Compound Document

The ensuing exercise creates the compound document in Figure 4.10 using WordPerfect as the word processor. You can, however, do the exercise with any Windows word processor that supports OLE.

HANDS-ON EXERCISE 3:

Object Linking and Embedding

Objective To create a compound document consisting of a memo and chart. The exercise is written for WordPerfect for Windows version 6.0 but will work with any Windows word processor that supports Object Linking and Embedding.

Step 1: Copy the spreadsheet to the clipboard
➤ Load Lotus. If necessary, click the maximize button so that Lotus takes the entire screen.
➤ Pull down the **File menu** and click **Open** (or click the **open folder SmartIcon**) to retrieve the **MYCHART2.WK4** spreadsheet.
➤ Click on the border of the chart to select it as shown in Figure 4.11a.
➤ Pull down the **Edit menu.**
➤ Click **Copy.** You will see the message, Select destination and choose Edit Paste in the upper left corner of the spreadsheet.

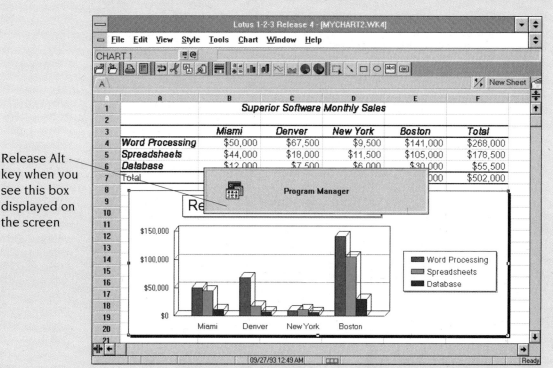

Release Alt key when you see this box displayed on the screen

(a) Switch to Program Manager (steps 1 and 2)

FIGURE 4.11   Hands-on Exercise 3

Step 2: Switch to Program Manager
➤ Press and hold the **Alt key** while you press and release the **Tab key** repeatedly to cycle through the open applications. Release the Alt key when you see Program Manager displayed in a box in the middle of your screen as shown in Figure 4.11a
➤ If necessary, open the **group window** for WordPerfect within Program Manager. Double click on the **program icon** for **WordPerfect.** Click the maximize button so that WordPerfect takes the entire screen.
➤ Pull down the **File menu.** Click **Open** to produce the dialog box in Figure 4.10b.
➤ Change to the LOTDATA subdirectory. Double click **MEMO.WPD** to open the word processing document.

Step 3: The Paste Special command
➤ Press **Ctrl+End** to move the insertion point to the end of the document. Press the **enter key** three times.
➤ Pull down the **Edit menu.**
➤ Click **Paste Special** to produce the dialog box in Figure 4.11c.

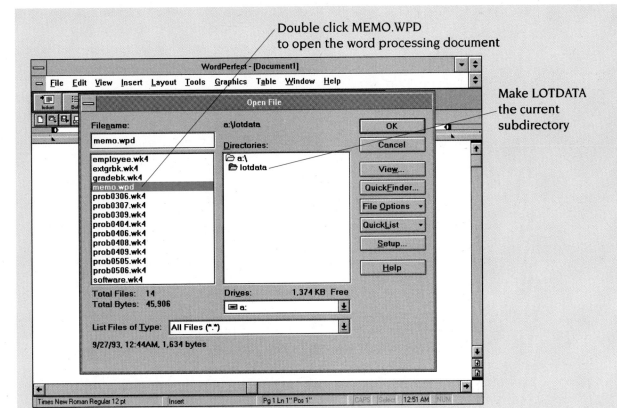

Double click MEMO.WPD
to open the word processing document

Make LOTDATA
the current
subdirectory

(b) Open the word processing document (step 2)

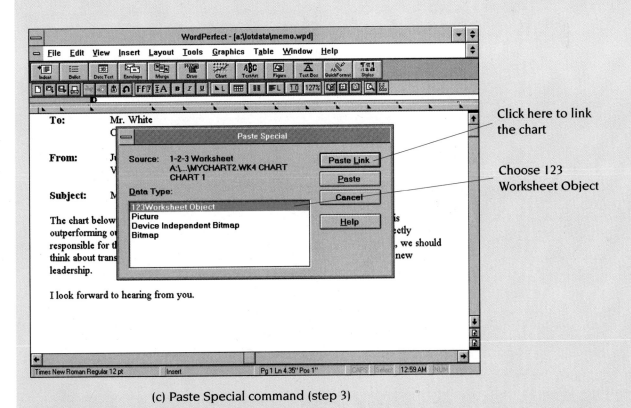

Click here to link
the chart

Choose 123
Worksheet Object

(c) Paste Special command (step 3)

FIGURE 4.11 Hands-on Exercise 3 (continued)

➤ Choose **123 Worksheet Object** as the data type as shown in the figure.
➤ Click **Paste Link.** The chart will be brought into the document as shown in Figure 4.11d.
➤ Pull down the **File menu.** Click **Save** to save the memo with the chart.

Step 4: Modify the chart
➤ Press and hold the **Alt key** while you press and release the **Tab key** repeatedly to cycle through the open applications. Release the Alt key when you see Lotus displayed in a box in the middle of your screen as in Figure 4.11d.
➤ Check that the chart is still selected.
➤ Pull down the **Chart menu.** Click **Type.** Click the **Stacked bar icon** as shown in Figure 4.11e.
➤ Click **OK.**

Step 5: Return to the word processing document
➤ Use **Alt+Tab** to return to WordPerfect.
➤ The chart has changed automatically to a stacked bar as shown in Figure 4.11f.
➤ Press **Ctrl+Home** to move to the beginning of the memo. Add **your name** as Vice President of Marketing.
➤ Save the memo.
➤ Print the memo.
➤ Exit WordPerfect
➤ Exit Lotus.
➤ Exit Windows.

Release Alt key when you see this box displayed on the screen

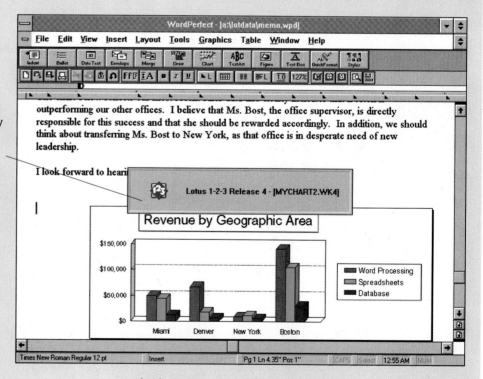

(d) The compound document (step 3)

FIGURE 4.11   Hands-on Exercise 3 (continued)

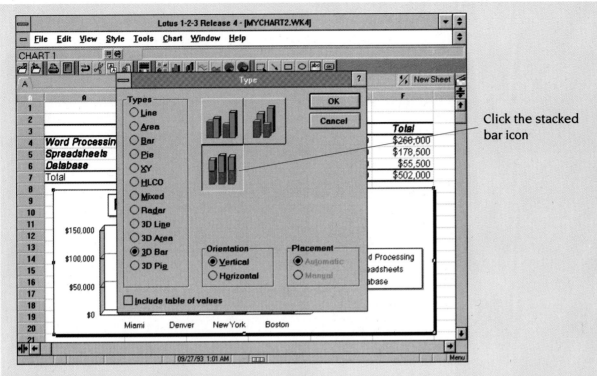

Click the stacked
bar icon

(e) Modify the chart (step 4)

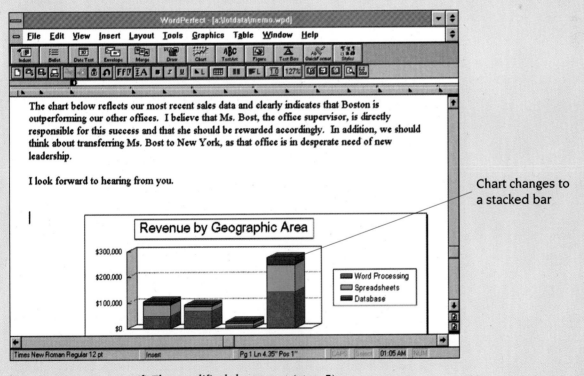

Chart changes to
a stacked bar

(f) The modified document (step 5)

FIGURE 4.11 Hands-on Exercise 3 (continued)

Lotus offers a total of 12 chart types, each with several formats. The chart types are displayed in the Chart Type dialog box (see Figure 4.6d) and are listed here for convenience. The chart types are line, area, bar, pie, XY (scatter), HLCO, mixed, radar, 3D line, 3D area, 3D bar, and 3D pie.

It is not possible to cover every type of chart and so we concentrate on the most common. We have already presented the bar and pie charts, and continue with the line and mixed charts. We use a different example, the spreadsheet in Figure 4.12a, which plots financial data for the National Widgets Corporation.

	A	B	C	D	E	F
1		National Widgets Financial Data				
2		1989	1990	1991	1992	1993
3	Revenue	$50,000,000	$60,000,000	$70,000,000	$80,000,000	$90,000,000
4	Income	$10,000,000	$8,000,000	$6,000,000	$4,000,000	$2,000,000
5	Stock price	$40	$35	$36	$31	$24

(a) The Spreadsheet

FIGURE 4.12   National Widgets Financial Data

Line Chart

A *line chart* is appropriate for any message associated with time-related information—for example, the five-year trend of revenue and income in Figure 4.12b. A line chart plots one or more data series (e.g., revenue and income) against a descriptive category (e.g, year). As with a bar chart, the quantitative values are plotted along the vertical scale (Y axis) and the descriptive category along the horizontal scale (X axis). The individual data points are connected by a straight line, and a legend is used to distinguish one data series from another.

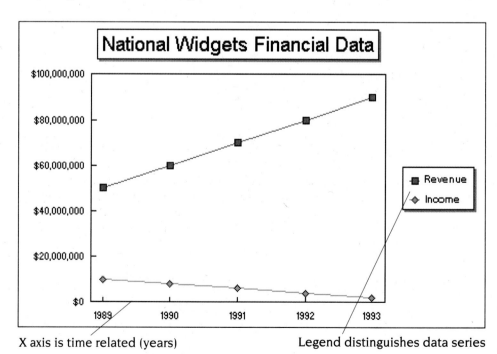

X axis is time related (years)   Legend distinguishes data series

(b) Line Chart

FIGURE 4.12   National Widgets Financial Data (continued)

Mixed Chart

A *mixed chart* is used when different scales are required for multiple data series that are plotted against the same descriptive variable. The chart in Figure 4.12c plots revenue, income, and stock price over the five-year period. The same scale can be used for revenue and income (both are in millions of dollars), but an entirely different scale is needed for the stock price. Note, too, how a line chart showing the declining price of the stock is imposed on the bar chart showing the increased revenue. A picture is indeed worth a thousand words, and investors in National Widgets can see at a glance the true status of their company.

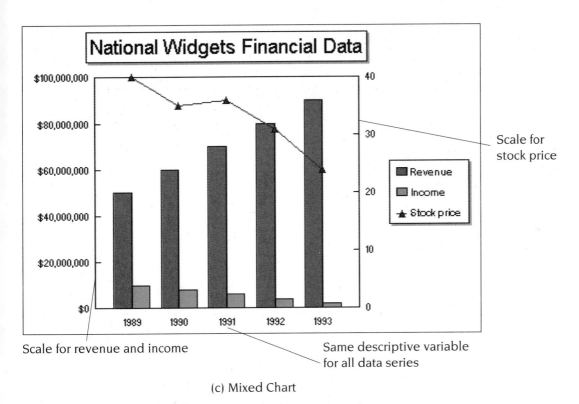

(c) Mixed Chart

FIGURE 4.12   National Widgets Financial Data (continued)

Fill by Example Command

The *Fill by Example command* was presented as a tip in Chapter 3 and is repeated here because of its applicability with charts. Fill by Example is the quickest way to enter a series into a spreadsheet for subsequent use as labels on a chart. You can use it to enter the years in a financial report as in the spreadsheet of Figure 4.12, the months of the year, or the days of the week. You can also create a series of labels with numeric entries, such as Quarter 1, Quarter 2, or Division 1, Division 2.

In essence, the Fill By Example command creates a series of values based on the initial value(s) you supply. If, for example, you want the months of the year in 12 successive cells, all you do is enter January (or Jan) in the first cell, select the 12 cells (including the one containing January), then execute the Fill By Example command. Lotus guesses at the type of series you want to create and fills in the rest of the cells accordingly. Thus you can type Monday (rather than January) and Lotus will return the days of the week; you can also enter a literal and numeric combination; for example, Quarter 1 would yield the series Quarter 1, Quarter 2, and so on.

USE AND ABUSE OF CHARTS

The hands-on exercises in the chapter demonstrate how easily numbers in a spreadsheet may be converted to their graphic equivalent. *The numbers can, however, just as easily be converted into erroneous or misleading charts, a fact too often overlooked.*

Unfortunately, many students are often so delighted to obtain the charts, that they accept the data entirely without question. The general public is also much too unquestioning in examining the barrage of statistical and graphical data with which it is confronted on a daily basis. Accordingly, we present two examples of statistically accurate, yet entirely misleading graphical data, drawn from charts submitted by our students in response to homework assignments.

> Lying graphics cheapen the graphical art everywhere. . . . When a chart on television lies, it lies millions of times over; when a *New York Times* chart lies, it lies 900,000 times over to a great many important and influential readers. The lies are told about the major issues of public policy—the government budget, medical care, prices, and fuel economy standards, for example. The lies are systematic and quite predictable, nearly always exaggerating the rate of recent change.
>
> **Edward Tufte**

Improper (omitted) Labels

The difference between *unit sales* and *dollar sales* is a concept of great importance, yet one which is often missed. Consider, for example, the two pie charts in Figures 4.13a and 4.13b, both of which are intended to identify the leading sales person based on the underlying spreadsheet in Figure 4.13c. The charts yield two different answers, Jones and Smith, respectively, depending on which chart you use.

Omitted titles can lead to incorrect conclusions

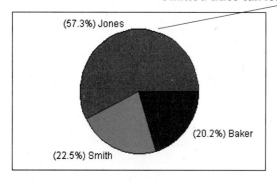

(a) Units

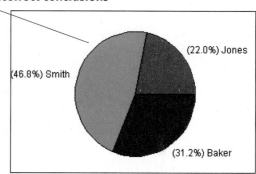

(b) Dollars

Sales Data - First Quarter							
		Units				Dollars	
		Jones	Smith	Baker	Jones	Smith	Baker
Product 1	$1	200	20	30	$200	$20	$30
Product 2	$5	50	30	30	$250	$150	$150
Product 3	$20	5	50	30	$100	$1,000	$600
	Totals:	255	100	90	$550	$1,170	$780

(c) Underlying Spreadsheet

FIGURE 4.13 Omitted Labels

As you can see, the two charts reflect different percentages and would appear therefore to contradict each other. Both charts, however, are technically correct as the percentages depend on whether they express unit sales or dollar sales. *Jones is the leader in terms of units, whereas Smith is the leader in terms of dollars.* The latter is generally more significant, and hence the measure which is probably most important to the reader. Neither chart, however, was properly labeled (there is no indication of whether units or dollars are plotted), which in turn may lead to erroneous conclusions on the part of the reader.

Adding Dissimilar Quantities

The conversion of a side-by-side bar chart to a stacked bar chart is a simple matter, requiring only a few keystrokes. Because the procedure is so easy, however, it is often done without thought and in situations where the stacked bar chart is inappropriate.

Consider, for example, Figures 4.14a and 4.14b, which contain a multiple bar and a stacked bar chart, respectively. The chart of Figure 4.14a shows steadily increasing sales in conjunction with decreasing profits. The chart does provide a realistic picture of the company's performance; it is becoming less efficient because profits are decreasing as sales are increasing

The stacked bar chart in Figure 4.14b plots the identical numbers, yet portrays a deceptively optimistic trend because the stacked columns reflect a nonsensical addition. In other words, even though sales and profits are both measured in dollars, they should not be added together, because the sum does not represent a meaningful concept. The stacked bar chart is misleading and provides no useful information.

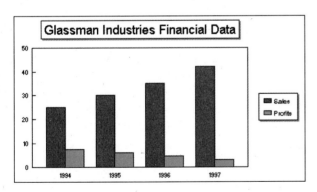

(a) Multiple Bar Chart

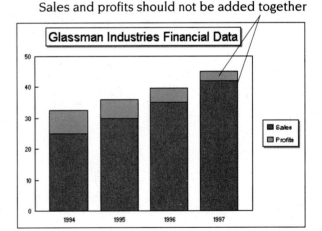

Sales and profits should not be added together

(b) Stacked Bar Chart

FIGURE 4.14 Adding Dissimilar Quantities

SUMMARY

A chart is a visual representation of numerical data within a spreadsheet and is often more effective in conveying the underlying information. Lotus offers 12 different types of charts, each with several formats. Multiple charts may be embedded in the same spreadsheet. All charts are linked directly to the spreadsheet so that changes in the data are automatically reflected in the corresponding charts.

Once a chart has been created, it can be moved elsewhere within a spreadsheet by selecting it, then dragging it to its new location; the chart may be sized by dragging any of the eight sizing handles in the desired direction. You can also change the type of chart, add a legend, text, or arrows for emphasis, and/or change colors, patterns, axes, and gridlines.

Multiple data series (ranges) may be plotted on the same chart and specified in rows or columns. Lotus will choose the first row or column, as appropriate, for the category names on the X axis and also add legends to differentiate the series.

Object Linking and Embedding enables the creation of a compound document containing data (objects) from multiple applications. Linking is dynamic in nature; that is, a change in the source document is automatically reflected in the destination document.

 ## Key Words and Concepts

Bar chart
Category label
Client application
Compound document
Data series
Destination
    document
Embedded chart
Exploded pie chart

Fill by Example
    command
Legend
Line chart
Mixed chart
Multibar chart
Multiple data series
Object Linking and
    Embedding (OLE)

Pie chart
Server application
Sizing handles
Source document
Stacked bar chart
X axis
Y axis

 ## Multiple Choice

1. Which type of chart is best to portray proportion or market share?
   (a) Pie chart
   (b) Line chart
   (c) Bar chart
   (d) Mixed chart

2. Which type of chart is the best to display time-related data?
   (a) Pie chart
   (b) Line chart
   (c) Bar chart
   (d) Mixed chart

3. Which type of chart is *not* suitable to display multiple data series?
   (a) Pie chart
   (b) Horizontal bar chart
   (c) Vertical bar chart
   (d) All of the above are equally suitable

4. Which of the following is best to display *additive information* from multiple data series?
   (a) A bar chart with the series stacked one on top of another
   (b) A bar chart with the data series side by side
   (c) Both (a) and (b) are equally appropriate
   (d) Neither (a) nor (b) is appropriate

5. Which of the following is true with respect to printing a chart?
  (a) It may be printed in landscape or portrait orientation
  (b) It may be printed as a selected object without printing the data in the spreadsheet on which it is based
  (c) Both (a) and (b)
  (d) Neither (a) nor (b)

6. Which of the following is true regarding an embedded chart?
  (a) It can be moved to a different location within the spreadsheet
  (b) It can be made larger or smaller
  (c) It can be copied elsewhere within the spreadsheet
  (d) All of the above

7. Which of the following best describes how multiple charts can be derived from a single spreadsheet?
  (a) Multiple charts can be derived from a single spreadsheet provided that all the charts are contained within the WK4 file for that spreadsheet
  (b) Multiple charts can be derived from a single spreadsheet with each chart saved in its own CH4 file
  (c) Multiple charts can be derived from a single spreadsheet, and further every chart must be printed whenever the spreadsheet is printed
  (d) Multiple charts can never be derived from a single spreadsheet

8. Which of the following is the default chart created by Lotus?
  (a) Pie
  (b) Bar
  (c) 3D Pie
  (d) 3D Bar

9. Which of the following will display sizing handles when selected?
  (a) The border of the chart when the chart is selected
  (b) An arrow added to the chart
  (c) A text box added to the chart
  (d) All of the above

10. Which of the following is true about a mixed chart that plots two data series against a single descriptive variable?
  (a) It can plot one series as a line chart and one series as a bar chart, but must use the same scale for each chart
  (b) It can use a different scale for each series, but must use the same type of chart for both series
  (c) It can plot one series as a line chart and one series as a bar chart and can use a different scale on the Y axis for each chart
  (d) None of the above

11. Which of the following is true regarding the compound document (the memo and chart) that was created in the chapter?
  (a) The spreadsheet is the source document and the memo is the destination document
  (b) Lotus is the server application and the word processor (e.g., WordPerfect) is the client application
  (c) Both (a) and (b) above
  (d) Neither (a) nor (b)

12. In order to represent multiple data series on the same chart,
- (a) The data series must be in rows and the rows must be adjacent to one another on the spreadsheet
- (b) The data series must be in columns and the columns must be adjacent to one another on the spreadsheet
- (c) The data series may be in rows or columns so long as they are adjacent to one another
- (d) The data series may be in rows or columns with no requirement to be next to one another

13. If multiple data series are selected and rows are specified,
- (a) The first row will be used for the category (X-axis) labels
- (b) The first column will be used for the legend
- (c) Both (a) and (b)
- (d) Neither (a) nor (b)

14. If multiple data series are selected and columns are specified,
- (a) The first column will be used for the category (X-axis) labels
- (b) The first row will be used for the legend
- (c) Both (a) and (b)
- (d) Neither (a) nor (b)

15. Which of the following is true about the scale on the Y axis in a bar chart that plots multiple data series side by side versus one that stacks the values one on top of another?
- (a) The scale for the stacked columns will contain larger values than if the columns are plotted side by side
- (b) The scale for the side-by-side columns will contain larger values than if the columns are stacked
- (c) The values on the scale will be the same regardless of whether the columns are stacked or side by side
- (d) The values on the scale will be different, but it is not possible to tell which chart will contain the higher values

ANSWERS

1. a
2. b
3. a
4. a
5. c
6. d
7. a
8. b
9. d
10. c
11. c
12. d
13. c
14. c
15. a

EXPLORING LOTUS

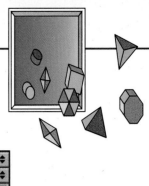

1. Use Figure 4.15 to match each action with its result; a given action may be used more than once or not at all.

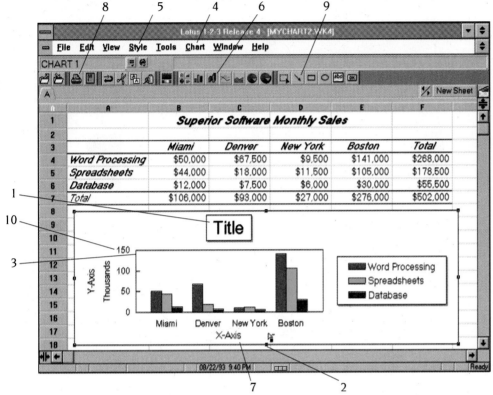

FIGURE 4.15 Screen for Problem 1

a. Click at 1, type Revenue by Geographic Area

b. Click and drag at 2

c. Click at 3, then click at 4

d. Click at 4

e. Click at 5

f. Click at 6

g. Click at 7, then press the Del key

h. Click at 8

i. Click at 9

j. Click at 10, then click at 5

_____ Change the chart to a 3D bar chart

_____ Create an appropriate title for the chart

_____ Add an arrow to reinforce the chart's message

_____ Delete the X axis

_____ Print the spreadsheet and embedded chart

_____ Resize the chart (make it larger)

_____ Format the numbers on the Y axis as currency with no decimals

_____ Add grid lines to the Y axis

_____ Change the orientation of the chart so that the data series are in columns

_____ Enhance the chart with a designer border

2. The value of a chart is aptly demonstrated by writing a verbal equivalent to a graphic analysis. Accordingly, write the corresponding written description of the information contained in Figure 4.7a. Can you better appreciate the effectiveness of the graphic presentation?

3. The spreadsheet of Figure 4.16c is the basis for the two charts of Figures 4.16a and 4.16b. Although the charts may at first glance appear to be satisfactory, each reflects a fundamental error. Discuss the problems associated with each.

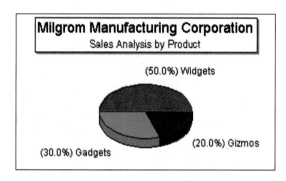

(a) Error 1

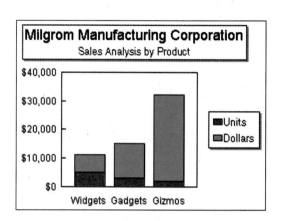

(b) Error 2

Milgrom Manufacturing Corporation Sales Analysis by Product			
	Unit Price	Units Sold	Revenue
Widgets	$1.25	5,000	$6,250
Gadgets	$4.00	3,000	$12,000
Gizmos	$14.99	2,000	$29,980

(c) The Spreadsheet

FIGURE 4.16   Spreadsheet for Problem 3

4. Using the data disk: Answer the following with respect to the spreadsheet and embedded chart in Figure 4.17, which are found on the data disk in the file PROB0404.WK4.

a. Retrieve the spreadsheet from the data disk.

b. Change the number in cell B8 to 6,000,000. What corresponding changes take place in the chart?

c. Change the format for cells B5 to F9 to comma with no decimals. How do you change the format in the chart?

d. Change the entry in cell A5 to Madrid. What corresponding changes take place in the chart?

e. Change the chart to a three-dimensional pie chart.

f. Use the text and arrow tools to add an appropriate callout.

g. Type your name in cell A11 of the spreadsheet.

h. Print the spreadsheet and embedded chart.

i. What would happen if you press the Del key when the chart is selected? Is there any way to retrieve the chart after it has been deleted?

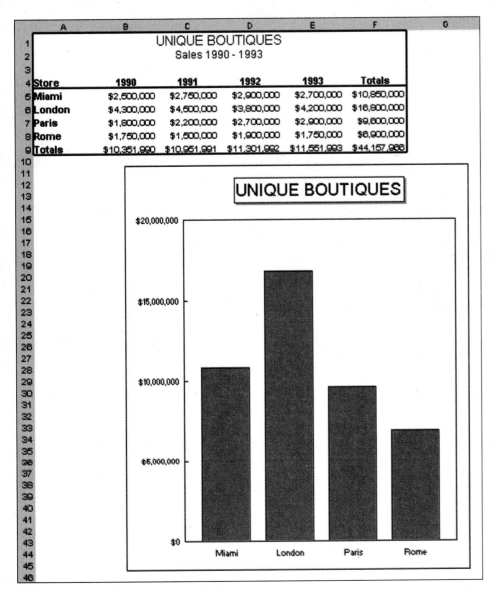

Store	1990	1991	1992	1993	Totals
		UNIQUE BOUTIQUES			
		Sales 1990 - 1993			
Miami	$2,500,000	$2,750,000	$2,900,000	$2,700,000	$10,850,000
London	$4,300,000	$4,500,000	$3,800,000	$4,200,000	$16,800,000
Paris	$1,800,000	$2,200,000	$2,700,000	$2,900,000	$9,600,000
Rome	$1,750,000	$1,500,000	$1,900,000	$1,750,000	$6,900,000
Totals	$10,351,990	$10,951,991	$11,301,992	$11,551,993	$44,157,966

FIGURE 4.17 Spreadsheet and Graph for Problem 4

5. Answer the following with respect to the spreadsheet and embedded chart of Figure 4.18.

   a. Are the data series in rows or columns?

   b. How many data series are there?

   c. Which cells contain the category names?

   d. Which cells contain the legends?

   e. How do you reverse the data series; that is, how do you switch rows to columns or vice versa?

   f. Create the spreadsheet in Figure 4.18, then create the two charts. Add your name to the spreadsheet. Print the spreadsheet and each chart on a separate piece of paper, then submit all three pages to your instructor.

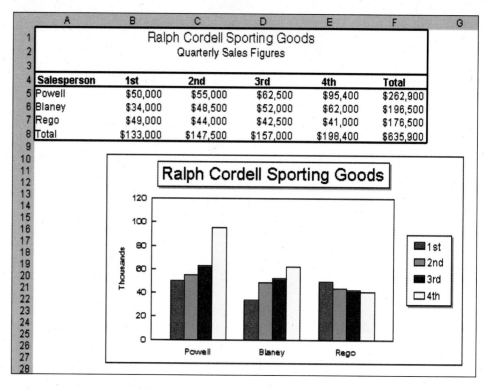

	A	B	C	D	E	F	G
1	Ralph Cordell Sporting Goods						
2	Quarterly Sales Figures						
3							
4	Salesperson	1st	2nd	3rd	4th	Total	
5	Powell	$50,000	$55,000	$62,500	$95,400	$262,900	
6	Blaney	$34,000	$48,500	$52,000	$62,000	$196,500	
7	Rego	$49,000	$44,000	$42,500	$41,000	$176,500	
8	Total	$133,000	$147,500	$157,000	$198,400	$635,900	

FIGURE 4.18 Spreadsheet and Graph for Problem 5

6. Using the data disk: The spreadsheet in Figure 4.19 is to be used as the basis for several charts depicting information on hotel capacities.

a. What type of chart is best to show the proportion of total capacity for each hotel?

b. Which data range(s) should be selected to create the chart of part a?

c. What type of chart is best to compare the capacities of the individual hotels to one another?

d. Which data range(s) should be selected to create the chart of part c?

e. What type of chart is best to show the comparison of the standard and deluxe room rates for all of the hotels, with the two different rates side-by-side for each hotel?

f. Which data range(s) should be selected to create the chart of part e?

g. Could the information in part e be conveyed in a stacked bar chart?

	A	B	C	D
1	Hotel Capacities and Room Rates			
2				
3		Total	Standard	Deluxe
4	Hotel	Rooms	Rate	Rate
5	Holiday Inn	250	$100	$150
6	Hyatt	450	$120	$175
7	Ramada Inn	300	$115	$190
8	Sheraton	750	$95	$150
9	Marriott	575	$100	$175
10	Hilton	600	$80	$120
11	Best Western	350	$75	$125
12	Days Inn	750	$50	$100

FIGURE 4.19 Spreadsheet for Problem 6

h. The spreadsheet in Figure 4.19 exists on the data disk as PROB0406.WK4. Create the three charts in parts a, c, and e as separate files, then print each chart and submit all three pages to your instructor.

7. Fill by example: Create the spreadsheet in Figure 4.20, then do each of the following:

a. Select cells A1 through A12. Pull down the Range menu and click the Fill by Example command. What are the contents of cells A2 through A12 after the command has been executed?

b. Select cells B1 through B12 and repeat the Fill by Example command. Do you see how easy it is to enter the months of the year into a spreadsheet?

c. Select cells C1 through C7 and execute the Fill by Example command, then select cells D1 through D7 and execute the command once again. What can you conclude about entering the days of the week?

d. Select cells E1 through E4 and execute the Fill by Example command. Now select cells E1 through E12 and execute the command again. What can you conclude about a repeating series? Would the command work just as well if the entry in cell E1 were Division 1 instead of Quarter 1?

e. Select cells F1 through F10 and execute the Fill by Example command. What are the contents of cells F2 through F10 after the command has been executed?

	A	B	C	D	E	F
1	January	Jan	Monday	Mon	Quarter 1	1992
2						
3						
4						
5						
6						
7						
8						
9						
10						
11						
12						

FIGURE 4.20   Fill by Example

8. Using the data disk: Figure 4.21 contains a spreadsheet with sales data for the chain of four Michael Moldof clothing boutiques. Use the spreadsheet to develop the following charts:

a. A pie chart showing the percentage of total sales attributed to each store

b. Redo part a as a bar chart

	A	B	C	D	E	F
1		Michael Moldof Men's Boutique - January Sales				
2						
3		Store 1	Store 2	Store 3	Store 4	Total
4	Slacks	$25,000	$28,750	$21,500	$9,400	$84,650
5	Shirts	$43,000	$49,450	$36,900	$46,000	$175,350
6	Underwear	$18,000	$20,700	$15,500	$21,000	$75,200
7	Accessories	$7,000	$8,050	$8,000	$4,000	$27,050
8						
9	Total:	$93,000	$106,950	$81,900	$80,400	$362,250

FIGURE 4.21   Spreadsheet for Problem 8

c. A stacked bar chart showing total dollars for each store, broken down by clothing category

d. A stacked bar chart showing total dollars for each clothing category, broken down by store

e. The spreadsheet in Figure 4.21 exists on the data disk as PROB0408.WK4. Create the charts in parts a, b, c, and d, then print each chart and submit all four pages to your instructor.

9. Using the data disk: The compound document in Figure 4.22 contains a memo and mixed chart and is an excellent way to review the entire chapter. Retrieve the **PROB0409.WK4** spreadsheet from the data disk, then follow the steps below:

a. Create the mixed chart:

➤ Select cells A2 through F5.

➤ Click the **Chart SmartIcon** to create the chart as a bar chart.

➤ Select the chart. Pull down the **Chart menu.** Click **Type.** Click **Mixed.** Click **OK.** You will not, however, be able to see the line chart for the stock prices until you designate a second scale on the Y axis.

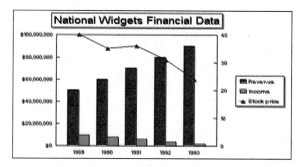

Steven Stocks
Financial Investments
100 Century Tower
New York, New York 10020

To: Carlos Rosell

From: Steven Stocks

Subject: Status Report on National Widgets Corporation

I have uncovered some information that I feel is important to the overall health of your investment portfolio. The graph below clearly shows that while revenues for National Widgets have steadily increased since 1989, income (profits) have steadily decreased. In addition, the stock price is continuing to decline. Although at one time I felt that a turnaround was imminent, I am no longer so optimistic and I am advising you to cut your losses and sell your National Widget stock as soon as possible.

FIGURE 4.22 Compound document for Problem 9

- ➤ Pull down the **Chart menu.** Click **Ranges.** Select the **D-range** (Stock Price) in the series list box, then check the box to plot on a second Y axis. Click **OK.**
- ➤ You will also have to use the **Chart Ranges** command a second time to designate cells B2 through F2 for the X-axis labels to plot the years along the X axis.
- ➤ Save the spreadsheet.

b. Create the memo:
- ➤ Use **Alt+Tab** to switch to Program Manager. Open the program group that contains WordPerfect 6.0 (or any other OLE-capable word processor). Double click on the program icon to open the word processor.
- ➤ Enter the text of the memo as shown in Figure 4.22. Add your name as the financial consultant.
- ➤ Save the word processing document as **PROB0409.WPD.**

c. Create the compound document:
- ➤ Use **Alt+Tab** to return to Lotus.
- ➤ Click just inside the border of the chart to select it.
- ➤ Pull down the **Edit menu.** Click **Copy.**
- ➤ Use **Alt+Tab** to return to WordPerfect. Place the insertion point at the end of the document.
- ➤ Pull down the **Edit menu.** Click **Paste Special.** Select **123 Worksheet Object** as the data type from the list box. Click **Paste Link** to bring the chart into the memo.
- ➤ Save the memo. Print the memo and submit it to your instructor.

Case Studies

University Enrollments

Your assistantship next semester has placed you in the Provost's office, where you are to help create a presentation for the Board of Trustees. The Provost is expected to make recommendations to the Board regarding the expansion of some programs and the reduction of others. You are expected to help the Provost by developing a series of charts to illustrate enrollment trends. The Provost has provided you with a spreadsheet (ENROLMNT.WK4, which is found on the data disk) with summary data over the last several years.

The Budget

Deficit reduction or not, the Federal Government spends billions more than it takes in; for example, in fiscal year 1992, government expenditures totaled $1,380 billion versus income of only $1,090, leaving a deficit of $290 billion. Thirty percent of the income came from social security and medicare taxes, 35% from personal income taxes, 7% from corporate income taxes, and 7% from excise, estate, and other miscellaneous taxes. The remaining 21% was borrowed.

Social security and medicare accounted for 33% of the expenditures and the defense budget another 24%. Social programs, including medicare and aid to dependent children, totaled 17%. Community development (consisting of agricultural, educational, environmental, economic, and space programs) totaled 10%

of the budget. Interest on the national debt amounted to 14%. The cost of law enforcement and government itself accounted for the final 2%.

Use the information contained within this problem to create the appropriate charts to reflect the distribution of income and expenditures. Do some independent research and obtain data on the budget, the deficit, and the national debt for the years 1945, 1967, and 1980. The numbers may surprise you; for example, how does the interest expense for the current year compare to the total budget in 1967 (at the height of the Viet Nam war)? to the total budget in 1945 (at the end of World War II)? Create charts to reflect your findings, then write your representative in Congress. We are in trouble!

The Annual Report

Corporate America spends a small fortune to produce its annual reports, which are readily available to the public at large. Choose any company and obtain a copy of its most recent annual report. Consolidate the information in the company's report to produce a two-page document of your own. Your report should include a description of the company's progress in the last year, a spreadsheet with any data you deem relevant, and at least two charts in support of the spreadsheet or written material. Formatting is important, and you are expected to use a word processor in addition to the spreadsheet to present the information in an attractive manner.

One Step Beyond

What exactly is a macro? More importantly, how can macros help you be more productive in using a spreadsheet? How do you create a macro? What is the difference between playing and recording a macro? How can you assign a macro to a button that appears on the spreadsheet? Use the on-line help facility and/or the reference manual to teach yourself the basics of macros, then create three macros in conjunction with creating, displaying, and/or modifying a chart.

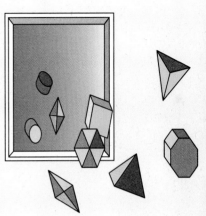

5

Data Management:
File Maintenance, Queries,
and Cross-tabulations

After reading this chapter you will be able to:

1. Create a database table within Lotus; explain the importance of proper planning and design prior to creating the database.

2. Add, edit, and delete records in an existing database table; explain the significance of data validation.

3. Distinguish between data and information; describe how one is converted to the other.

4. Use the Sort command; distinguish between an ascending and a descending sort, and among primary, secondary, and tertiary keys.

5. Define a range name; explain how range names facilitate the execution of database commands and functions.

6. Use the DSUM, DAVG, DMAX, DMIN, and DCOUNT functions.

7. Create a cross-tabulation table.

OVERVIEW

All businesses maintain data of one kind or another. Companies store data on their employees; magazines and newspapers keep data on their subscribers; political candidates monitor voter lists, and so on. While each of these examples refers to different types of data, they all operate under the same principles of record keeping, regardless of whether they use manual or computer-based systems.

This chapter presents the fundamentals of data management, showing how the principles of a computerized system parallel those of manual record keeping. We begin with the definition of basic terms such as field and record, then cover the commands to add a new record or modify or delete an existing record. We distinguish between data and information, and emphasize the importance of proper design so that the system is capable of producing the desired information.

All of this is accomplished within Lotus, and although it may eventually be necessary for you to use a dedicated database program (e.g., Paradox for Windows or Microsoft Access), you will be pleased at what you can do with a spreadsheet.

The chapter contains three hands-on exercises, each of which focuses on a different aspect of data management.

DATA MANAGEMENT

Imagine, if you will, that you are the personnel director of a medium-sized company with offices in several cities, and that you manually maintain employee data for the company. Accordingly, you have recorded the specifics of every individual's employment (the name, salary, location, title, and so on) in a manila folder, and you have stored the entire set of folders in a file cabinet. You have also written the name of each employee on the label of his or her folder and have arranged the folders alphabetically in the filing cabinet.

The manual system illustrates the basics of data management terminology. The set of manila folders is called a *file* with each individual folder known as a *record.* Each data item within a folder is called a *field.* The folders are arranged alphabetically in the file cabinet (according to the employee name on the label of each folder) to simplify the retrieval of any given folder. The records in a computer-based system are also in sequence, according to a specific field known as a *key.*

A *database table,* as used in Lotus, is an area in a spreadsheet. The first row in the database range contains the *field names,* which identify the data in those fields. Each additional row contains a record. Each column represents a field, and thus every record contains the same fields in the same order. The *record structure* (the order of fields within a record) is identical for every record in the file.

	A	B	C	D
1	**Name**	**Location**	**Title**	**Salary**
2	Adams	Atlanta	Trainee	$19,500
3	Adamson	Chicago	Manager	$52,000
4	Brown	Atlanta	Trainee	$18,500
5	Charles	Boston	Account Rep	$40,000
6	Coulter	Atlanta	Manager	$100,000
7	Frank	Miami	Manager	$75,000
8	James	Chicago	Account Rep	$42,500
9	Johnson	Chicag	Account Rep	$47,500
10	Manin	Boston	Accout Rep	$49,500
11	Marder	Chicago	Account Rep	$38,500
12	Milgrom	Boston	Manager	$57,500
13	Rubin	Boston	Account Rep	$45,000
14	Smith	Atlanta	Account Rep	$65,000

FIGURE 5.1   The Employee Database

Figure 5.1 shows a database table with 13 records. There are four fields in every record, and the arrangement of the fields within a record is consistent from record to record—name, location, title, and salary. The employee name was chosen as the key, and the records are shown in alphabetical order.

Normal business operations will require you to make repeated trips to the filing cabinet to maintain the accuracy of the data. You will have to add a folder whenever a new employee is hired, and in similar fashion, you will have to delete the folder of any employee who leaves the company, or modify the folder of any employee who receives a raise, changes location, and so on.

Changes of this nature (additions, deletions, and modifications) are known as *file maintenance* and constitute a critical activity within any system. Indeed, without adequate file maintenance, the data in a system quickly becomes obsolete and the information useless. Imagine, if you will, the consequences of producing a payroll based on data that is six months old.

Nor is it sufficient to simply add (edit or delete) a record without adequate checks on the validity of the data. Look carefully at the entries in Figure 5.1 and ask yourself if a computer-generated report listing employees in the Chicago office will include Johnson? Will a report listing account reps include Manin? The answer to both questions is *no* because the data for these employees were entered incorrectly. Chicago is misspelled in Johnson's record (the "o" was omitted), as is Manin's title. You know that Johnson works in Chicago but the computer does not, because it is searching for the correct spelling. It also will omit Manin from a listing of account reps because of the misspelled title.

GARBAGE IN, GARBAGE OUT (GIGO)

A computer does exactly what you tell it to do, which is not necessarily what you want it to do. It is absolutely critical, therefore, that you validate the data that goes into a system or else the associated information will not be correct. No system, no matter how sophisticated, can produce valid output from invalid input. In other words, garbage in—garbage out.

File Design

Implicit in the process of file maintenance is the all-important decision as to which fields to include in the record structure. Ask yourself precisely what information you expect from a system, so that you can determine the data necessary to produce that information. Create a rough draft of any reports you will need, then check the record structure to be sure it contains the data (fields) to produce those reports; if not, modify the *file design.*

The data in Figure 5.1 is sufficient to calculate the annual payroll. It could also be used to select the employees earning more than $50,000 or less than $25,000, or to provide a list of all employees in ascending (descending) sequence by salary. You could not, however, determine the amount of an employee's last salary increase because the record structure does not contain the employee's previous salary. Nor could you inquire about the date an employee received an increase because that field is also missing. Whether or not these omissions are important depends on the objectives of the system; suffice it to say that you must plan a system carefully, so that you are not disappointed when it is implemented.

CITY, STATE, AND ZIP CODE—ONE FIELD OR THREE?

The answer depends on whether the fields are referenced as a unit or accessed individually. However, given the almost universal need to sort or select on zip code, it is invariably defined as a separate field. An individual's last name, first name, and middle initial are defined as individual fields for the same reason.

IMPLEMENTATION IN LOTUS

Creating and maintaining a database table is easy because you use ordinary spreadsheet commands to enter and edit the data. You start by choosing the area in the spreadsheet that will contain the table, then you enter the *field names* in the first row of the designated area. Each field name must be unique, and further, each field name must be a label rather than a number or formula. The data for the individual records is entered in the rows immediately below the row of field names.

Once a database table has been created, you can change the entry in any field of any record just as you would change the cells in an ordinary spreadsheet—that is, click on the cell to enter a new value or double click to edit the existing entry. You use the *Edit Insert command* to add new rows (records) or columns (fields) just as you can use the *Edit Delete command* to delete an existing record or field. You can also use quick menus to execute the commands more quickly. And finally, you can also format the entries within a database table just as you do the entries in any spreadsheet.

FORMAT THE DATABASE

Formatting has no effect on the success or failure of database commands and thus you can format the entries in a database to any extent you like. You should, however, use the same data type and format for all entries within a column; for example, do not enter zip code as a number for some employees and a label for others. Remember, too, that the accuracy of the data is much more important than its appearance.

The Sort Command

The *Sort command* arranges the records within a database table according to the value of one (or more) field(s) within that table. You can, for example, list employees alphabetically, or you can list them by location and then alphabetically within each location. You can list the employees in *ascending* (low to high) or *descending* (high to low) *sequence* according to whichever field you choose. The field on which you sequence the table is known as the key, and as indicated, you can sequence on multiple keys at the same time.

The records in Figure 5.2a are listed alphabetically, that is, in ascending sequence according to employee name. Adams comes before Adamson, who comes before Brown, and so on. Figure 5.2b displays the identical records but in descending sequence by employee salary. The employee with the highest salary is listed first and the employee with the lowest salary is last.

Records in ascending (alphabetical) order by name field

	A	B	C	D
1	**Name**	**Location**	**Title**	**Salary**
2	Adams	Atlanta	Trainee	$19,500
3	Adamson	Chicago	Manager	$52,000
4	Brown	Atlanta	Trainee	$18,500
5	Charles	Boston	Account Rep	$40,000
6	Coulter	Atlanta	Manager	$100,000
7	Frank	Miami	Manager	$75,000
8	James	Chicago	Account Rep	$42,500
9	Johnson	Chicago	Account Rep	$47,500
10	Manin	Boston	Account Rep	$49,500
11	Marder	Chicago	Account Rep	$38,500
12	Milgrom	Boston	Manager	$57,500
13	Rubin	Boston	Account Rep	$45,000
14	Smith	Atlanta	Account Rep	$65,000

(a) Ascending Sequence (by name)

FIGURE 5.2   The Sort Command

	A	B	C	D
1	**Name**	**Location**	**Title**	**Salary**
2	Coulter	Atlanta	Manager	$100,000
3	Frank	Miami	Manager	$75,000
4	Smith	Atlanta	Account Rep	$65,000
5	Milgrom	Boston	Manager	$57,500
6	Adamson	Chicago	Manager	$52,000
7	Manin	Boston	Account Rep	$49,500
8	Johnson	Chicago	Account Rep	$47,500
9	Rubin	Boston	Account Rep	$45,000
10	James	Chicago	Account Rep	$42,500
11	Charles	Boston	Account Rep	$40,000
12	Marder	Chicago	Account Rep	$38,500
13	Adams	Atlanta	Trainee	$19,500
14	Brown	Atlanta	Trainee	$18,500

Records in descending sequence by salary field

(b) Descending Sequence (by salary)

	A	B	C	D
1	**Name**	**Location**	**Title**	**Salary**
2	Coulter	Atlanta	Manager	$100,000
3	Smith	Atlanta	Account Rep	$65,000
4	Adams	Atlanta	Trainee	$19,500
5	Brown	Atlanta	Trainee	$18,500
6	Milgrom	Boston	Manager	$57,500
7	Manin	Boston	Account Rep	$49,500
8	Rubin	Boston	Account Rep	$45,000
9	Charles	Boston	Account Rep	$40,000
10	Adamson	Chicago	Manager	$52,000
11	Johnson	Chicago	Account Rep	$47,500
12	James	Chicago	Account Rep	$42,500
13	Marder	Chicago	Account Rep	$38,500
14	Frank	Miami	Manager	$75,000

Records in descending order by salary within like values of location, making salary the secondary key

(c) Primary and Secondary Keys (by location and descending salary within location)

FIGURE 5.2   The Sort Command (continued)

Figure 5.2c sequences the employees on two keys, by location, and by descending salary within location. Location is the more important or ***primary key.*** Salary is the less important or ***secondary key.*** The Sort command groups employees according to like values of the primary key (location), then within the primary key arranges them in descending (ascending could have been chosen just as easily) sequence according to the secondary key (salary). Lotus provides a maximum of 255 keys, but we suggest you do not go beyond three—primary, secondary, and tertiary.

The Range Name Command

The ***Range Name command*** equates a mnemonic name such as *database* to a cell range such as *A1..D14,* then enables you to use the mnemonic name to reference that range in all subsequent commands. If, for example, you wanted to print only a portion of a spreadsheet, you could specify the range name in the dialog box of the Print command instead of the specific cell addresses.

Range names adjust automatically to accommodate insertions and/or deletions *within* the range, but do not accommodate changes outside that range. Thus, if you were to add a new employee in row 15, which is *outside* the range name (*database* was defined as cells A1 through D14), the definition of the range name would not change. If, however, you were to add the employee by inserting a row within the range name—for example, between existing rows 7 and 8—the range name would be modified to cells A1 through E15.

A range name can be also used in any formula or function instead of a cell address, such as @SUM(SALES) instead of @SUM(M1..M10), where the range name *sales* has been defined as cells M1 through M10. Note, too, that after a range name has been defined, all existing formulas and functions that reference the associated cell range will be changed to reflect the range name. Range names can also be used in the Edit Go To command to move directly to the first cell in the range and simultaneously select the entire range.

The exercise that follows shows you how to create and maintain a database table within a spreadsheet. The exercise uses range names as appropriate, and also reviews shortcuts from earlier chapters, including quick menus, fill by example, and the Copy Down command.

HANDS-ON EXERCISE 1:

Database Tables

Objective: To create a database table within a spreadsheet; to add, edit, and delete records to an existing database table; to sort a database; to use the range selector and quick menus.

Step 1: Open the employee spreadsheet
➤ Pull down the **File menu** and click **Open** (or click the **Open folder SmartIcon**).
➤ Open the **EMPLOYEE.WK4** spreadsheet as shown in Figure 5.3a.

Incorrect spelling located

Click here to select correct spelling

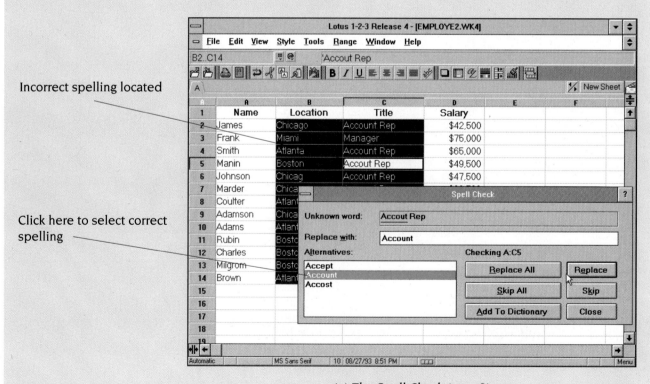

(a) The Spell Check (step 2)

FIGURE 5.3   Hands-on Exercise 1

➤ Pull down the **File menu.**
➤ Click **Save As.** Save the spreadsheet as **EMPLOYE2.WK4**

Step 2: The spell check
➤ Select cells **B2..C14** as in Figure 5.3a.
➤ Pull down the **Tools menu** and click **Spell Check.**
➤ If necessary, click **Range** to restrict the spell check to columns B and C, containing the employees' locations and titles, respectively.
➤ Click **OK** to begin the spell check.
➤ Account is misspelled in cell C5 and flagged accordingly. Click **Account** in the Alternatives box, then click the **Replace command button** to correct the misspelling.
➤ Correct the misspelling of Chicago in cell B6 in similar fashion.
➤ Lotus will indicate that it has finished checking the selected cells. Click **OK** to return to the spreadsheet.
➤ Save the spreadsheet.

Step 3: Add a record
➤ Records are added to a database table through the Edit Insert command or more quickly through a quick menu; we will add two records using the latter technique.
➤ Click in the **row label** for **row 14,** the row containing the last record.
➤ Click the **right mouse button** to produce the quick menu in Figure 5.3b. Click **Insert.**

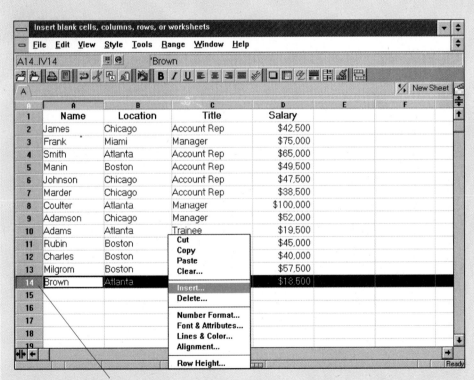

Click here to select row, then click right
mouse button to produce quick menu

(b) Adding a Record (step 3)

FIGURE 5.3 Hands-on Exercise 1 (continued)

- Enter data for **Elofson,** who works in **Miami** as an **Account Rep** with a salary of **$47,500.**
- Click in the **row label** for **row 15,** the row that now contains the last record.
- Add a record for **Gillenson,** who works in **Miami** as an **Account Rep** with a salary of **$55,000.**
- Save the spreadsheet.

Step 4: Delete a record
- Records are deleted through the Edit Delete command or more quickly through a quick menu; we will delete the record for Frank using a quick menu.
- Click the **row label** in **row 3,** the row containing the record slated for deletion.
- Click the **right mouse button** to produce the quick menu. Click **Delete.** The record for Frank has been deleted from the database.
- Click the **Undo SmartIcon** or pull down the **Edit menu** and click **Undo.** Frank's record has been restored to the database.
- Delete Frank's record a second time. The names in the database should match those in Figure 5.3c.
- Save the spreadsheet.

Select A1..D15 (range includes field names) to assign name to database table

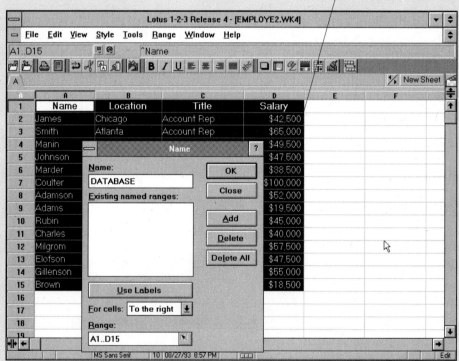

(c) The Range Name Command (step 5)

FIGURE 5.3   Hands-on Exercise 1 (continued)

Step 5: The Range Name command
- Click cell **A1.** Drag the mouse to select the range **A1 through D15.**
- Pull down the **Range menu.** Click **Name** to produce the dialog box in Figure 5.3c.
- Click the **Name** text box. Type **DATABASE.** Click **OK.**

➤ Click in cell **A2.** Drag the mouse to select the range **A2 through D15.**

➤ Pull down the **Range menu.** Click **Name** to produce the dialog box in Figure 5.3c.

➤ Click the **Name** text box. Type **SORTRANGE.** Click **OK.**

➤ You have defined two range names, Database and Sortrange, which will be referenced in subsequent steps in this and other exercises.

➤ Save the spreadsheet.

KEYBOARD SHORTCUTS

The keyboard is faster than the mouse if your hands are already on the keyboard and you know the menu shortcuts. Press the **Alt key** plus the underlined letter to pull down the menu—for example **Alt+R** to pull down the **Range menu**—then type the underlined letter in the desired command, such as **N** for Name. In other words, **Alt+R,** then the letter **N,** executes the Range Name command.

Step 6: The Edit Go To command

➤ Click anywhere in the spreadsheet outside the database table.

➤ Pull down the **Edit menu** and click **Go To** (or press the **F5 key**) to produce the dialog box in Figure 5.3d.

➤ Click **SORTRANGE,** one of the range names you created in step 5.

➤ Click **OK.** Cells A2 through D15 (the cells within the name SORTRANGE) are selected.

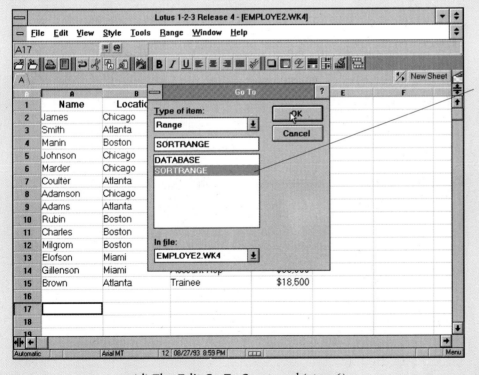

(d) The Edit Go To Command (step 6)

FIGURE 5.3   Hands-on Exercise 1 (continued)

Step 7: Sort the database

➤ Save the spreadsheet.

➤ Pull down the **Range menu.** Click **Sort** to produce the dialog box in Figure 5.3e.

➤ All parameters have already been set. The Sort by text box references cell A2, the Ascending button is checked, and the Range text box indicates cells A2 through D15.

➤ Click **OK** to accept these parameters for the Sort command.

➤ The employees will be rearranged in alphabetical order. If you made a mistake, pull down the **Edit menu** and click **Undo** to cancel the sort and begin again.

Click here to accept defaults

A2 is the primary key

Sort range does not
include field names

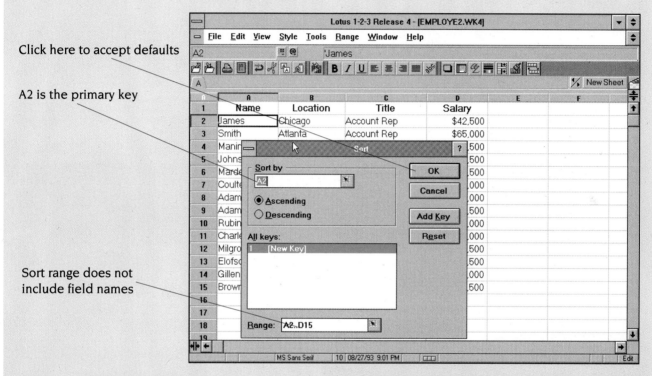

(e) The Sort Command (step 7)

FIGURE 5.3   Hands-on Exercise 1 (continued)

THE SORT RANGE

The sort range includes every field in every record, but does not include the field names in the first row of the database; if the field names are erroneously included, they would be interspersed with the records in the database. Use the **Undo command** immediately after executing the Sort command if you specify the range incorrectly.

Step 8: Insert a field

➤ Click the **column label** in column D.

➤ Click the **right mouse button** to produce a quick menu.

➤ Click **Insert** to insert a new column for the employee's hire date, which in turn moves the employee salaries to column E as can be seen in Figure 5.3f.

➤ Click cell **D1.** Type **Hire Date** and adjust the column width if necessary.

HIRE DATE VERSUS LENGTH OF SERVICE

An individual's date of hire and length of service provide equivalent information as one is calculated from the other. It might seem easier, therefore, to store the length of service in the database table and avoid the calculation, but this would be a mistake. The length of service changes continually, whereas the hire date remains constant; thus the date, not the length of service, should be stored. Similar reasoning applies to a person's birth date and age.

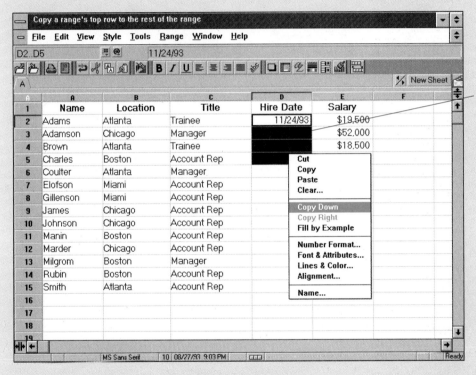

Selected range includes source and destination cells for Copy Down command

(f) Inserting a Field (step 8)

FIGURE 5.3   Hands-on Exercise I (continued)

Step 9: Enter the hire dates

➤ For ease of data entry we will assume that the first four employees were hired on the same day, November 24, 1993. We will enter the date for the first employee, then use the Copy Down command to copy the date from cell D2 to cells D3 through D5.

— Click in cell **D2.** Enter **11/24/93.**

— Select cells **D2 through D5** as shown in Figure 5.3f. (The Copy Down command requires that you select the source *and* destination ranges.)

— Click the **right mouse button** to produce the quick menu shown in the figure. Click **Copy Down** to complete the copy operation.

➤ Again, for ease of data entry, assume that the next several employees were hired on the same day, March 16, 1992.
— Click in cell **D6.** Type **3/16/92.** Press **enter.**
— Select cells **D6 through D10.**
— Click the **right mouse button** to produce the quick menu. Click **Copy Down** to complete the copy operation.
➤ The last five employees were hired one year apart beginning October 31, 1989.
— Click in cell **D11** and type **10/31/89.**
— Click in cell **D12** and type **10/31/90.**
— Select cells **D11 through D15.**
— Pull down the **Range command.** Click **Fill by Example.** The remaining dates have been entered and are one year apart.
➤ The completed spreadsheet is shown in Figure 5.3g.
➤ Save the spreadsheet.

Step 10: The range selector
➤ Click the **range selector icon** on the edit line to produce the list of range names in Figure 5.3g.
➤ Click **Database.** Cells A1 through E15 are highlighted and reflect the cells in the database table; note that the cells within the range name have expanded automatically to include the column of hire dates.
➤ Click the **range selector icon** a second time. Click **Sortrange,** which highlights cells A2 through E15.
➤ Save the spreadsheet. Exit Lotus.

Range selector icon

	A	B	C	D	E	F
1	**Name**	**Location**	**Title**	**Hire Date**	**Salary**	
2	Adams	Atlanta	Trainee	11/24/93	$19,500	
3	Adamson	Chicago	Manager	11/24/93	$52,000	
4	Brown	Atlanta	Trainee	11/24/93	$18,500	
5	Charles	Boston	Account Rep	11/24/93	$40,000	
6	Coulter	Atlanta	Manager	03/16/92	$100,000	
7	Elofson	Miami	Account Rep	03/16/92	$47,500	
8	Gillenson	Miami	Account Rep	03/16/92	$55,000	
9	James	Chicago	Account Rep	03/16/92	$42,500	
10	Johnson	Chicago	Account Rep	03/16/92	$47,500	
11	Manin	Boston	Account Rep	10/31/89	$49,500	
12	Marder	Chicago	Account Rep	10/31/90	$38,500	
13	Milgrom	Boston	Manager	10/31/91	$57,500	
14	Rubin	Boston	Account Rep	10/31/92	$45,000	
15	Smith	Atlanta	Account Rep	10/31/93	$65,000	

(g) The Completed Database (step 9)

FIGURE 5.3 Hands-on Exercise 1 (continued)

DATA VERSUS INFORMATION

Data and information are not synonymous. **Data** refers to a fact or facts about a specific entity, such as an employee's name, title, or salary. **Information,** on the other hand, is data that has been rearranged into a form perceived as useful by the recipient, such as a list of employees earning more than $35,000 or a total of all employee salaries. Put another way, data is the raw material and information is the finished product.

Decisions in an organization are based on information rather than raw data; for example, in assessing the effects of a proposed across-the-board salary increase, management needs to know the total payroll rather than individual salary amounts. In similar fashion, decisions about next year's hiring will be influenced, at least in part, by knowing how many individuals are currently employed in each job category.

Data is converted to information through a combination of database commands and functions whose capabilities are illustrated in Figure 5.4. The reports are based on the employee database as it existed at the end of the hands-on exercise. Each report presents the data in a different way, according to the information requirements of the end-user. As you view each report, ask yourself how it was produced; what was done to the data to produce the information?

Figure 5.4a contains a master list of all employees, listing employees by location, and alphabetically within location. The report was created by sorting the database on two keys, location and name. Location is the more important or primary key. Name is the less important or secondary key. The sorted report groups employees according to like values of the primary key (location), then within the primary key sequences the records according to the secondary key (name).

Location Report

Name	Location	Title	Hire Date	Salary
Adams	Atlanta	Trainee	11/24/93	$19,500
Brown	Atlanta	Trainee	11/24/93	$18,500
Coulter	Atlanta	Manager	03/16/92	$100,000
Smith	Atlanta	Account Rep	10/31/93	$65,000
Charles	Boston	Account Rep	11/24/93	$40,000
Manin	Boston	Account Rep	10/31/89	$49,500
Milgrom	Boston	Manager	10/31/91	$57,500
Rubin	Boston	Account Rep	10/31/92	$45,000
Adamson	Chicago	Manager	11/24/93	$52,000
James	Chicago	Account Rep	03/16/92	$42,500
Johnson	Chicago	Account Rep	03/16/92	$47,500
Marder	Chicago	Account Rep	10/31/90	$38,500
Elofson	Miami	Account Rep	03/16/92	$47,500
Gillenson	Miami	Account Rep	03/16/92	$55 000

(a) Employees by Location and Name within Location

Employees Earning Between $40,000 and $60,000

Name	Location	Title	Hire Date	Salary
Smith	Atlanta	Account Rep	10/31/93	$65,000
Milgrom	Boston	Manager	10/31/91	$57,500
Gillenson	Miami	Account Rep	03/16/92	$55,000
Adamson	Chicago	Manager	11/24/93	$52,000
Manin	Boston	Account Rep	10/31/89	$49,500
Johnson	Chicago	Account Rep	03/16/92	$47,500
Elofson	Miami	Account Rep	03/16/92	$47,500
Rubin	Boston	Account Rep	10/31/92	$45,000
James	Chicago	Account Rep	03/16/92	$42,500
Charles	Boston	Account Rep	11/24/93	$40 000

(b) Employees Earning between $40,000 and $60,000

Summary Statistics:

Total Salary for Account Reps:	$430,500
Average Salary for Account Reps	$47,833
Maximum Salary for Account Reps	$65,000
Minimum Salary for Account Reps	$38,500
Number of Account Reps	9

(c) Account Rep Summary Data

FIGURE 5.4 Data versus Information

The report in Figure 5.4b contains only some of the records in the database; that is, it selects the employees that meet a specific criterion. The criteria can be based on any field, or combination of fields; in this case employees whose salary is between $40,000 and $60,000. Note, too, that the employees are shown in descending order of salary; the employee with the highest salary is listed first.

The report in Figure 5.4c displays summary statistics for the selected employees—in this example, the salaries for the account reps within the company. Reports of this nature omit the salaries of individual employees (known as detail lines), in order to present an aggregate view of the organization.

IMPLEMENTATION IN LOTUS

Lotus provides a special set of commands and functions for use with a database table that are described in conjunction with the spreadsheet in Figure 5.5. Cells A1 through A15 contain the database table we have been using throughout the chapter in which three records have been selected; the selected records are Account Reps earning more than $47,500. Summary statistics have been computed for the selected records and are displayed in rows 17 through 22. The selected records have also been copied into a table of their own in rows 24 through 27.

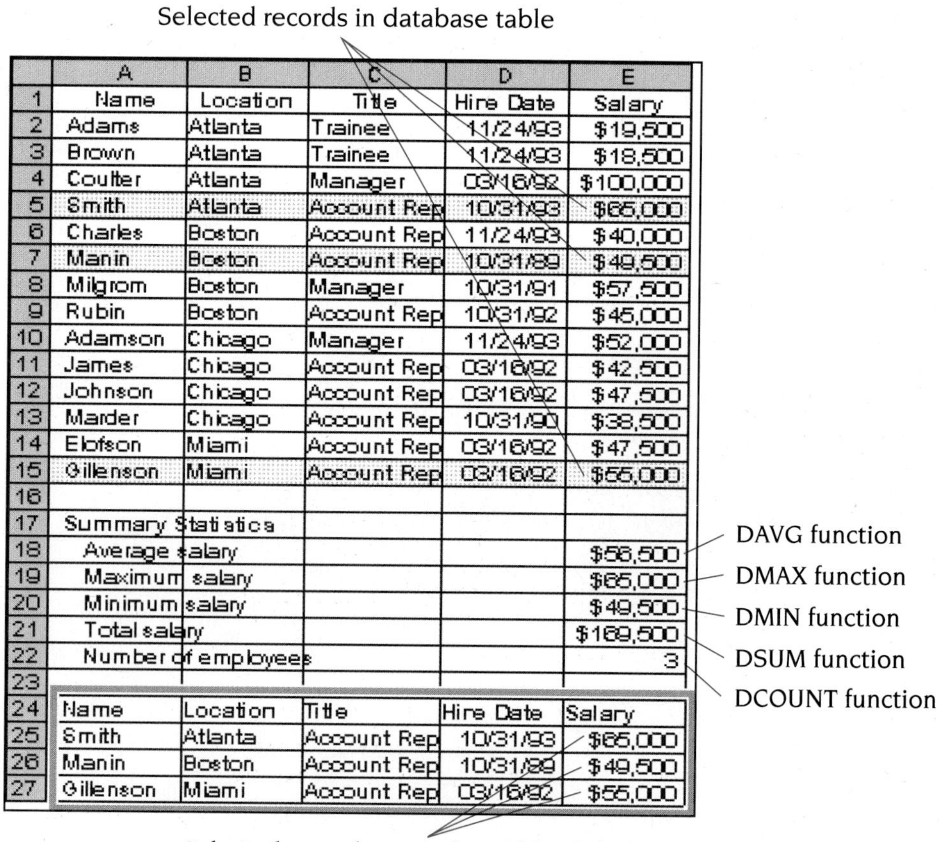

Selected records in database table

	A	B	C	D	E
1	Name	Location	Title	Hire Date	Salary
2	Adams	Atlanta	Trainee	11/24/93	$19,500
3	Brown	Atlanta	Trainee	11/24/93	$18,500
4	Coulter	Atlanta	Manager	03/16/92	$100,000
5	Smith	Atlanta	Account Rep	10/31/93	$65,000
6	Charles	Boston	Account Rep	11/24/93	$40,000
7	Manin	Boston	Account Rep	10/31/89	$49,500
8	Milgrom	Boston	Manager	10/31/91	$57,500
9	Rubin	Boston	Account Rep	10/31/92	$45,000
10	Adamson	Chicago	Manager	11/24/93	$52,000
11	James	Chicago	Account Rep	03/16/92	$42,500
12	Johnson	Chicago	Account Rep	03/16/92	$47,500
13	Marder	Chicago	Account Rep	10/31/90	$38,500
14	Elofson	Miami	Account Rep	03/16/92	$47,500
15	Gillenson	Miami	Account Rep	03/16/92	$55,000
16					
17	Summary Statistics				
18	Average salary				$56,500
19	Maximum salary				$65,000
20	Minimum salary				$49,500
21	Total salary				$169,500
22	Number of employees				3
23					
24	Name	Location	Title	Hire Date	Salary
25	Smith	Atlanta	Account Rep	10/31/93	$65,000
26	Manin	Boston	Account Rep	10/31/89	$49,500
27	Gillenson	Miami	Account Rep	03/16/92	$55,000

DAVG function
DMAX function
DMIN function
DSUM function
DCOUNT function

Selected records copied to table of their own

FIGURE 5.5   Implementation in Lotus

The concept of *criteria* is essential to all parts of Figure 5.5, as it is to database commands and functions in general. The criteria determine which records are selected and are specified in different ways. The dialog box in Figure 5.6a is used with the Data Find command to select individual records; it is also used with the Data Query command to copy the selected records to a separate table. The example in Figure 5.6b shows a database function in which the criteria are specified as part of the function itself.

Either way, the same rules are followed in building the criteria. A *simple condition* compares a field name to a label or a value, using one of the standard relational operators (=, <>, >, <, >=, or <=). The criterion TITLE="Account Rep" will select all employees who are Account Reps, while the criteria SALARY>47500 selects any employee whose salary is above this amount. A field that contains a label (e.g., TITLE) is compared to a character string enclosed in quotation marks; a field that contains a number (e.g., SALARY) is compared to a numeric value without the quotation marks.

A *compound condition* is created by combining simple conditions with either AND or OR. Two simple conditions joined by AND must both be true for the compound condition to be true; when they are joined by OR, only one of the conditions need be true for the compound condition to be true. Lotus syntax requires that AND and OR be delimited by #s as can be seen in Figure 5.6b.

Data Find Command

The *Data Find command* selects the records in the database table that satisfy the criteria specified in the command, such as Account Reps earning more than $47,500. The selected records will be affected by any subsequent command(s) as

Compound condition

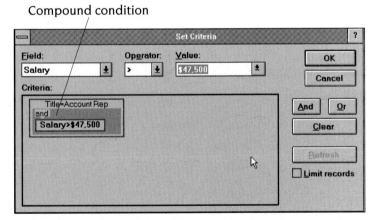

(a) The Set Criteria Command

@DAVG(DATABASE,"Salary",Title="Account Rep"#AND#Salary>47500)

(b) Criteria Specified within the Database Function

FIGURE 5.6   Criteria

long as the selection is active. You can move from one record to the next within the selected range by pressing Ctrl+Enter; press Shift+Ctrl+Enter to return to the previous record. You can move from field to field within a record with Enter (or Shift+Enter) to edit data as needed.

Query Tables

The *New Query Command* copies all records that satisfy the specified criteria to a separate *query table* elsewhere in the spreadsheet. The query table is similar to a database table except that it contains only a subset of the records in the table. The first row of the query table contains the field names, but you need not include every field from the database table. Each additional row in the query table contains a record satisfying the criteria.

The query table is automatically linked to the original database table and can be refreshed to reflect changes in the database table. In similar fashion, the database table can be updated to reflect changes made to records in the query table.

Database Functions

The database functions, *DSUM, DAVG, DMAX, DMIN,* and *DCOUNT,* operate on the *selected* records in a database. The database functions parallel the statistical functions presented in Chapter 3 (SUM, AVG, MAX, MIN, and COUNT) except that they process only the records that satisfy the current criteria.

The summary statistics in Figure 5.5 are based on the account reps earning more than $47,500, rather than the database as a whole. The DAVG function returns the average salary for the selected employees, whereas the DMAX and DMIN functions display the maximum and minimum salaries, respectively. The DSUM function computes the total salary, and the DCOUNT function indicates the number of employees who meet the criteria.

Each database function has three arguments: the database range, the field to be processed, and the criteria. Consider, for example, the DAVG function as shown below:

@DAVG(database range,"field",criteria)

The criteria can be entered in the command—for example, LOCATION="Atlanta"—or it can be entered as a cell range—for instance, A17..E18—or as a named range, such as, CRITERIA

The field to be processed; the field name is enclosed in quotes—for example, "SALARY"

The database range can be entered as a cell range—for example, A1..E15—or as a name assigned to a cell range—for example, DATABASE.

The other database functions have identical arguments. The criteria can appear in the function itself as in the example of Figure 5.6b, or in an independent criteria range elsewhere in the spreadsheet. The advantage of the latter approach is that multiple database functions can reference the *identical* criteria range so that changes in the criteria are made in only one place. A criteria range also accepts *wild cards*, whereas the individual functions do not.

The Criteria Range

The *criteria range* is an integral part of a database function as it determines which records will be included in the associated calculation. It can be entered as a specific cell range (e.g., A17..E18) or, preferably, as a range name (e.g., CRITERIA). Either way, the criteria range is defined independently of the database table on which it operates. The criteria range must be at least two rows deep and one column wide, but it can be as large as necessary.

The simplest criteria range consists of two rows and as many columns as there are fields in the database. The first row contains the field names as they appear in the database. The second row holds the value(s) you are looking for; for example, the criteria range in Figure 5.7a selects the employees who work in Atlanta. Values can be entered under several fields to select records that meet more than one condition or to select records that meet one of several conditions.

Multiple values in the same row are connected by an AND and imply that the selected records meet *all* of the specified criteria. The criteria range in Figure 5.7b identifies the Account Reps in Atlanta; that is, it selects any record in which the location field is Atlanta *and* the title field is Account Rep.

Values entered in multiple rows are connected by an OR in which the selected records satisfy *any* of the indicated criteria. The criteria range in Figure 5.7c will identify employees who work in Atlanta *or* whose title is Account Rep.

Name	Location	Title	Hire Date	Salary
	Atlanta			

(a) Employees Who Work in Atlanta

Name	Location	Title	Hire Date	Salary
	Atlanta	Account Rep		

(b) Account Reps in Atlanta (AND condition)

Name	Location	Title	Hire Date	Salary
	Atlanta			
		Account Rep		

(c) Employees Who Work in Atlanta or
Who Are Account Reps (OR condition)

FIGURE 5.7   The Criteria Range

Name	Location	Title	Hire Date	Salary
			<1/1/93	

(d) Employees Hired Before January 1, 1993

Name	Location	Title	Hire Date	Salary
				>$40,000

(e) Employees Who Earn More Than $40,000

Repeat field name to establish an upper and lower boundary

Name	Location	Title	Hire Date	Salary	Salary
				>$40,000	<$60,000

(f) Employees Who Earn More Than $40,000 but Less Than $60,000

Name	Location	Title	Hire Date	Salary

(g) All Employees (a blank row)

FIGURE 5.7   The Criteria Range (continued)

Relational operators such as the greater than or less than sign may be used with date or numeric fields to return records within a designated range. The criteria range in Figure 5.7d selects the employees hired before January 1, 1993. The criteria range in Figure 5.7e returns employees whose salary is greater than $40,000.

An upper and lower boundary may be established for the same field by repeating the field name within the criteria range. This was done in Figure 5.7f, which returns all records in which the salary is greater than $40,000, but less than $60,000.

An empty row in the criteria range returns *every* record in the database as shown in Figure 5.7g.

WHERE IS THE < SYMBOL?

To enter the less than symbol in a cell, you *must* begin the cell with a label prefix; you cannot simply press the Shift key in conjunction with the key containing the less than symbol. Omitting the label prefix produces the Lotus classic menu, which existed in the DOS version of Lotus.

HANDS-ON EXERCISE 2:

Data Versus Information

Objective   To use multiple keys within the Sort command; to define a criteria range for use with the DSUM, DAVG, DMAX, DMIN, and DCOUNT functions; to create and modify a query table.

Step 1: Sort the database
➤ Open the **EMPLOYE2.WK4** spreadsheet created in the previous exercise.

- ➤ Click the **range selector icon** on the edit line to display the named ranges.
- ➤ Click **Sortrange** to select cells **A2 through E15.** (Cell A2 becomes the active cell.)
- ➤ Pull down the **Range menu.** Click **Sort** to produce the dialog box similar to Figure 5.8a.
- ➤ Check that the appropriate range, A2..E15 (or the equivalent Sortrange range name), is entered in the range text box at the bottom of the Sort dialog box.
- ➤ Clear any existing keys that already exist in the All keys list box by clicking the **Reset command button;** you should then see [New key] next to key one.
- ➤ Click the **range selector icon** in the Sort by text box to (temporarily) return to the spreadsheet.
- ➤ Click in cell **B2** to designate Location as the primary key and return to the dialog box. Click the **Add Key command button.**
- ➤ Click the **range selector icon** a second time, then click cell **A2** to designate Name as the secondary key. Click the **Add Key command button.**
- ➤ Check that the settings in your dialog box match those in Figure 5.8a. Click **OK** to sort the file and return to the spreadsheet. The employees are listed by location and alphabetically within location.
- ➤ Click outside the selected cells.

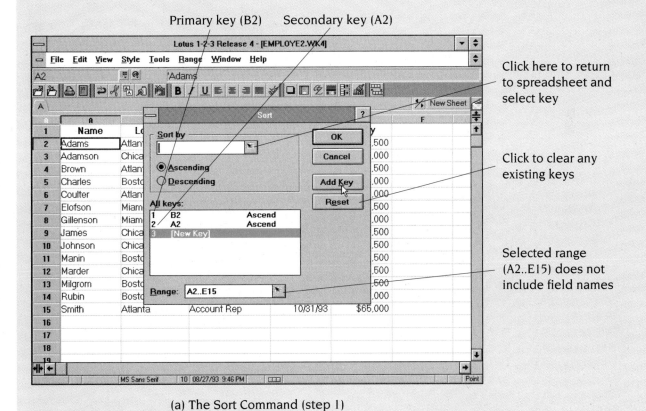

(a) The Sort Command (step 1)

FIGURE 5.8 Hands-on Exercise 2

Step 2: Define the criteria range
- ➤ The field names in the criteria range must be spelled *exactly* the same way as in the database. The best way to ensure that the names are the same is to copy the entries from one range to the other.

— Click in cell **A1.** Drag the mouse over the cells **A1 through E1.**
— Pull down the **Edit menu.** Click **Copy.**
— Click in cell **A17.** Pull down the **Edit menu.** Click **Paste.**

➤ Click in cell **A17.** Drag the mouse over cells **A17 through E18** to highlight these cells as shown in Figure 5.8b.

➤ Pull down the **Range menu.** Click **Name** to produce the dialog box in Figure 5.8b.

➤ Type **Criteria** in the Name text box. Click **OK.**

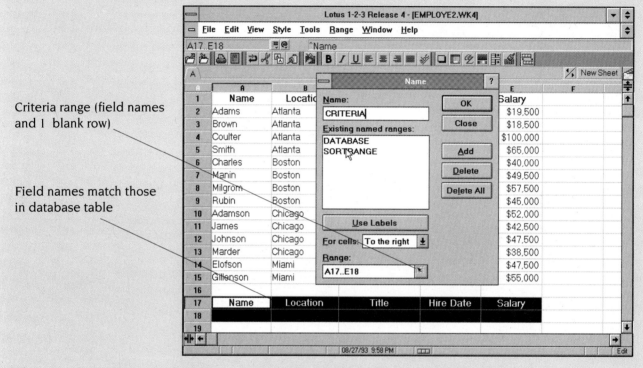

Criteria range (field names and 1 blank row)

Field names match those in database table

(b) Defining the Criteria Range (step 2)

FIGURE 5.8   Hands-on Exercise 2 (continued)

DRAG-AND-DROP TO NONADJACENT RANGES

You can use the mouse to copy selected cells to a *nonadjacent* range provided the source and destination ranges are the same size and shape. Select the cells to be copied, then point to any border of the selected range (the mouse pointer changes to an *open hand*). Click and continue to press the left mouse button (the mouse pointer changes to a *closed fist),* then press and hold the **Ctrl** key (a plus sign appears within the fist) as you drag the selection to its destination. Release the mouse to complete the operation. Follow the same procedure, but do not press the Ctrl key, to move rather than copy the selected cells to a nonadjacent range.

Step 3: The DAVG function
➤ Click in cell **A21.** Type **Summary Statistics** as shown in Figure 5.8c.
➤ Click in cell **A22.** Press the space bar four times, then type **Average salary.**
➤ Click in cell **E22.** Type **@DAVG(DATABASE,"SALARY",CRITERIA)** and

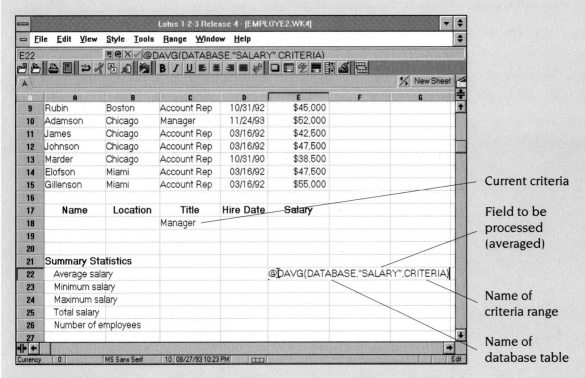

Lotus 1-2-3 Release 4 - [EMPLOYE2.WK4]

File Edit View Style Tools Range Window Help

E22   @DAVG(DATABASE,"SALARY",CRITERIA)

	A	B	C	D	E	F	G
9	Rubin	Boston	Account Rep	10/31/92	$45,000		
10	Adamson	Chicago	Manager	11/24/93	$52,000		
11	James	Chicago	Account Rep	03/16/92	$42,500		
12	Johnson	Chicago	Account Rep	03/16/92	$47,500		
13	Marder	Chicago	Account Rep	10/31/90	$38,500		
14	Elofson	Miami	Account Rep	03/16/92	$47,500		
15	Gillenson	Miami	Account Rep	03/16/92	$55,000		
16							
17	**Name**	**Location**	**Title**	**Hire Date**	Salary		
18			Manager				
19							
20							
21	Summary Statistics						
22	Average salary				@DAVG(DATABASE,"SALARY",CRITERIA)		
23	Minimum salary						
24	Maximum salary						
25	Total salary						
26	Number of employees						
27							

Current criteria

Field to be processed (averaged)

Name of criteria range

Name of database table

Currency 0   MS Sans Serif   10 08/27/93 10:23 PM   [   ]   Edit

(c) The DAVG Function (steps 3 and 4)

FIGURE 5.8   Hands-on Exercise 2 (continued)

press the **enter key.** You will see $48,429, the average salary of all employees. (No specific values have as yet been entered into the criteria range, and hence the DAVG function reflects every record in the database table.)

➤ Click in cell **C18.** Type **Manager** (be sure you spell it correctly) and press the **enter key.**

➤ Cell E22 contains $69,833, the average salary for all records satisfying the current criteria—that is, the average salary for all managers.

➤ Save the spreadsheet.

Step 4: Change the criteria

➤ Click in cell **B18.**

➤ Type **Chicago.** Press **enter.**

➤ The average salary changes to $52,000, reflecting the one employee (Adamson) who meets the current criteria (a manager in Chicago).

➤ Click in cell **C18.**

➤ Press the **Del key.**

CLEAR THE CRITERIA RANGE

Clear the existing values within the criteria range before you enter new values, especially when the selection criteria are based on different fields. If, for example, you are changing from managers in any location, to employees in Chicago, you must clear the title field, or else you will get employees who are managers and work in Chicago.

- The average salary changes to $45,125, reflecting all employees in Chicago.
- Click in cell **B18.** Press the **Del key.**
- The criteria range is now empty. The DAVG function again displays $48,429, which is the average salary of all employees in the database.
- Click in cell **C18.** Type **Manager.** The average salary is $69,833, the average salary for all managers.

Step 5: The DMAX, DMIN, and DCOUNT functions
- Enter the rest of the labels for cells **A23 through A26** as shown in Figure 5.8c.
- Click in cell **E23.** Type **@DMIN(DATABASE,"SALARY",CRITERIA).** Press **enter.** Cell E23 should display $52,000, the minimum salary for managers.
- Click in cell **E24.** Type **@DMAX(DATABASE,"SALARY",CRITERIA)** to compute the minimum salary for managers. Press **enter.** Cell E24 should display $100,000, the maximum salary for managers.
- Click in cell **E25.** Type **@DSUM(DATABASE,"SALARY",CRITERIA)** to compute the total salary for all managers. Press **enter.** Cell E24 should display $209,500, the total salary for all managers.
- Click in cell **E26.** Type **@DCOUNT(DATABASE,"SALARY",CRITERIA).** Press **enter.** Use the status bar to change to a fixed rather than a currency format. Cell E26 should display 3, the number of managers.
- Save the spreadsheet.

REDEFINE THE CRITERIA RANGE

Multiple rows within the criteria range implement an OR condition in which the selected records need to satisfy only one of several conditions. You must, however, use the Range Name command to redefine the criteria range whenever you increase (decrease) the number of rows to add (remove) a condition. Do not include a blank row in the criteria range unless you want to select every record in the database.

Step 6: The Database Find command
- Pull down the **Tools menu.** Click **Database.** Click **Find Records** to produce the dialog box in Figure 5.8d.
- Type **Database** in the Find records text box to select the database table, cells A1 through E15.
- Click the **down arrow** in the field list box. Click **Title.**
- Click the **down arrow** in the value list box. Click **Manager.** Click **OK.**

NAME VERSUS SOCIAL SECURITY NUMBER

If you want to be sure of finding a specific record, you must search on a unique field, such as social security or account number, rather than name. Although smaller databases may not require the presence of the additional field, it is wise to include one anyway.

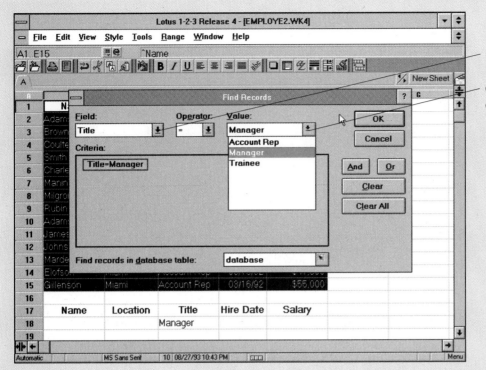

Click here to select field

Click here to select comparison value

(d) The Find Records Command (step 6)

FIGURE 5.8 Hands-on Exercise 2 (continued)

➤ You are back in the spreadsheet with the records for the managers highlighted.
➤ Press **Enter** (Shift+Enter) to move to the next (previous) field in the current record.
➤ Press **Ctrl+Enter** (Shift+Ctrl+Enter) to move to the first field in the next (previous) record.
➤ Click anywhere to deselect the Managers and return to the Ready mode.

Step 7: Create a query table
➤ Pull down the **Tools menu.** Click **Database.** Click **New Query** to produce the dialog box in Figure 5.8e.
➤ Type **Database** in the Select Database text box.
➤ Type **A28** in the Select location text box to specify the location for the query table. Do not press the enter key.
➤ Click the **Set Criteria command button** to produce the second dialog box in Figure 5.8e.

NAME THE QUERY TABLE

A query table can be named, then subsequently referenced by name for easy reference. (See the following tip on the Edit Go To command.) Select the query table, then pull down the Query menu (which appears instead of the Range menu when a query table is selected). Click Name, enter a name for the query table, then click the Rename command button. The name can be up to 15 characters long and should consist entirely of numbers and/or letters; spaces are not allowed.

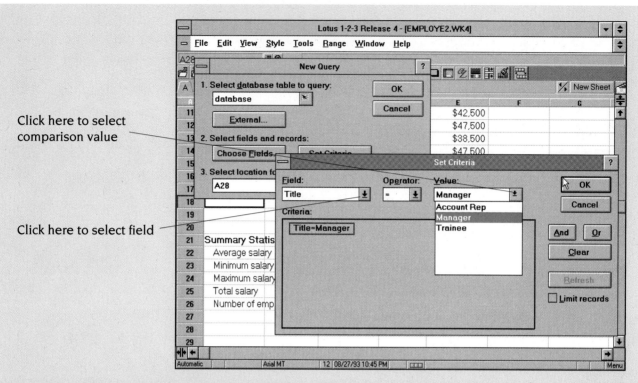

Click here to select comparison value

Click here to select field

(e) Creating a Query (step 7)

FIGURE 5.8 Hands-on Exercise 2 (continued)

> Click the **down arrow** in the field list box. Click **Title.**
> Click the **down arrow** in the value list box. Click **Manager.** Click **OK.** Click **OK** a second time.
> A query table, containing the records for all managers, has been created as shown in Figure 5.8f.
> Save the spreadsheet.

Step 8: Update the query table
> Click in cell **C15.** Type **Manager** to change Gillenson's title. Press **enter.**
> Point to any border of the query table until the mouse pointer changes to an arrow and a solid square.
> Click the **right mouse button** to produce the quick menu in Figure 5.8f.
> Click **Refresh Now.** The contents of the query table are changed automatically to reflect the change in the database table; that is, the query table contains a fourth record for Gillenson, who is now a manager.

THE EDIT GO TO COMMAND

The **Edit Go To command** (or equivalent F5 key) is the easiest way to select a query table. Press the **F5** key to produce a dialog box. Click the down arrow in the Type of item list box and click Query table. Click the table you want (the tables have default names of Query 1, Query 2, and so on), then click OK. You can use the Query Name command (see previous tip) to substitute a meaningful name for each table, such as CHICAGOMGRS instead of Query 1.

Change Gillenson's title

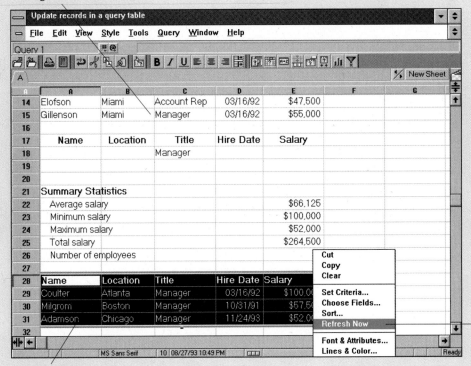

Query table

(f) Updating a Query Table (step 8)

FIGURE 5.8 Hands-on Exercise 2 (continued)

Step 9: Change the criteria
- ➤ Check that the query table is still selected.
- ➤ Click the **right mouse button.** Click Set Criteria to produce a dialog box similar to Figure 5.8g, which contains the current criterion (Title=Manager).
- ➤ Click the **And command button.**
- ➤ Click the arrow on the **Field list box.** Click **Salary.**
- ➤ Click the arrow on the **Operator list box.** Click the **less than sign.**
- ➤ Click the arrow on the **Value list box.** Click **$57,500.** The criteria are now complete and will select managers who earn less than $57,500.
- ➤ Click **OK.** The query table is updated automatically to reflect the new criteria and now contains only two records, Adamson and Gillenson.

PRESS TAB, NOT ENTER

Press the **Tab** key to move to the next field within a dialog box. Press **Shift+Tab** to move to the previous field. Press the enter key (or click the OK command button) only after the last entry has been completed.

Step 10: Update the query table
- ➤ Select the entire query table. Pull down the **Query menu.**
  - — Click **Set Options** if Update Database Table is not available, then click

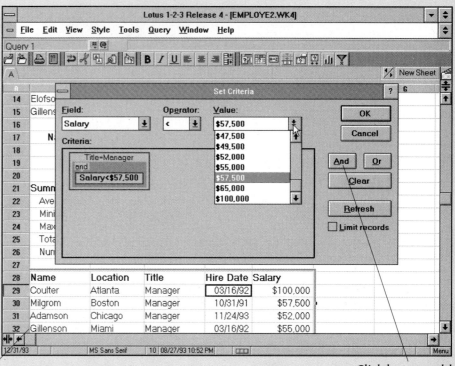

Gillenson added to Query Table

Click here to add second condition

(g) The Set Criteria Command (step 9)

Click here to set Allow Updates option on

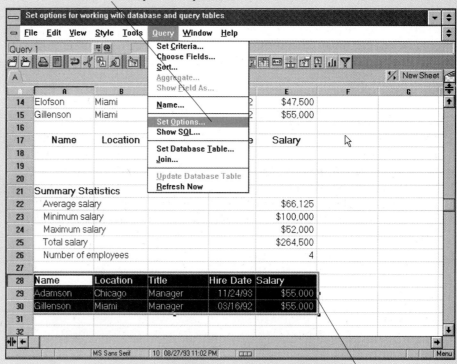

Change Adamson's salary to $55,000

(h) Update the Database Table (step 10)

FIGURE 5.8   Hands-on Exercise 2 (continued)

the check box to Allow updates to database table. Click **OK** to exit the dialog box, then click **OK** a second time in response to the message that follows.

➤ Click in the cell in the query table that contains Adamson's salary. Change the value to $55,000.

➤ Select the query table, pull down the **Query menu,** and click **Update Database Table.**

➤ Click in cell **E10,** the cell containing Adamson's salary within the database table. The value has been updated to reflect the change from the query table.

➤ Save the spreadsheet.

Step 11: Print the spreadsheet and/or the query table

➤ To print the entire spreadsheet, pull down the **File menu,** click **Print,** select **Current worksheet,** then click **OK** as you have throughout the text.

➤ To print only a portion of the spreadsheet—for example, just the query table—you first select the specific range. Press the **F5** (GoTo) key, then use the dialog box to select the query table. (Click the arrow in the Type of item list box and select Query Table. Query 1 is highlighted. Click **OK.**)

➤ Pull down the **File menu.** Click **Print.** Click **OK** to print the selected range.

➤ Exit Lotus.

CROSS-TABULATIONS

A *cross-tabulation* or *crosstab table* extends the capability of individual database functions by presenting the data in summary form. It organizes the records in a database table into categories, then computes summary statistics for those categories. The table is created through the Database Crosstab command, which prompts the user for the row and column headings, the field in the database table on which the calculation is to be performed, and the means of calculation (sum, average, count, etc.).

The crosstab table in Figure 5.9a was created according to the dialog boxes in Figures 5.9b and 5.9c. It displays the total salary for all employees in each job location according to job title; each cell in the table displays the total salary for a different location-title combination. Cell B6, for example, displays the total salaries for the Account Reps in Miami.

The crosstab table in Figure 5.9a was produced by the Database Crosstab command with no additional commands from the user. The table in Figure 5.9d has been enhanced by the user to include row and column totals (computed through @SUM functions) and additional formatting.

B	A	B	C	D	E
1	Crosstab Table For Total Salary by Location and Title				
2		Account Rep	Manager	Trainee	
3	Atlanta	$65,000	$100,000	$38,000	
4	Boston	$134,500	$57,500	$0	
5	Chicago	$128,500	$55,000	$0	
6	Miami	$47,500	$55,000	$0	

(a) Cross-tabulation Table

FIGURE 5.9   Cross-tabulation tables

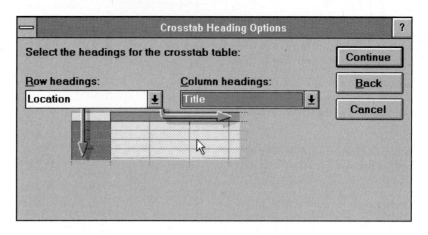

(b) Row and Column Headings

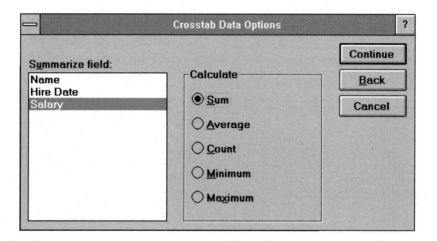

(c) Data Options

Title enhanced

B	A	B	C	D	E
1	Crosstab Table For Total Salary by Location and Title				
2		Account Rep	Manager	Trainee	Totals
3	Atlanta	$65,000	$100,000	$38,000	$203,000
4	Boston	$134,500	$57,500	$0	$192,000
5	Chicago	$128,500	$55,000	$0	$183,500
6	Miami	$102,500	$0	$0	$102,500
7	Totals	$375,500	$267,500	$38,000	$681,000

Totals added

(d) Modified cross-tabulation Table

FIGURE 5.9 Cross-tabulation tables (continued)

The Crosstab command prompts you for the information it needs to develop the cross-tab table. You supply the row and column headings by selecting a field from the drop-down list boxes in Figure 5.9b. You choose the field on which the calculation is based and the means of calculation from the dialog box in Figure 5.9c. Lotus does the rest as you will see in the ensuing hands-on exercise.

There is, however, one subtlety in that the cross-tabulation table is placed in a *different* worksheet from the database table on which it is based. Look carefully at the worksheet grid in Figures 5.9a and 5.9d and note the indication of worksheet B, rather than worksheet A. In other words, the address of the cross-tabulation table in Figure 5.9d is really B:A1 through B:D6. The database table on which it is based is the same table we have been using throughout the chapter and is located in worksheet A in cells A:A1 through A:E15. Both worksheets are stored in the same WK4 file—for example, the EMPLOYE2.WK4 file used in the second hands-on exercise.

THE THIRD DIMENSION

A Lotus spreadsheet can be extended to a third dimension with up to 256 worksheets stored in a single WK4 file. Each worksheet is identified with a letter from A to Z, then continuing with AA to AZ, BA to BZ, etc. The complete cell address includes the worksheet letter followed by a colon, such as A:A1 to indicate cell A1 in worksheet A. Omission of the worksheet letter in the cell address (as has been done throughout the text) assumes worksheet A.

HANDS-ON EXERCISE 3:

A Cross-tabulation Table

Objective To create a cross-tabulation table from a database table, then modify the table with additional formatting; to view multiple worksheets within the same WK4 file.

Step 1: Retrieve the EMPLOYE2 spreadsheet
➤ Open the **EMPLOYE2** spreadsheet from the previous exercise.
➤ Pull down the **File menu.**
➤ Click **Save As.** Save the spreadsheet as **EMPLOYE3.WK4.**
➤ Pull down the **Tools menu.** Click **Database** as shown in Figure 5.10a.
➤ Click **Crosstab** to produce the first dialog box in Figure 5.10b.

Step 2: Create the cross-tabulation table
➤ Type **Database** (the range name for the database table) in the text box to select the database range as shown in Figure 5.10b.
➤ Click the **Continue Command button.**
➤ Click the drop-down list box for the Row headings. Click **Location.**
➤ Click the drop-down list box for Column headings. Click **Title.**
➤ Click the **Continue Command button.**
➤ Click **Salary** in the Summarize field list box. If necessary, click the **Sum button.**
➤ Click the **Continue Command button.**
➤ The crosstab table is created in worksheet B of the EMPLOYE3.WK4 file as shown in Figure 5.10c.

Step 3: The Third Dimension
➤ Look carefully at the screen in Figure 5.10c. The title bar indicates EMPLOYE3.WK4, the same WK4 file we have been using throughout the exercise; the selection indicator, however, displays B:B5 to indicate that the active cell is in worksheet B.

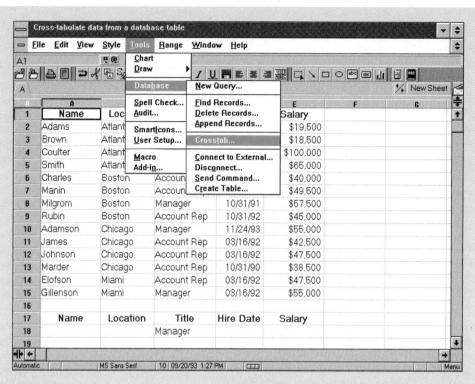

(a) The Crosstab Command (step 1)

Click here to produce next dialog box

Enter name of database table

(b) Creating the Table (step 2)

FIGURE 5.10 Hands-on Exercise 3

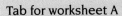

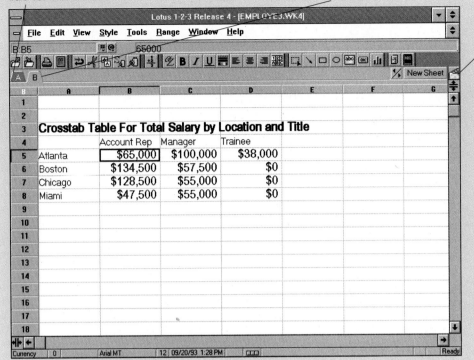

(c) The Third Dimension (step 3)

FIGURE 5.10 Hands-on Exercise 3 (continued)

➤ Click on any cell in the worksheet and note that the new active cell is always prefaced by B: to indicate worksheet B of the EMPLOYE3.WK4 spreadsheet.
➤ Look for the worksheet tabs in the upper-left portion of the spreadsheet. The tab for worksheet B is in front to indicate you are in worksheet B. (If you cannot see the tabs, click the tabbing icon above the vertical scroll bar at the right of the window, which toggles the tabs on and off.)
➤ Click the **tab for worksheet A** and you once again see the database table. The selection indicator prefaces the cell address with A: to indicate you are in worksheet A.
➤ Click the **tab for worksheet B** and you see the crosstab table.

WORKSHEET TABS AND THE QUICK MENU

A quick menu contains context-sensitive commands for the selected item, which may be a cell or cell range, a chart, a query table, or a worksheet. Point to a worksheet tab (or the worksheet letter in the space between the row and column labels), then click the **right mouse button** to select the entire worksheet and display the associated quick menu.

Step 4: Complete the cross-tabulation table
➤ The cross-tabulation table in Figure 5.10d reflects the following modifications to the original version.

Row totals added; shaded and formatted for emphasis

Title moved to row 2

Locations and job titles bolded for emphasis

Column totals added; shaded and formatted for emphasis

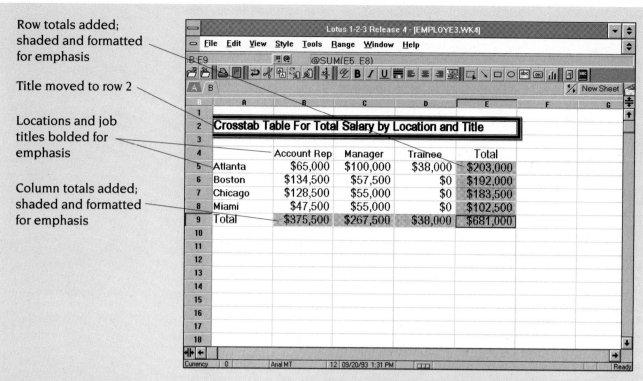

(d) The Completed Table (step 4)

FIGURE 5.10 Hands-on Exercise 3 (continued)

— Row and column totals were added for each location and job title; the totals are in currency format and have been shaded for emphasis; the word Total is entered in cells E4 and A9.
— The title of the table has been moved to row two and enclosed in a designer frame.
— The location names and job titles have been changed to boldface for emphasis.
➤ Implement these and/or other modifications as you see fit.

THE SMARTSUM ICON

The fastest way to compute the row and column totals for a cross-tabulation table is to use the Summation SmartIcon which sums the (selected) elements above and to the left of the active cell. Select all values in the cross-tabulation table, but include in the selection an extra row at the bottom of the table and an extra column to the right of the table. Click the Summation SmartIcon in the default set of SmartIcons.

Step 5: The Print Preview command
➤ Pull down the **File menu.** Click **Print.**
➤ Click the **All worksheets button** to print the database table in worksheet A and the crosstab table in worksheet B.
➤ Click the **Page Setup command button** to establish the printing parameters. We have included the worksheet frame and grid lines and modified the header.

- Click **OK** to exit the Page Setup dialog box.
- Click the **Preview command button** to preview the spreadsheet as shown in Figure 5.10e and consider the implications. You are printing two worksheets on the same page, and further, both worksheets are stored in the EMPLOYE3.WK4 file.
- Print the spreadsheet.
- Save the spreadsheet a final time.
- Exit Lotus.
- Exit Windows.

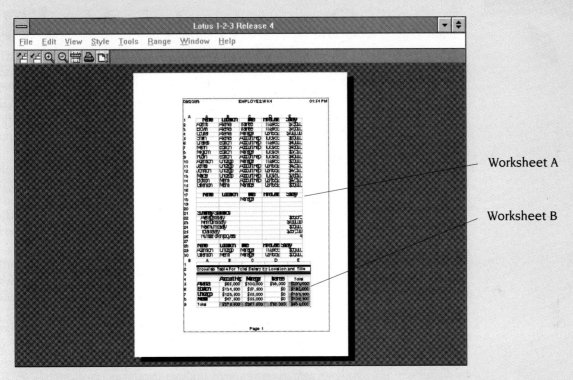

(e) The Print Preview Command (step 5)

FIGURE 5.10 Hands-on Exercise 3 (continued)

A WISH LIST FOR LOTUS

It was a complete surprise to us that changes to a database table were not reflected in the corresponding cross-tabulation table, but that is precisely what happens; any change in the database requires you to recreate the cross-tabulation table from scratch. To make matters worse, the new table is placed in worksheet C (unless you first delete the old table in worksheet B) so that the WK4 file contains both the old and new versions of the cross-tabulation table. We hope this will be fixed in a future release, but the problem existed in version 4.0. To determine the version of Lotus you are using, pull down the Help menu and click About 1-2-3.

SUMMARY

A database table, as the term is used in Lotus, is an area in a spreadsheet. The first row in the database contains the field names. Each additional row contains a record and each column represents a field.

Data and information are not synonymous; information is data that has been rearranged into a form perceived as useful by the recipient. The data within a system must be sufficient to produce the required information.

The DSUM, DAVG, DMAX, DMIN, and DCOUNT functions each have three arguments: the database range, the field on which the function is to operate, and the criteria. The criteria can be entered in the function itself, or preferably, in an independent criteria range.

The Data Find command selects the records in the database table that satisfy the criteria specified in the command. The Query Command copies all records that satisfy the criteria specified in the command to a separate query table elsewhere in the spreadsheet. The query table is similar to a database table except that it contains only a subset of the records in the table.

A cross-tabulation or crosstab table extends the capability of individual database functions by presenting the data in summary form. It organizes the records in a database table into categories, then computes summary statistics for those categories. The crosstab table is placed in a different worksheet from the database table on which it is based.

 Key Words and Concepts

Ascending sequence	DMIN function	Primary key
Compound condition	DSUM function	Query table
Criteria	Edit Delete command	Range Name command
Criteria range	Edit Insert command	Range selector
Cross-tabulation table	Field	Record
Data	Field name	Record structure
Database table	File	Secondary key
Data Find command	File design	Simple condition
DAVG function	File maintenance	Sort command
Descending sequence	Information	Tertiary key
DCOUNT function	Key	Wild card
DMAX function	New Query command	Worksheet

 Multiple Choice

1. Which of the following best describes the implementation of data management within a spreadsheet?
   (a) The columns in a spreadsheet correspond to records in a file
   (b) The rows in a spreadsheet correspond to fields in a record
   (c) Both (a) and (b)
   (d) Neither (a) nor (b)

2. A social security number is often used to identify a specific employee rather than the employee's name because:
   (a) The social security number is numeric whereas the name is not

(b) The social security number is unique whereas the name is not

(c) The social security number is a shorter field consisting of only nine digits whereas the name contains many more characters

(d) All of the above

3. Assume that cells A21..B22 have been defined as the criteria range for a database function; that cells A21 and B21 contain the field names City and Title, respectively; and that cells A22 and B22 contain New York and Manager. The records used in the function will consist of:

(a) All employees in New York

(b) All managers

(c) Only the managers in New York

(d) All employees in New York and all managers

4. Assume that cells A21..B23 have been defined as the criteria range for a database function; that cells A21 and B21 contain the field names City and Title, respectively; and that cells A22 and B23 contain New York and Manager, respectively. The records used in the function will consist of:

(a) All employees in New York

(b) All managers

(c) Only the managers in New York

(d) All employees in New York and all managers

5. If employees are to be listed so that all employees in the same city appear together in alphabetical order by the employee's last name,

(a) City and last name are both considered to be the primary key

(b) City and last name are both considered to be the secondary key

(c) City is the primary key and last name is the secondary key

(d) Last name is the primary key and city is the secondary key

6. Which field—age or birth date—should be stored within a database table, given the need to reference an employee's age?

(a) Age, and not birth date, since age is required and birth date is not

(b) Birth date, not age, since the age can be calculated from the birth date

(c) There is no preference between the two since an individual's age can always be calculated from the birth date

(d) Both fields must be stored since they contain entirely different values

7. How are the criteria entered in a database function?

(a) Directly in the function

(b) As a named range

(c) Either (a) or (b)

(d) Neither (a) nor (b)

8. Which of the following best describes the range associated with a Sort command intended to resequence the records in a database table?

(a) The sort range should include the entire database table, including the row containing the column headings (field names)

(b) The sort range should include the entire database table, *except for* the row containing the column headings (field names)

(c) The sort range should include all rows in the database but only those columns that are referenced as keys

(d) The sort range should include only the row of column headings and only those columns referenced as keys

9. Which of the following can be used to add records to a database table?
   (a) Click in the last row of the existing table, pull down the Edit menu, click Insert, then enter the data
   (b) Click in the row label of the last row in the table, click the right mouse button, click Insert, then enter the data
   (c) Both (a) and (b)
   (d) Neither (a) nor (b)

10. Assume that a range name has been defined for a database table, which is presently in cells A1 through D24. The Edit Insert command has been used to add a new field in column C and again to add a new employee in row 15. The range name now includes:
    (a) Cells A1 through E25
    (b) Cells A1 through E24
    (c) Cells A1 through D25
    (d) Cells A1 through D24

11. Which of the following is true of the Data Sort command?
    (a) It provides a maximum of two keys: a primary key and a secondary key
    (b) The primary key must be in the same sequence as the secondary key; that is, both keys must be ascending or descending
    (c) Both (a) and (b)
    (d) Neither (a) nor (b)

12. Which of the following can be used to select a named range?
    (a) The Edit Go To command or equivalent F5 key
    (b) The range selector
    (c) Both (a) and (b)
    (d) Neither (a) nor (b)

13. Under which circumstances would you include a blank row within the criteria range?
    (a) To select every record within the database
    (b) To ensure that records added with the Insert command are included in the database without having to redefine the database
    (c) Both (a) and (b)
    (d) Neither (a) nor (b)

14. The Undo command will reverse the effect of
    (a) The Range Sort command
    (b) The Edit Insert and Edit Delete commands
    (c) Both (a) and (b)
    (d) Neither (a) nor (b)

15. A cross-tabulation table is
    (a) Placed in a different worksheet than the database table on which it is based
    (b) Saved in the same WK4 file as the database table on which it is based
    (c) Both (a) and (b)
    (d) Neither (a) nor (b)

ANSWERS

1. d	**3.** c	**5.** c
2. b	**4.** d	**6.** b

7. c   **10.** a   **13.** a

8. b   **11.** d   **14.** c

9. c   **12.** c   **15.** c

EXPLORING LOTUS

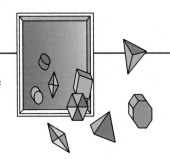

1. Use Figure 5.11 to match each action with its result; a given action may be used more than once or not at all.

a. Click at 1
b. Click at 2
c. Click at 3
d. Click at 4
e. Click at 5, drag to 6, click at 7, then specify A2 as the first key
f. Click at 5, drag to 6, click at 7, then specify H2 as the first key and A2 as the second key
g. Click at 8, drag to 6, click at 7
h. Click at 9, click at 10
i. Click at 11, click at 10
j. Click at 12

_____ Add a field to the database

_____ Sort the database in alphabetical order by name

_____ Find the records that match the specified criteria

_____ Create a crosstab table

_____ Sort the database by name within loan type

_____ Print the database

_____ Delete records that meet specified criteria

_____ Add a record to the database

_____ Create a query table

_____ Assign a name to the database

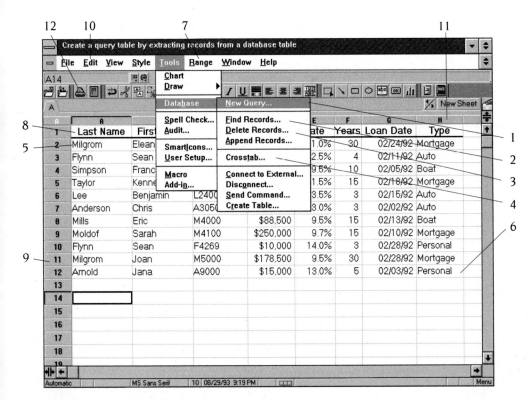

FIGURE 5.11 Screen for Problem 1

2. Careful attention must be given to designing a database, or else the resulting system will not perform as desired. Consider the following:

   a. An individual's age may be calculated from his or her birth date, which in turn can be stored as a field within a record. An alternate technique would be to store age directly in the record and thereby avoid the calculation. Which field—that is, age or birth date—would you use? Why?

   b. Social security number is typically chosen as a record key in lieu of a person's name. What attribute does the social security number possess that makes it the superior choice?

   c. Zip code is normally stored as a separate field to save money at the post office in connection with a mass mailing. Why?

   d. An individual's name is normally divided into two (or three) fields corresponding to the last name and first name (and middle initial). Why is this done; that is, what would be wrong with using a single field consisting of the first name, middle initial, and last name, in that order?

3. Show the criteria needed to produce the following reports using the employee database presented in the chapter.

   a. All trainees

   b. All trainees in Chicago

   c. Employees who are managers or trainees

   d. Managers in Chicago or trainees in Atlanta

   e. Employees hired before January 1, 1992, earning less than $50,000

   f. All employees in the company

4. Trouble shooting: The informational screens in Figure 5.12 appeared (or could have appeared) in response to various commands introduced in the chapter. Indicate a command that could have produced each message and suggest the appropriate corrective action.

(a) Informational Message 1

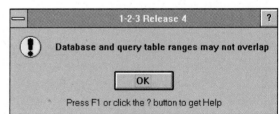

(b) Informational Message 2

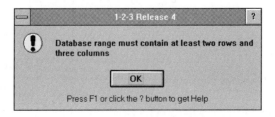

(c) Informational Message 3

FIGURE 5.12 Informational Messages for Problem 4

5. Figure 5.13 is a revised version of the EMPLOYEE spreadsheet containing an employee's previous salary as well as two additional fields that reflect calculations based on the previous salary. The database has been redefined to include cells A1 through H15.

a. In which order are the employees listed? What is the primary key? Is the sequence ascending or descending? What is the sort range?

b. What formula (function) should be entered into cell G2 to compute the amount of the increase for those employees who actually have an increase? (Employees who were recently hired do not have a previous salary, and hence they should not show a salary increase. Remove the check in the Displays Zeros check box in the Worksheet Defaults command in the Styles menu to suppress the display of zero values.)

c. What formula (function) should be entered into cell H2 to compute the percentage increase for those employees who have had an increase?

d. What would be the effect of removing the >0 entry from cell G18?

e. What is the entry in cell G22? in cell H22?

f. Retrieve the spreadsheet PROB0505.WK4 from the data disk, which is a partially completed version of Figure 5.13. The file contains the data in column F, but you will have to complete the entries in columns G and H, and define various ranges needed for the database commands and functions. When you are finished, type your name and title (compensation analyst) in cells A22 and A23, then print the spreadsheet and submit it to your instructor.

	A	B	C	D	E	F	G	H
1	Name	Location	Title	Hire Date	Salary	Previous Salary	Increase	Percentage
2	Johnson	Chicago	Account Rep	03/16/92	$47,500	$40,000	$7,500	18.8%
3	Rubin	Boston	Account Rep	10/31/92	$45,000	$40,000	$5,000	12.5%
4	Coulter	Atlanta	Manager	03/16/92	$100,000	$90,000	$10,000	11.1%
5	Manin	Boston	Account Rep	10/31/89	$49,500	$45,000	$4,500	10.0%
6	Marder	Chicago	Account Rep	10/31/90	$38,500	$35,000	$3,500	10.0%
7	Elofson	Miami	Account Rep	03/16/92	$47,500	$45,000	$2,500	5.6%
8	Gillenson	Miami	Account Rep	03/16/92	$55,000	$52,500	$2,500	4.8%
9	Milgrom	Boston	Manager	10/31/91	$57,500	$55,000	$2,500	4.5%
10	James	Chicago	Account Rep	03/16/92	$42,500	$41,000	$1,500	3.7%
11	Adams	Atlanta	Trainee	11/24/93	$19,500			
12	Brown	Atlanta	Trainee	11/24/93	$18,500			
13	Smith	Atlanta	Account Rep	10/31/93	$65,000			
14	Charles	Boston	Account Rep	11/24/93	$40,000			
15	Adamson	Chicago	Manager	11/24/93	$52,000			
16								
17	Name	Location	Title	Hire Date	Salary	Previous Salary	Increase	Percentage
18							>0	
19								
20								
21					Evaluation of Salary Increase:			
22					Average Increase:		$4,389	9.0%
23					Maximum Increase:		$10,000	18.8%
24					Minimum Increase:		$1,500	3.7%
25					Number of employees:		9	9

FIGURE 5.13 Spreadsheet for Problem 5

6. Using the data disk: The spreadsheet in Figure 5.14 exists on the data disk as PROB0506.WK4. Retrieve the spreadsheet, then implement the following changes:

a. Delete the record for Julie Rubin, who has dropped out of school.

	A	B	C	D	E	F
1	Academic advisor					
2						
3	Last Name	First Name	Major	Quality Points	Credits	GPA
4	Moldof	Alan	Engineering	60	20	3.00
5	Stutz	Joel	Engineering	180	75	2.40
6	Rubin	Julie	Liberal Arts	140	65	2.15
7	Milgrom	Richard	Liberal Arts	400	117	3.42
8	Grauer	Jessica	Liberal Arts	96	28	3.43
9	Moldof	Adam	Business	160	84	1.90
10	Grauer	Benjamin	Business	190	61	3.11
11	Rudolph	Eleanor	Liberal Arts	185	95	1.95
12	Ford	Judd	Engineering	206	72	2.86
13	Fegin	Rick	Communications	190	64	2.97
14	Flynn	Sean	Business	90	47	1.91
15	Coulter	Maryann	Liberal Arts	135	54	2.50
16						
17						
18	The Deans' List (GPA > 3.0)					
19						
20						
21						
22						
23						
24						
25						
26						
27						
28						
29	Academic Probation (GPA < 2.0)					
30						
31						
32						
33						
34						
35						

FIGURE 5.14 Spreadsheet for Problem 6

b. Change the data in Rick Fegin's record to show 193 quality points.

c. Add a transfer student, Jimmy Flynn, majoring in Engineering. Jimmy has completed 65 credits and has 200 quality points.

d. Sort the database so that the students are listed in alphabetical order. Specify last name and first name as the primary and secondary key, respectively.

e. Does the sort you just performed explain why the last name and first name were defined as separate fields within the database? Would the students still be in alphabetical order if you had defined the name as a single field consisting of the first name followed by the last name and you used the combined name as the primary key?

f. Save the spreadsheet.

g. Create a query table for students on the Dean's List (with a grade point average of 3.00 or higher).

h. Create a second query table starting in cell A30 for students on academic probation (with a grade point average less than 2.00).

i. Add your name as the academic advisor in cell C1. Print the spreadsheet with both lists of students and submit it to your instructor.

Soleil Shoes, Inc.
Italy, Brazil, Spain

Dear John,

Enclosed please find the information on our managers earning less than $57,500 (Adamson and Gillenson). If you need further information, please don't hesitate to ask.

Name	Location	Title	Hire Date	Salary
Adamson	Chicago	Manager	11/24/93	$55,000
Gillenson	Miami	Manager	03/16/92	$55,000

Bob

FIGURE 5.15   Compound document for Problem 7

7. Object Linking and Embedding: The compound document in Figure 5.15 consists of a memo produced by a word processor and a portion of the spreadsheet created in the second hands-on exercise. The document was created in such a way that any change in the spreadsheet will be automatically reflected in the memo. The exercise below is written for WordPerfect for Windows but will work equally well within any Windows word processor that supports OLE.

a. Copy the query table to the clipboard.
   - Open the EMPLOYE2.WK4 as it existed at the end of the second hands-on exercise.
   - Select the query table. Pull down the **Edit menu.** Click **Copy** to copy the selected cells to the Windows clipboard.

b. Open a Windows word processor.
   - Press and hold the **Alt key,** while you press and release the **Tab key** repeatedly to cycle through the open applications. Release the Alt key when you see Program Manager displayed in a box in the middle of your screen.
   - Open the Windows word processor—perhaps WordPerfect for Windows. Type the text of the memo shown in Figure 5.15.

c. Link the spreadsheet to the word processing document.
   - The specific commands to complete the link between the spreadsheet and the word processing document depend on the word processor. In WordPerfect for Windows: pull down the **Edit menu,** click **Paste Special,** then click **Paste Link.**
   - The spreadsheet data should appear within the word processing document as shown in Figure 5.15.

d. Change the underlying spreadsheet data.
   - Use **Alt+Tab** to return to Lotus. Click in cell **E10** of the **EMPLOYE3** spreadsheet. Type **65000** to change Adamson's salary.
   - The database functions are updated automatically to reflect Adamson's new salary, but the query table is not. Accordingly, select the query table, then press the right mouse button to produce a quick menu. Click **Refresh Now** to update the query table.

e. Return to the Word Processing document.

> ➤ Use **Alt+Tab** to return to the word processing document.
> ➤ The spreadsheet data within the document no longer includes Adamson.
> ➤ Save the document. Exit WordPerfect. Exit Lotus. Exit Windows.

 Case Studies

The United States of America

What is the total population of the United States? What is its area? Can you name the 13 original states or the last five states admitted to the Union? Do you know the 10 states with the highest population or the five largest states in terms of area? Which states have the highest population density (people per square mile)?

The answers to these and other questions are readily available, provided you can analyze the data in the USADBASE.WK4 spreadsheet that is available on the data disk. This assignment is completely open ended and requires only that you print out the extracted data in a report on the United States database. Format the reports so that they are attractive and informative.

The Super Bowl

How many times has the NFC won the Super Bowl? When was the last time the AFC won? What was the largest margin of victory? What was the closest game? What is the most points scored by two teams in one game? How many times have the Miami Dolphins appeared? How many times did they win? Use the data in the SUPERBWL spreadsheet to prepare a trivia sheet on the Super Bowl, then incorporate your analysis into a letter addressed to NBC Sports. Convince them you are a super fan and that you merit two tickets to next year's game.

Personnel Management

You have been hired as the Personnel Director for a medium-sized firm (500 employees) and are expected to implement a system to track employee compensation. You want to be able to calculate the age of every employee as well as the length of service. You want to know each employee's most recent performance evaluation. You want to calculate the amount of the most recent salary increase, in dollars as well as a percentage of the previous salary. You also want to know how long the employee had to wait for that increase—that is, how much time elapsed between the present and previous salary.

Design a spreadsheet capable of providing this information. Enter test data for at least five employees to check the accuracy of your formulas. Format the spreadsheet so that it is attractive and easy to read.

Equal Employment Opportunity

Are you paying your employees fairly? Is there any difference between the salaries paid to men and women? between minorities and nonminorities? between minorities of one ethnic background versus those of another ethnic background? Use the EEO.WK4 spreadsheet to analyze the data for the listed employees. Are there any other factors not included in the database that might be reasonably expected to influence an employee's compensation? Write your findings in the form of a memo to the Vice President for Human Resources.

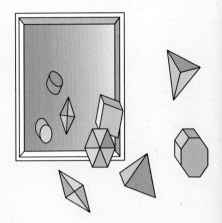

Appendix A
SmartIcons

Lotus for Windows provides approximately 200 SmartIcons, grouped into a series of palettes, which can be used to quickly and easily execute a command or perform a task. The default palette that appears when you first load Lotus contains icons that perform the most commonly executed tasks. As you work, Lotus automatically switches to the palette appropriate to the task being performed. For example, when you are working with charts, the Chart palette is displayed; when you are working with objects, the Arrange palette is displayed; and when you are working with query tables, the Table palette is displayed. In addition, you can explicitly change the displayed palette to one of eight available palettes and/or customize the SmartIcons displayed on these palettes.

The eight available palettes include the Default, Editing, Formatting, Goodies, Macro Building, Printing, Sheet Auditing, and Working Together palettes. You may work with these palettes as follows:

➤ To hide (show) a palette, pull down the View menu, click Set View Preferences, and deselect (select) the SmartIcons check box. Alternatively, you can click the SmartIcons selector on the Status bar and click Hide (Show) SmartIcons.

➤ To execute the task associated with a SmartIcon, point to the icon and click the left mouse button. Clicking with the right mouse button will cause a description of the icon to appear in the title bar.

➤ To switch the currently displayed palette, pull down the Tools menu, click Smart-Icons, and select the desired palette from the drop-down list at the top of the dialog box. Alternatively, you can click the SmartIcon selector on the Status bar and click the desired palette.

➤ To customize a palette, pull down the Tools menu, click SmartIcons, and select the palette that you wish to modify from the drop-down list at the top of the dialog box. Then:

● To add an icon, find the icon in the Available Icons list and drag it to the selected palette list, dropping it in the position you wish it to appear.

● To delete an icon, drag it out of the selected palette list and release the mouse button.

● To reposition an icon, drag it to a new location on the selected palette list.

(You may also reposition icons directly on the displayed palette without pulling down the Tools menu by pressing the Ctrl key as you drag the icon to the desired position on the palette.)

- To separate the SmartIcons into logical groups on the selected palette, drag the Spacer SmartIcon found at the top of the Available Icons list to the selected palette list.
- To save the changes made, click the Save Set command button, assigning a new name to the palette if you so desire.

➤ To change the display size of the SmartIcons, pull down the Tools menu, click SmartIcons, click the Icon Size command button, and then click either Medium or Large.

➤ To change the position of the palette, pull down the Tools menu, click SmartIcons, pull down the Position drop-down list, and select the desired location. If you choose Floating, you may move or size the SmartIcon window as you would any window (i.e., drag the title bar to move it and drag a border or corner to size it).

1-2-3 FOR WINDOWS SMARTICON PALETTES

Default Sheet Palette

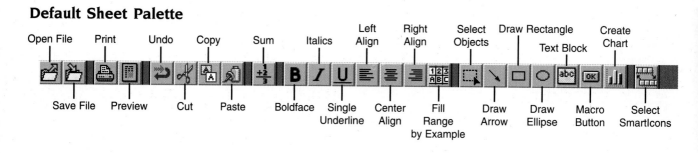

Editing Palette

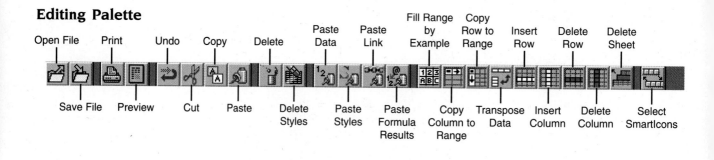

Formatting Palette

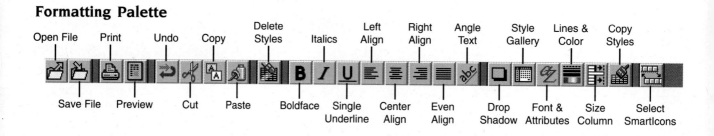

Goodies Palette

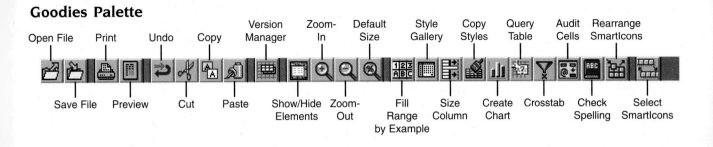

Open File · Print · Undo · Copy · Version Manager · Zoom-In · Default Size · Style Gallery · Copy Styles · Query Table · Audit Cells · Rearrange SmartIcons

Save File · Preview · Cut · Paste · Show/Hide Elements · Zoom-Out · Fill Range by Example · Size Column · Create Chart · Crosstab · Check Spelling · Select SmartIcons

Macro Building Palette

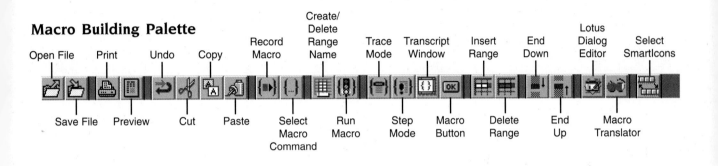

Open File · Print · Undo · Copy · Record Macro · Create/Delete Range Name · Trace Mode · Transcript Window · Insert Range · End Down · Lotus Dialog Editor · Select SmartIcons

Save File · Preview · Cut · Paste · Select Macro Command · Run Macro · Step Mode · Macro Button · Delete Range · End Up · Macro Translator

Printing Palette

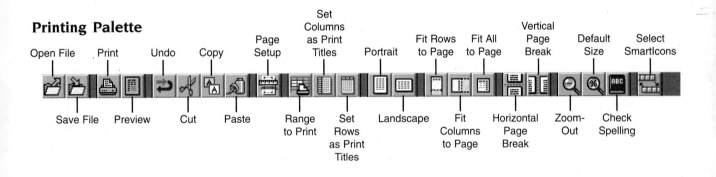

Open File · Print · Undo · Copy · Page Setup · Set Columns as Print Titles · Portrait · Fit Rows to Page · Fit All to Page · Vertical Page Break · Default Size · Select SmartIcons

Save File · Preview · Cut · Paste · Range to Print · Set Rows as Print Titles · Landscape · Fit Columns to Page · Horizontal Page Break · Zoom-Out · Check Spelling

Sheet Auditing Palette

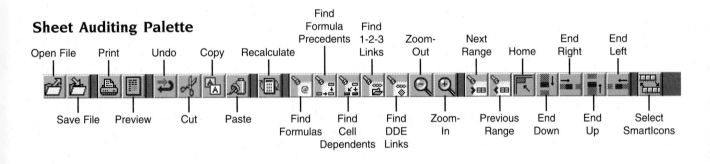

Open File · Print · Undo · Copy · Recalculate · Find Formula Precedents · Find 1-2-3 Links · Zoom-Out · Next Range · Home · End Right · End Left

Save File · Preview · Cut · Paste · Find Formulas · Find Cell Dependents · Find DDE Links · Zoom-In · Previous Range · End Down · End Up · Select SmartIcons

Working Together Palette

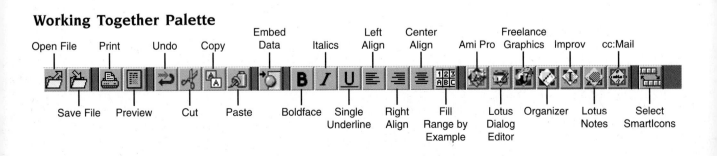

Open File · Print · Undo · Copy · Embed Data · Italics · Left Align · Center Align · Ami Pro · Freelance Graphics · Improv · cc:Mail

Save File · Preview · Cut · Paste · Boldface · Single Underline · Right Align · Fill Range by Example · Lotus Dialog Editor · Organizer · Lotus Notes · Select SmartIcons

Default Chart Palette

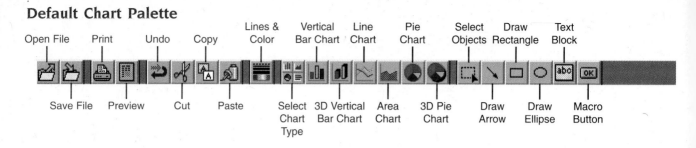

Open File — Print — Undo — Copy — Lines & Color — Vertical Bar Chart — Line Chart — Pie Chart — Select Objects — Draw Rectangle — Text Block

Save File — Preview — Cut — Paste — Select Chart Type — 3D Vertical Bar Chart — Area Chart — 3D Pie Chart — Draw Arrow — Draw Ellipse — Macro Button

Default Arrange Palette

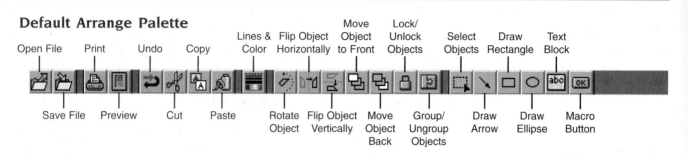

Open File — Print — Undo — Copy — Lines & Color — Flip Object Horizontally — Move Object to Front — Lock/Unlock Objects — Select Objects — Draw Rectangle — Text Block

Save File — Preview — Cut — Paste — Rotate Object — Flip Object Vertically — Move Object Back — Group/Ungroup Objects — Draw Arrow — Draw Ellipse — Macro Button

Default Table Palette

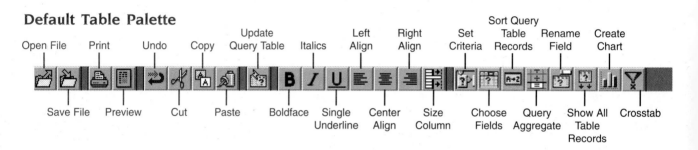

Open File — Print — Undo — Copy — Update Query Table — Italics — Left Align — Right Align — Set Criteria — Sort Query Table Records — Rename Field — Create Chart

Save File — Preview — Cut — Paste — Boldface — Single Underline — Center Align — Size Column — Choose Fields — Query Aggregate — Show All Table Records — Crosstab

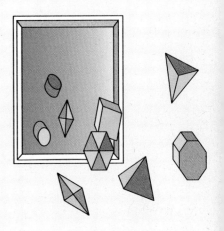

Index